DATE DUE

Demco, Inc. 38-293

G.

Gender and Development

Other books by IDE-JETRO

INDUSTRIAL CLUSTERS IN ASIA
Akifumi Kuchiki and Masatsugu Tsuji (*editors*)

SPATIAL STRUCTURE AND REGIONAL DEVELOPMENT IN CHINA
Nobuhiro Okamoto and Takeo Ihara (*editors*)

Gender and Development

The Japanese Experience in Comparative Perspective

Edited by Mayumi Murayama

58451964   4-1-09

HQ
1240.5
J3G46
2005

c.1

First published 2005 by
PALGRAVE MACMILLAN
Houndmills, Basingstoke, Hampshire RG21 6XS and
175 Fifth Avenue, New York, N. Y. 10010
Companies and representatives throughout the world

PALGRAVE MACMILLAN is the global academic imprint of the Palgrave Macmillan division of St. Martin's Press, LLC and of Palgrave Macmillan Ltd. Macmillan® is a registered trademark in the United States, United Kingdom and other countries. Palgrave is a registered trademark in the European Union and other countries.

ISBN-13: 978-1-4039-4944-8
ISBN-10: 1-4039-4944-1

This book is printed on paper suitable for recycling and made from fully managed and sustained forest sources.

A catalogue record for this book is available from the British Library.

Library of Congress Cataloging-in-Publication Data
Gender and development : the Japanese experience in comparative perspective / edited by Mayumi Murayama.
    p. cm.
  "Outcome of a research project conducted at the Institute of Developing Economies (IDE-JETRO) from 2002 to 2004"–Introd.
    Includes bibliographical references and index.
    ISBN 1-4039-4944-1
    1. Women in development–Japan. 2. Women–Japan–Social conditions–20th century. 3. Women–Japan–Economic conditions–20the century. 4. Social change–Japan. 5. Women in development–Developing countries. I. Murayama, Mayumi, 1961– II. Ajia Keizai Kenkyujo (Japan)
HQ1240.5.J3 G46 2005
305.48′8956′09045–dc22   200542931

10   9   8   7   6   5   4   3
14   13   12   11   10   09   08   07   06

Printed and bound in Great Britain by
Antony Rowe Ltd, Chippenham and Eastbourne

Contents

v

List of Figures

List of Tables

Glossary of Japanese Terms

chu-senkyoku-sei	multiple-seat constituency electoral system
daimyo	feudal lord
danson-johi	male chauvinism
dai-senkyoku-sei seigen-renki	limited plural ballot under large constituency system
Edo period	period between 1603 and 1867
fujin mondai	women question
hinoeuma	the year of the Fire Horse under the Chinese lunar calendar, during which it is believed to be inauspicious to bear a daughter
ie	literally 'dwelling house', a derivation used to signify the members of a patrilineal family, sometimes including non-kin members
joko	female factory worker
kaizen	improvement through innovative thinking
kazoku	family
katei	hearth/home
kokka	states, country, nation
kou	a traditional rotating credit system
Meiji period	period between 1868 and 1912
michi-no-eki	roadside station
ryosai kenbo	'good wife, wise mother'
seikatsu	livelihood
sensei	teacher
shufu	housewife
shujin	master
Taisho period	period between 1912 and 1926
Tokugawa period	same as Edo period
tsubo	unit of area, approximately 3.3 square metres

Acknowledgements

This book was made possible by the contributions of many people. I would like to express my deep gratitude to the Institute of Developing Economies (IDE), which allowed us to conduct our research project. The liberal as well as stimulating environment offered by IDE was a continuous source of inspiration. The participation of colleagues – Koichi Usami, Miwa Tsuda, Soya Mori, Yuka Kodama, Kumiko Izumisawa and Rie Takahashi – in the discussions added a variety of perspectives to the research agenda. The administrative support given by Fusako Hirata was an indispensable part of the project. Masahiro Okada, Ritsuko Takakusagi and Yumiko Ishikawa gave needed suggestions for publications based on their professional expertise.

Valuable comments were received from the anonymous referees, their suggestions were taken into account whenever possible. I hope this book will be of use for those who are interested in Japanese experiences in the areas of gender and development, and will provide some inputs that will lead to further investigations.

The English-language editorial support given by Lingua Guild was most helpful. I am personally indebted to Junko Yamaka, who had an intangible but great influence on me in my student days. I am also grateful to Amanda Hamilton, Katie Button and Keith Povey who offered valuable support throughout the publication process. Through this project, there was interaction with many people, both in Japan and in the other countries studied. Although not all can be mentioned, each of them made important contributions to the completion of this book. I am ever grateful to them all for sharing their life experiences by way of providing vital information. Of course, the contributing authors, are solely responsible for any shortcomings in the book.

MAYUMI MURAYAMA

Notes on the Contributors

Kuniko Funabashi is a Professor at Wako University, where she teaches women/gender studies. She is not only a scholar but also a feminist activist, and has been actively involved in the women's movement for more than twenty years. Prior to her current post, she worked on a project to create a curriculum entitled 'Building Women's Studies Curriculum in Asia' as a senior researcher at Osaka Women's University. Her areas of interest include the history of the women's movement, the theory of social movements, and public policies for gender equality.

Yasuko Hayase is a former Senior Researcher at the Institute of Developing Economies (IDE-JETRO). She currently teaches as lecturer, in the Faculty of Economics at Meikai University. She received her PhD in Sociology from Japan Women's University. She is a member of the Population Association of Japan and worked as a member of the board of the Association in 2001–4. She is a member of the gender analysis group on the '2004 National Public Opinion Survey on Population, Family, Generation,' carried out by the Mainichi Newspapers. She has published widely on a range of topics including population and development in Africa, population in Asia, China's population change, international migration in Asia, and gender and population issues.

Kazuko Kano is a Senior Technical Adviser for Social Development at the Japan Bank for International Co-operation (JBIC). She worked previously as the Country Director of the United Nations Population Fund (UNFPA) in Malaysia, Indonesia and Thailand. She has been trying to integrate soft components with hard infrastructure. One recent example is the introduction and promotion of roadside stations (*michi-no-eki*), for the purpose of rural women's empowerment as well as the invigoration of rural areas in countries such as Thailand, China and India. She teaches at Nagoya University and presents various training courses for rural women's empowerment supported by the Japan International Cooperation Agency (JICA).

Kaoru Murakami is a Research Fellow at IDE-JETRO. Her specialization is Turkish Studies, and Gender and Family Studies. She lived in Ankara for two years from 1994 to 1996. While doing graduate studies at Ankara University, she conducted field surveys on female labour in small-scale factories in Izmir. She is the editor of a book entitled *Women's Labour and Social Policies in Developing Countries* published by IDE-JETRO (in Japanese). The book focused on women's labour, which embodies state interventions in the familial as well as gender relations of individual societies.

Mayumi Murayama is Director of the South Asian Studies Group, Area Studies Center at IDE-JETRO. She has written extensively on development issues concerning Bangladesh, where she spent six years in various capacities including as a student at Dhaka University and a research expert at the Japanese Embassy in Dhaka. Her recent interest in female factory workers has expanded to cover other countries, including Japan. She is currently concerned about the issue of informalization of employment in both South Asia and Japan, and is interested in finding common ground for women in the different countries to work together to resist the trend.

Hiroki Nogami is Senior Research Fellow at IDE-JETRO. His main research interest is issues related to human development and well-being in developing countries. He has many publications to his credit including *Identity of Development Economics*, published by IDE-JETRO (in Japanese). He also regularly teaches at the IDE Advanced School and is actively engaged in fostering development experts in Japan.

Hiroshi Kan Sato is a Senior Researcher in development sociology at the Development Studies Center of IDE-JETRO. Recently, he has three main research topics; the first focuses on the social impacts of development aid projects in the recipient societies. He has edited several books on this matter, covering a variety of areas of development aid such as social capital, community organizations, empowerment, and participatory development. His second topic is an area study of Yemen, where he spent five years. Third, he is concentrating on a re-evaluation of the social development process in postwar Japan. He is a pioneer of this issue and is trying to communicate these Japanese experiences to the outside world, especially to developing countries.

Kanako Yamaoka is an Associate Senior Research Fellow at IDE-JETRO. She has worked on Cuban studies for fifteen years, and written on Cuba–US and Cuba–Japan relations, Cuba's economic reform and its political impact, and Cuban social development. She spent two years in Havana as a visiting researcher at the Center for Studies on Asia and Oceania, a research institution under the Central Committee of the Cuban Communist Party. She has worked on Cuban social policy in recent years, and from 2005 will work as a visiting scholar at Harvard University to launch a new research project on comparative studies of the survival of the remaining socialist countries, based on case studies of Cuba and Vietnam. She will be back at IDE-JETRO in 2007.

Map of Japan

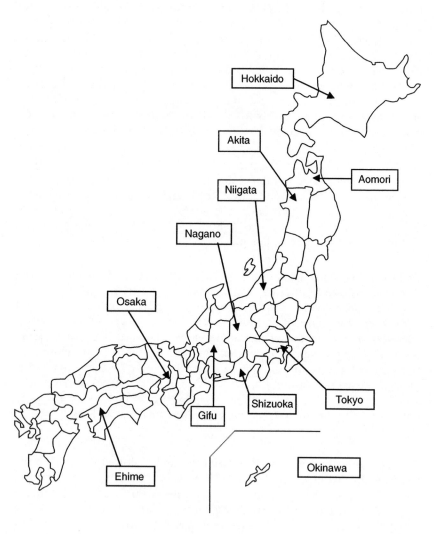

Map of Japan

Chronology of Related Events

Japanese period	Year	Events
Edo (Tokugawa) 1603–1867		
Meiji 1868–1912		
	1872	The first modern silk-reeling mill (*Tomioka seishi*) is established.
	1898	The Meiji Civil Code is enforced.
	1894–95	Sino-Japanese War
	1904–05	Russo-Japanese War
Taisho 1912–1926		
	1914–18	Japan joins allied forces in the First World War.
	1916	The Factory Act is enforced.
Showa 1926–1989		
	1937	Second Sino-Japanese War starts.
	1939	The Second World War starts.
	1941	Pacific War starts.
	1945	Japan surrenders to the Allied Forces.
	1945	The franchise is extended to women for the first time in Japan.
	1948	The Agricultural Improvement Promotion Law is enacted.
	1948	The Eugenic Protection Law is enacted.
	1952	The allied occupation of Japan ends.
	1952	The national family planning programme is formulated.
	1955	The New Life Movement starts.
	1961	The Agricultural Basic Law is enacted
	1965	The Maternal and Child Health Law is enacted.
	1975	The international year of women.
	1979	Ochanomizu University opens the first women's study course.
	1985	Japan ratifies the Convention for the Elimination of All Forms of Discrimination against Women.
	1985	The Equal Employment Opportunity Law is enacted.

Heisei 1989

	1990	The research group on Women and Development is constituted at JICA.
	1995	The fourth world conference on women is held in Beijing
	1997	The Equal Employment Opportunity Law is amended.
	1999	The Basic Law for a Gender-equal Society is enacted.
	1999	The Basic Law on Food, Agriculture and Rural Areas is enacted.

List of Abbreviations

ASEAN	Association of South East Asian Nations
BAAC	Bank for Agriculture and Agricultural Cooperatives
CEM	Centro de Estudios de la Mujer (Center of Woman Studies)
CIEM	Centro de Investigaciones de la Economía Mundial (Center for World Economy Studies)
CMEA/ COMECON	Council for Mutual Economic Assistance
DHS	Demographic and Health Surveys
FAO	Food and Agriculture Organization
FDI	foreign direct investment
FEEM	Federación de Estudiantes de la Enseñanza Media (Federation of Secondary-School Students)
FMC	Federación de Mujeres Cubanas (Federation of Cuban Women)
GAD	Gender and Development
GDI	Gender Development Index
GEM	Gender Empowerment Measure
GHQ	General Headquarters of the Allied Forces
GSP	Generalized System of Preference
HDI	Human Development Index
HLIESP	Home Living Improvement Extension Service Programme
ICPD	International Conference on Population and Development
IPP	Institute of Population Problems
IPU	Inter-Parliamentary Union
JA	Japan Agricultural Cooperatives
JBIC	Japan Bank for International Cooperation
JICA	Japan International Cooperation Agency
LIM	Livelihood Improvement Movement
LIP	Livelihood Improvement Programme
MAFEZ	Masan Free Export Zone
METI	Ministry of Economy, Trade and Industry
MFA	Multi-Fibre Agreement
NGO	non-governmental organization
NHK	Nippon Hoso Kyokai (Japan Broadcasting Corporation)
NIDL	New International Division of Labour
NIEs	Newly industrializing economies
NPO	non-profit organization
NWEC	National Women's Education Center

ODA	Official Development Assistance
ONE	Oficina Nacional de Estadísticas (National Office of Statistics)
OTOP	One Tambon (village) One Product
SLA	Sustainable Livelihood Approach
TFR	total fertility rate
TQC	Total Quality Control
UJC	Unión de Jóvenes Comunistas (The Communist Youth Union)
UNDP	United Nations Development Programme
UNFPA	United Nations Population Fund
USAID	US Agency for International Development
WID	Women in Development
WINWIN	Women in New World International Network

Introduction: An Attempt to Integrate Gender and Development Issues of Japan and Developing Countries

Mayumi Murayama

This book is the outcome of a research project conducted at the Institute of Developing Economies (IDE-JETRO) between 2002 and 2004. Each contributor had different interests and motives for joining the project. However, we all shared a common goal: to review the issues of gender and development with two fields of research in mind: Japan and developing countries.[1] On the basis of this approach, we adopted two objectives: first, to draw some implications from Japanese past and present experiences applicable to gender and development problems in today's developing countries, and second to reflect on the situations of gender and development in Japan from examining the experiences of developing countries. Thus the two objectives have had opposite orientations, assigning different weights to Japan and the developing countries. Through both approaches, however, we have sought new insights for issues of gender and development.

Before describing the rationale, limitations and findings of our project, it should be mentioned that in this book, 'gender and development' is used in a broad term, not limited to Gender and Development (GAD), which refers to an academic discipline as well as practices related to development assistance to developing countries. The term as we use it indicates economic, political and social changes that take place in relation to gender perspectives. Thus, for example, in some chapters, it implies the relationship between the nation-building process and gender ideology, while in others, female political participation has been analysed within the broad perspective of gender and development.

Reviewing Japanese experiences from a gender and development perspective

The rationale of the project

In April 2002, we embarked on a rather ambitious project, considering that few of the members had any experience of research about Japan. The majority of the contributors, including myself, as professional researchers at a research organization specializing in social science research on developing countries and regions, have been engaged in research on the developing countries, ranging from Asia and the Middle East to Latin America. It should be noted that the researchers of our institute have worked on various issues of developing countries, but that for most members, this was the first time that gender issues had been the central theme of research. Nevertheless, with an awareness of the importance of doing so, through our perennial encounters with gender-related issues in academia as well as practical experiences, we decided to address the issues squarely, setting up a project with like-minded colleagues.

In order to compensate for our lack of research experience on the gender situation in Japan, we invited two outside researchers to participate. They benefited the project greatly, bringing their knowledge as well as their experiences as activists in the gender and development context in Japan. They also became a bridge, linking the experiences of women in Japan and developing countries, since they each had considerable experience of working or networking with women in developing countries. Their broad perspectives and ability to articulate the differentiated experiences of women in a common language underpinned the fundamental tenet of our project.

Despite our lack of experience and institutional opportunities to do field research in Japan, we decided to look into the gender and development situation there, primarily because of our expectation that we could draw useful implications from these experiences. As is well known, Japan lagged behind other developed countries in the West in its industrialization, and succeeded in carrying out economic and social development in a relatively short time span. It is no exaggeration that people outside Japan, especially those treading the thorny path of development, have a great interest in its experiences. Needless to say, the experiences of each country are individual, taking place under different conditions and at different times. Moreover, there are no doubt many unsolved as well as newly emerging problems in Japan as a whole. Nevertheless, both the 'successes' and 'failures' experienced by any society can provide a reference point for others by increasing the available options for developmental thinking.

Recently, some initiatives have been carried out, mainly by official donor agencies, to review Japanese development experiences within the framework of aid research and to draw upon new insights to deal with the problems of developing countries (JICA, 2003b, 2003c, 2003d; Sato *et al.*, 2003). Although various areas such as population, education, regional development and livelihood improvement are covered in these initiatives, they appear to share a common stance: being fully aware of the different and specific conditions in which Japan and the individual developing countries are embedded, they deny the viability of the outright application of Japanese experiences. On the basis of this assumption, however, they still find it relevant to review the experiences of Japan. Each research initiative has tried to learn what could be of use in the problems developing countries face today. The justification for such research can also be applied to issues related to gender. However, there are few research undertakings reviewing the gender problems of Japan and developing countries on the basis of their having a common footing. One significant reason for this seems to be the gap between women/gender studies and Gender and Development studies in Japan. Women/gender studies and GAD studies in Japan have separate origins and, in my opinion, had few linkages, at least until the latter half of the 1990s.

Women/gender studies, and Gender and Development studies in Japan

Women's studies in Japan emerged at the end of the 1970s (Sechiyama, 1995). The first course on the women question began at the leading women's university in 1979. At that time, there were several groups of women who tried to institutionalize women's studies in Japanese academia (Iwao and Hara, 1979; Josei-gaku kenkyukai, 1981). The rise of women's studies in Japan was bolstered, first by the blossoming of women's studies in the USA, which preceded Japan by about a decade, and second by the International Year of Women in 1975, which became a milestone for making women's issues public. Against this backdrop were set the changing realities of women's lives at that time. Iwao and Hara (1979) in particular shed light on the issue of housewives. The high economic growth in the 1960s and early 1970s produced a large mass of white-collar employee-husband and housewife couples. However, despite the size of this 'housewife' population, the category was not given the same attention as prewar factory women or women in villages, who were quite commonly written about. Iwao and Hara argue that the 'housewife' as a social construct necessarily reflects the problems facing other categories of women as well as society as a whole, including men.

As in other sciences, the methodologies and concepts of women's studies in Japan have been influenced heavily by those developed in the USA and Europe. The emphasis on housewives by Iwao and Hara also seems to have been stimulated partly by Betty Friedan's seminal work, *The Feminine Mystique*, published in 1963. However, it should be noted that they suggest that women's studies in Japan should not be limited by American models, but should also include the rich collection of ethnological as well as historical studies in Japan. On the other hand, they call simultaneously for a comparative framework so that women's studies in Japan would not be isolated from the world. Since the advent of women's studies in Japan in the late 1970s, the academic field has grown phenomenally, adopting different titles such as feminism studies and gender studies (Sechiyama, 1995). The subjects of research have expanded significantly beyond the housewife and family, to include males and other social spaces, such as workplaces and communities, and theoretical and methodological refinement has been pursued vigorously. Nevertheless, it remains questionable how far the suggestions raised by Iwao and Hara at the end of the 1970s have been achieved today.

Although it is beyond my ability to overview the vast literature of women and gender studies in Japan, it seems that the comparative framework adopted by the majority of studies has primarily been a comparison between Japan and the developed Western countries. There are understandable reasons for this. First, there is the massive academic influence of US and European academia. Second, the availability of data related to various gender situations limits the scope of comparative studies. Third, and most important, women's/gender studies, which are inextricably linked with movements for gender equality, prefer to look toward the West, which is considered to be better-off in that respect, for the sake of emphasizing the 'backwardness' of Japan and calling for solutions.

Another critique of the current feminist debate in Japan is raised by Miyake (2001). Miyake states that women's/gender studies in Japan, as in other academic fields, have been preoccupied with absorbing new theories produced in the USA and Europe. Consequently, there has not been a search for methodologies that could be applied to analyse gender issues in the Japanese historical as well as contemporary context. I find those problems in women's and gender studies also to be present in studies of Gender and Development in slightly different forms.

The institutionalization of Women in Development (WID)/Gender and Development (GAD) in Japan dates back to the early 1990s, and was thus lagging by two decades compared to developed Western countries. Internationally, women's issues and development were first linked at the beginning of the 1970s. It is not only in terms of the time lag, but also the main actors who promoted its institutionalization, that marked a distinctive difference between WID/GAD in the USA and some European countries, and in Japan. In the former, the growing strength of the women's movement took an instrumental role by influencing women in the United Nations system and national aid agencies. Through their efforts, women's issues have gained a place in development thought (Tinker, 1990; Young, 1993; Kabeer, 1994). As early as 1973, the US Senate adopted the Percy Amendment to the Foreign Assistance Act under pressure from the WID lobby. This amendment added a provision to 'encourage and promote the integration of women' into all aspects of development planning and into policy-making bodies (Young, 1993 p. 24).

In contrast, in Japan, it was primarily through government initiatives, and aid practitioners in particular, encouraged by policy calls in international forums concerned with Official Development Assistance (ODA) that opened the field for WID/GAD as a policy agenda as well as a subject of research. In the background, there was tacit international pressure on Japan, which in 1989 overtook the USA to become the largest provider of ODA. In 1990, a research group on Development and Women was set up within the auspices of the Japan International Cooperation Agency (JICA), one of the state aid agencies. It was the first time that WID/GAD was incorporated as an important dimension worthy of research in the Japanese aid regime. Subsequently, Japan's 1992 ODA Charter stipulated that 'full consideration will be given to the active participation of women in development, and to their obtaining benefits from development'. Further, the Japanese government announced 'Japan's Initiative on WID' at the Fourth World Conference on Women held in Beijing in 1995.[2] Although gender mainstreaming, even at state level, leaves much scope for improvement,[3] through those policy measures, WID/GAD has gained some measure of publicity in Japan.

Ito and Fujikake (2003) state categorically that in Japan there is no strong movement to support WID/GAD apart from among the aid agencies. There is a need to explore further whether women's groups in Japan have shown a lack of interest in the impact of Japanese ODA on women in developing countries and, if so, what the reasons are for this. Nevertheless, it is true that their involvement in WID/GAD has not been substantial compared with other developed countries. Ito and Fujikake (2003) also point out that most research on WID/GAD in Japan has been carried out by practitioners and a handful of researchers as individual efforts. Thus, it can be concluded that there is a lack of links among the three actors – activists/advocates, practitioners and scholars – in Japan in the field of WID/GAD. This is considered to be one of the critical factors hindering gender mainstreaming. Moreover, in relation to our project, it seems to be an important reason for the isolation of WID/GAD research from women/gender studies in Japan. Although WID/GAD research has grown gradually in Japan, the literature has been written mainly by researchers and practitioners who studied on related courses in the USA and Europe, since there were no courses on Gender and Development in Japan until Ochanomizu University launched one in 1997. Here, I do not intend to argue that it is wrong to conduct research based on the framework developed in the West. What I would like to emphasize is that we could have benefited greatly by integrating the perspectives of developing countries, as well as of Japan and other developed countries, in order to deepen our knowledge of both Japan itself and developing countries. Even after acknowledging the different origins of women's/gender studies and WID/GAD studies, it seems bizarre that the Gender and Development concept is referred to only in relation to development assistance to developing countries. There are other areas that the concept could be applied even within Japanese society in the twenty-first century.

Nevertheless, various efforts have been made since the latter half of the 1990s. As mentioned above, the Gender and Development course was started in 1997 at Ochanomizu University. The University has been working to build a network of women/gender research institutes in the Asia-Pacific region. Hara *et al.* (1996) is an outcome of the networking promoted jointly by Ochanomizu University and the National Women's Education Centre (NWEC).[4] In their Introduction, Hara and Osawa expressed concern for the fact that the generally recognized history of women's studies and the women's movement was only depicted with a limited number of American and European cases in mind. In order to fill this perception gap, they analyse the situations of women/gender research, education and policies in eight countries in the Asia-Pacific region, including Japan. This work can be cited as the first large-scale comparative study in this particular field. The foreign participants of the project also mention an interest in carrying out comparative work. Chung (1996) indicates in her article that since the 1980s in Korea, sociologists attempting to produce original theories based on the realities of life in Korea began to cast their eyes towards Japan. These studies on Japan were conducted primarily with the objective of creating a framework in which to analyse Korean society.

Reviewing the Japanese experience from the perspective of developing countries

The second objective in examining the gender and development experiences of Japan and developing countries simultaneously is to review the Japanese experience from the perspective of developing countries. This is intended as a reflection on the subjectivity and methodological bias of the researchers.

Most of all, what we are hoping to question is the unconscious assumption involved in our implicit comparative framework. When talking with people in developing countries, remarks are often heard – which can be a compliment or an accusation – that Japan is a rich country, and thus Japanese women are free from the problems that others face in developing countries. When confronted with this statement, we generally agree with it, but then add the reservation that the reality in Japan is very complex, and that there is diversity in life experiences in Japan as much as in any other country. Thus, we say, women are not totally free from problems. At that point, however, we stop reflecting on Japan and resume the unilateral relationship of questioning our 'respondents'.

There are two methodological issues that we should look into here. The first concerns the problem of objectivity and subjectivity. In recent debate, some schools of feminist epistemology[5] in particular have questioned critically the positivism and underlying assumptions of mainstream science and social science (Harding, 1987; Fonow and Cook, 1991; Wolf, 1996). According to Wolf (1996), positivist science is:

based on the tenet of value-free objectivity that can, should, and must be attained by the scientist or social scientist in order to uncover 'facts' and 'the truth.' Research must be completely replicable by others, and this entire endeavor is thought to further our knowledge of universal truth. This view of science entails and encourages distance and non-involvement between the researcher and researched and assumes that the researcher can objectively see, judge, and interpret the life and meanings of his/her subjects. (p. 4)

Wolf's critique can apply to our attitude towards 'subjects in developing countries'. Generally speaking, we often find ourselves acting unconsciously as though we were impersonal judges with no links to any worldly problems. We try to be as 'objective' as possible by drawing on 'academic' disciplines and approaches. But feminist scholars have argued that it is impossible to be objective and value-free, since our vision and interpretations are shaped by our own experiences and values, and because our very presence in the research field already influences the context in which 'the researched' live. Professional obsessiveness with 'scientific objectivity' is also considered to be undesirable, from several viewpoints, in that it has a sexist nature, involves the imposition of a hierarchical and controlling relationship upon the researcher–researched dyad, and tends to exclude personal, subjectively-based knowledge from 'science' (Jayaratne and Stewart, 1991). The false dualism between objectivity and subjectivity, or structure and agency, has been questioned by many others including Anthony Giddens and Pierre Bourdieu, as elucidated in their theories of structuration and practice. They state that the objective and subjective aspects of social life are bound together inescapably. Their central argument is that neither the experiences of individual actors, nor any form of structural totality, exist independently. There is a recursive relationship between subject and structure. Structure is recreated continually through the agency of subjects, while the subjective consciousness of agents is constructed and mediated by structure (Giddens, 1984; Bourdieu, 1990).

A second problem is our perceptional bias. As mentioned above, we evaluate a particular gender issue unconsciously on the basis of a continuum where Western societies and developing countries are placed at the two extremes. Without much reflection, we tend to draw the unexamined conclusion that Japan is situated in the middle of the continuum. This reveals our perceptional assumption that there is a linear path for the development of gender issues based on economic development or, more precisely, Westernization. In other words, we assume that, first, the gender situation in Japan is better than that in developing countries but worse than in developed Western countries such as the USA and Europe, and that, second, all gender-related problems are solved automatically as the economy

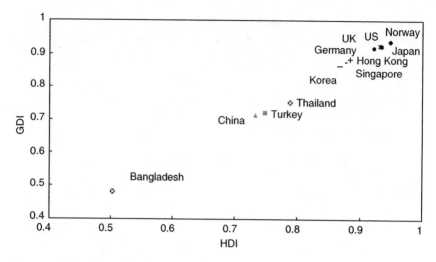

Source: Compiled from UNDP (2003) *Human Development Report 2003*.

Figure I.1   HDI and GDI of selected countries, 2001

and society become closer to the level and nature of Western countries. But to what extent is this true?

Figure I.1 shows the relative position of the Human Development Index (HDI) and Gender Development Index (GDI) of several countries, calculated by the United Nations Development Programme. In general, a positive linear relationship can be observed between HDI and GDI: countries with a higher HDI have a higher GDI. The distribution of the selected countries shows four clusters: the highest group (Norway, USA, UK, Japan and Germany); the second-highest group (Hong Kong, Korea and Singapore); the middle-range group (Thailand, Turkey and China); and the lowest group (Bangladesh). Among the twelve countries presented in the figure, Japan belongs to the highest group, along with the Western countries. This implies that Japan ranks above most countries in terms of human development (life expectancy at birth, education and GDP per capita) even after taking into account the factor of gender inequality.

However, if we look at gender disparities in the respective countries, a somewhat different picture emerges. Figure I.2 presents the differences between HDI and GDI in the countries that were placed in the highest and the second-highest group. With the exception of Germany, GDI is lower than HDI. Japan and Korea have a higher HDI–GDI gap than the others, as shown by the distance from the diagonal line. This fact is shown in absolute terms in Table I.1. Japan and Korea have the highest HDI–GDI gap in their respective groups, though the gaps are not as large as for countries such as Turkey and Bangladesh. Countries such as Thailand and China,

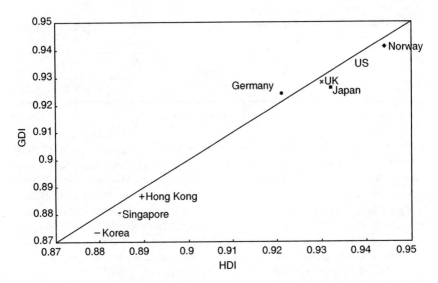

Source: As Figure I.1.

Figure I.2 Comparison of HDI and GDI for the highest and second-highest group, 2001

whose HDI and GDI are both lower in absolute terms than Japan and Korea, demonstrate lower gender gaps with respect to the indicators incorporated into GDI. Thus it is evident that higher HDI does not necessarily ensure gender equality.

Another aspect we should note is changes in the HDI–GDI gap over time. Table I.2 shows 1992 data for the four countries that recorded a relatively

Table I.1 HDI-GDI gap, 2001

	Norway	Japan	USA	UK	Germany	Hong Kong
HDI	0.944	0.932	0.937	0.93	0.921	0.889
GDI	0.941	0.926	0.935	0.928	0.924	0.886
HDI-GDI gap (%)	0.3	0.6	0.2	0.2	–0.3	0.3

	Singapore	Korea	Thailand	Turkey	China	Bangladesh
HDI	0.884	0.879	0.768	0.734	0.721	0.502
GDI	0.88	0.873	0.766	0.726	0.718	0.495
HDI-GDI gap (%)	0.5	0.7	0.3	1.1	0.4	1.4

Notes: HDI-GDI gap is calculated based on the following formula: (HDI-GDI)/HDI*100. The negative figure for Germany indicates that GDI is higher than HDI.

Source: Compiled and calculated based on the same data as Figure 1.1.

Table I.2   HDI-GDP gap for selected countries, 1992

	Japan	Korea	Turkey	Bangladesh
HDI	0.937	0.882	0.792	0.364
GDI	0.896	0.780	0.744	0.334
HDI-GDI gap (%)	4.4	11.6	6.1	8.2

Source: Compiled and calculated based on data in (UNDP 1995).

high HDI–GDI gap in 2001. A comparison with the data from 2001 presented in Table I.1 reveals that Korea, Turkey and Bangladesh achieved large reductions in the HDI–GDI gap over that period – of 10.9, 5.0 and 6.8 percentage points, respectively – whereas for Japan the reduction was 3.8 percentage points. Korea's success in narrowing the gap is particularly noteworthy. In 1992, it was one of two countries in Asia with an HDI–GDI gap of more than 10 per cent, along with Pakistan (25 per cent). What was behind this remarkable reduction? It is natural that we would like to know more than a simple analysis of the indices tells us.

While working in the developing countries, we are frequently impressed by the lived knowledge, practice and activism of the people. It seems obvious that they can provide new insights to the developed societies. If we are to draw lessons from their experiences for our own lives, we do not have to rely only on first-hand information or observation by ourselves. Contrary to the general impression that there is little research carried out into the situation and problems of developing countries, there is in fact an emerging body of literature because of global concern over development issues. No doubt there are many aspects that remain unexplored or neglected, given the fact that trends exist in development issues and discourses. Nevertheless, gender issues have been one of the most 'popular' subjects among both researchers and practitioners, irrespective of their country of origin. We can also learn a lot from this rich literature. Just as feminism has questioned the 'natural order of things' perceived by the individual and society, looking at our gender and development experiences in Japan from different perspectives can contribute to deconstructing our unquestioned ideas and expanding our knowledge and scope for tackling problems.

Structure of the book

The eight chapters that follow are grouped into three sections according to the approaches they adopt. These approaches are in line with the objectives mentioned at the beginning. The first approach is to draw implications from Japanese experiences, past and present, in relation to the gender and development problems in the present developing countries. The second involves reflecting on Japan's gender and development situation from the experiences of developing countries. Finally, one chapter discussing female factory work is placed in an independent section. The emphasis of the last chapter is on integrating Japanese case studies into the global debate on female factory work rather than focusing on either Japan or developing countries. The four chapters in the first section investigate Japanese experiences — both successes and failures – in order to draw implications, some practical and others theoretical, for gender and development issues at the time of writing. In Chapter 1, the author poses the question of how far economic development has benefited women's well-being. Starting from the assumption that there are similarities in the way that industrialization affects women across countries, the author looks at the history of Japanese industrialization. In an attempt to assess the level of human well-being in prewar Japan, he computes GDI with some modifications. We can recall here that Japan has been referred to by UNDP as a 'notorious' country characterized by relatively large and persistent gender gaps over time. This chapter attempts to elucidate the trend from a long-term perspective. One of the features of late industrialization, in the case of both Japan and the present developing countries, is the uneven and telescoped pattern of economic development. In analysing disparities among the various dimensions of human life, the author cites the necessity for multidimensional welfare indicators. Deconstructed indicators, namely health (life expectancy), education (school enrolment/average years of schooling) and income (daily wages of factory workers) provide a view of the smallest and largest improvements took in health and education. However, the author adds that there is a time lag between male and female achievements in terms of average years of schooling. In Japan, gender gaps in health and education persisted throughout the prewar period. In particular, the slowness in the improvement of health indicators for women was alarming. On the basis of these findings, the author emphasizes the importance of resource allocation for the improvement of women's health, an aspect that is likely to be omitted in the natural course of economic development. The article also suggests that there is scope for further refinements of GDI as a viable indicator in assessing the complexity of gender disparities as well as long-term standards of living.

Japan's experiences with respect to family planning are presented in Chapter 2. As we know, population is one of the fundamental problems in a large number of developing countries. Before the Second World War, Japan also had a problem of surplus population, but in subsequent years, a demographic transition has taken place within a very short period of time. After presenting an overview of the current situation with regard to family planning and gender relations in developing countries, this chapter provides an analysis of the causes of Japan's 'success'. The end of the Second World War brought with it a rapid increase in population because of net immigration and a resultant 'baby boom'. Although the concept of family planning was introduced to Japan in the 1920s, despite the efforts of birth-control advocates such as Margaret Sanger, few people had either accurate knowledge or the facilities for birth control. Moreover, the government adopted a pro-natalistic policy for military purposes. After the Second World War, the government adopted several measures, including the enactment of the Eugenic Protection Law (1948) and the launching of a national family planning programme (1952), with the main purpose of promoting proper contraception to combat the marked increase in induced abortions, which endangered both the lives and the health of mothers. However, these early governmental efforts were not very successful, largely because of a lack of institutional and financial support to spread family planning among the masses. The turning point came in 1955. A new family planning programme was launched along the lines recommended in the previous year by the Council for Population Problems, a governmental advisory body. The ideas presented by the recommendation represented a clear departure from the earlier government focus on the protection of mothers' health, and towards the implementation of a population policy. A special scheme was implemented targeting low-income families. They were provided not only with technical guidance but also with contraceptive devices at little or no charge. Also, with industrial workers as the main beneficiaries, the 'New Life Movement' was started by a private organization using state subsidies. After 1958, the administration of family planning programmes was transferred to local government, and maternal and child health centres began to provide health services including prenatal assistance. The author provides a detailed analysis of the work of the 'New Life Movement'. It was unique in the sense that the promoting organization worked together with employers and trade unions to promote family planning from the standpoint of 'workers' welfare'. The wives of employees were organized into small groups. Housewives were expected to contribute to raising company productivity by providing their husbands with a stable family life. Looking at the method of contraception, the high rate of condom usage is a special characteristic of Japan. Although a survey finds that males participate actively in family planning, important questions remain on the power between males and females. The chapter concludes with the presentation of several implications for developing countries. The author asserts that gender systems in each society interact with family planning programmes to determine their success.

The period covered by Chapter 3 overlaps to some extent with Chapter 2. In this chapter, the author reviews the Livelihood Improvement Programme (LIP), which also contributed to the spread of family planning in rural areas. The LIP was launched immediately after the Second World War under instructions from the General Headquarters of the Allied Forces (GHQ). It was a women-centred development programme, and achieved remarkable success, not only in alleviating poverty but also in raising the social and economic status of rural women. The author analyses its contemporary relevance for developing countries, not only from the historical record of 'success stories' but also in the context of current debates in development studies. The important elements of the LIP are conceptualized as the 'Sustainable Livelihood Approach' and 'participatory development', both of which have gained currency as dominant development concepts in recent years. Within the programme, extension workers, all of whom were women, played a pivotal part in encouraging women in rural areas to improve their livelihoods. However, they were never providers of solutions. They acted rather as facilitators or catalysts, motivating such women to identify their own problems and solutions. In addition to the LIP workers, there were several tools and methods that proved effective, such as the emphasis on a group approach rather than individual guidance, the promotion of improved cooking stoves, creative methods of fund-raising, and a model area approach. The reader can find practical suggestions in the author's account. Overall, the author argues that the LIP set the stage for the economic growth that followed by encouraging social development in rural areas. According to the author, the LIP can be regarded as a GAD rather than a WID approach. This opinion differs from the findings of earlier studies on the LIP, which found that it had only had limited effects in changing existing gender ideology. The author maintains that the LIP emphasized private home life not only for women and by women, but of all family members. It promoted the long-run modernization and democratization of home life, and through this process many young wives gained empowerment.

Chapter 4 analyses the issue of entrepreneurial activities and empowerment of women in rural areas. Some women's collective activities originated in the LIP groups discussed in the preceding chapter. People who joined LIP groups as young wives in the postwar period later grew into aged but active promoters of entrepreneurial activities. From this fact, we can observe the long-term impact of the LIP on women.

Despite their substantial contributions to agriculture, women have not received the recognition they deserve. In this regard, the author states that entrepreneurial activities can provide women with a chance to rectify this situation. In 2003, 8,186 activities of this type were carried out by women in rural Japan. The author examines the processes leading to the empowerment of these women through activities, by looking at case studies from Japan and Thailand. Based on interviews with women in rural businesses, and their families, and from observations of their activities, she delineates the process of empowerment into four stages: awareness and participation, capacity building, practice and effect, and transformation. The last stage, transformation, can take place at the level of individual women, families and communities. Empowerment can also be classified into three categories: economic, social and political. The case studies conducted by the author demonstrate vividly how the empowerment process in various dimensions took place through enterprising work. The author also uses practical examples that show how any woman or women's group can adopt and tailor activities to suit their own needs and conditions, irrespective of their country. The experience of Thailand mentioned in the article involves the application of the 'one village, one product' scheme in a Thai context. The author concludes that a similar process of empowerment has been taking place among rural Thai women as well.

The three chapters in the second section conduct comparative analyses between Japan and specific developing countries. Although they touch on the case of Japan to varying degrees, they do not try to draw implications unilaterally from Japan's case. Rather, they show that comparative studies on Japan and developing countries can be mutually beneficial in deepening our understanding of particular gender issues as well as providing alternative views to problems, and consequently can contribute academically to specific fields of knowledge.

Chapter 5 takes up the issue of political participation by women. As is well known, participation in the decision-making process by Japanese women, particularly in politics, is quite low. The author, who has long been involved in the women's movement, analyses the problem using first-hand information. The situation of Korean women is referred to for comparison. Although they generally have a low profile, the women's movements there have been trying to make inroads into the political arena. In recent years, women have gained ground in politics, especially in local assemblies. Chapter 5 looks at the case of Nagano Prefecture, where more women were elected to office in the first two elections after the Second World War than anywhere else in Japan, and where, after a low ebb lasting many years, the number of female assembly members is now higher again than in other regions of Japan. The author finds that activities led by voluntary groups of women have been instrumental to this success, and presents a detailed account of their groups. It should be noted that one of the two women's movements was originally a LIP group. Thus we can see again here the empowerment effects of the LIP. The chapter also discusses the impact that the entry of women into politics has had on the male-dominated political culture, gender relations at home, and the gender-based consciousness of individuals. In summary, the author finds that there have been positive changes in all aspects. Nevertheless, she maintains that the number of female politicians is still too small to allow women's voices to be heard. With this in mind, she looks into the case of Korea, which has made rapid progress in women's participation in politics. This was made possible mainly by the revision of the electoral system and the introduction of a quota for female candidates. The female quota is backed by incentives such as increased party subsidies and reduced election deposits. Such revisions of the electoral system are seen as an important achievement of the women's movement. In addition to elections, the women's movement in Korea has played a powerful role in institutionalizing women's demands. In contrast, Japanese women, in the absence of institutionalized support, face severe obstacles in increasing the number of female Diet members. The author suggests that the Japanese women's movement should learn from the experiences of its Korean counterparts while at the same time finding a way to overcome the problems it faces.

Chapter 6 investigates a very familiar issue – who performs domestic work – through a comparative study of Japan and a less familiar area, Cuba. Cuba has a very different environment from Japan, both culturally and politically. However, in terms of the female labour participation rate as well as the presence of a strong sense of male dominance, the two countries have somewhat parallel conditions. Under the socialist regime in Cuba, not only has female labour participation been encouraged, but the equal sharing of domestic work between husbands and wives was stipulated in the Family Code enacted in 1975. Nevertheless, contrary to the findings of earlier studies that mentioned changing gender roles, especially among younger generations, the author finds that this provision has not been realized as much as one might expect. She posits that the socialist revolution has failed to transform the old gender roles, and corroborates this supposition by piecing together the available statistical data. She states that Cuban state's socialist policy merely lessened men's obligations as breadwinners by providing social welfare services such as free education and medical care, along with subsidized food and low-cost housing, but did not do anything to ensure their participation in domestic work. In addition, the economic crisis in the mid 1990s, following the collapse of the Soviet Union, has affected women adversely by increasing the burden of domestic work as a result of the deteriorating public and social infrastructure and decreasing employment opportunities. In addition, high-income jobs require a stricter discipline from workers, and women may be unable to take advantage of such chances as they are heavily burdened by domestic work. This may lead to a rise in the husband's authority over the wife. Looking at the Japanese case, the author finds that the Gender Equality Law, promulgated in 1999, has not been very effective in promoting the equal sharing of domestic work, as it mentions only vaguely the problem of the traditional gender-based division of labour in the household. Moreover, a work culture with long working hours has impeded male involvement in domestic activities. In conclusion, the author remarks that, in Cuba, the Family Code has justified male engagement in domestic work, and thus at least has had some demonstrable effect. In Japan, in contrast, the country's capitalist economic development has made it possible for women to reduce the time they spend on domestic work through the provision of labour-saving devices and services. However, it has failed to convince men to share the work. Finally, the author anticipates that the growing role of the private sector in the economy in Cuba may lead to a revival of traditional gender relations along lines similar to those in Japan, because the business norms and institutions of the private sector demand long male working hours.

Chapter 7 is a comparative analysis of feminist studies in Japan and Turkey, looking at discourses on the nation-state, the modern family and the role of women. The two countries share a history of having transformed themselves into modern nation-states without losing political independence. Since the end of the 1980s, the relationship between modern nation-state building and family and gender issues has attracted the concern of feminist scholars in both countries. It is interesting to note, however, that the discussions carried out in each country have a different focus and line of argument. In the case of Japan, the discussions on the modern family have shifted from re-examining the characteristics of the institution of *ie* in modern Japan, to the relationship between the state and family as a system of control. It has been argued that it was not only the pre-modern family ethics as embodied in the *ie*, but also the newly-created family consciousness, similar to that of the modern family in Europe, that played an important role in the ideology supporting the state's authority. On the other hand, in Turkey, the Kemalist modernization, which in the past has been praised with respect to women's liberation, has more recently come under critical review. Scholars have pointed to its limitations in using women merely as symbols of a modern and democratic nation. Beneath this critical re-examination of women's liberation under the Kemalist reforms lay a search for a native feminism that reflects the cultural and political context of Turkey. Though different themes are discussed, reflecting their own historical experiences, the arguments in the two countries share common points of contention, such as the construction of the 'new family' concept, and the new role of women as mothers and wives of the nation. The arguments also share a standpoint, though to different degrees, that women were not always passive, but rather acted according to subjective choices. The emphasis on women's subjectivity is considered an academic undertaking by feminist scholars to rectify the male-biased historical perspectives of existing studies. However, the differing degree to which female subjectivity was highlighted in Japan and Turkey led the two arguments in different directions: in Japan, it led to questioning women's responsibility in supporting the Second World War, while in Turkey such complex feelings about the role of women in nation-building have yet to be observed.

In Chapter 8, in the last section, the author argues for the need to expand the scope of research beyond comparative studies of Japan and developing countries. The theme of the article is female factory work, which is of equal importance for both developing and developed countries, including Japan. From the time of the first Industrial Revolution in Britain, female factory work has been one of the most popular subjects in women/gender studies, and Japan is no exception here. There is a great volume of literature on female workers in the silk and cotton textile industries during the early stage of industrialization. Since the late 1970s, when multinational companies began to shift their production bases from their own countries, research fields have expanded to encompass developing countries, and this trend has accelerated during the 1990s, representing the most visible effect of globalization. While the developing countries are the central areas of research on this specific theme, there is growing interest in female factory work within Western developed countries as a result of the re-emergence of sweatshops and the presence of migrant workers. The findings of this chapter show clearly that problems at home and abroad are inseparably linked. On the other hand, looking at the academic situation in Japan, there is a dearth of research looking at the issue of female factory work in the contemporary context of Japan. The issue is a critical one, however, considering the fact that the exodus of Japanese factories to other Asian countries has taken place on a scale that will have a considerable effect on the host countries, including the workers there. We can assume there has been as much effect within Japan, in particular, in the form of displaced workers. The brief case studies presented on Japanese garment factories indicate that there are many similarities between the problems that the workers of developing and developed countries face. On the basis of this finding, the author questions the optimistic view that economic development, to which the factory workers in developing countries have been making crucial contributions, will bring them automatic benefits in return.

Concluding remarks

In the light of the research objectives, we have discussed the fact that Japanese experiences in family planning, LIP, rural women's entrepreneurial activities, and political networking among women may be useful development tools as well as case studies worthy of consideration for the benefit of developing countries. Also, the argument has been raised that women's health issues tend to be neglected in the process of industrialization, and thus there is a need for greater resource allocations by governments to improve the health levels of women and create better working conditions. On the other hand, the experiences of women's political participation and sharing of domestic work in Korea and Cuba suggest that the Japanese experiences do not show the only ways to cope with persistent problems. The different lines of argument developed in Japan and Turkey regarding the nation-state, the modern family and the role of women corroborate the differences in orientation and emphasis in both women's consciousness and activism between women in the two countries. Finally, the situation of contemporary factory women in Japan casts a shadow over the rosy picture that female workers in developing countries may have of the future.

Looking at the studies on Japanese women, three of the eight chapters (Chapters 3,4 and 5) happened to refer to LIP groups. They elaborate on the significance of those groups with respect not only to the livelihood improvement *per se* in the post-Second World War period, but also to the nurturing of women who have played a central role in rural entrepreneurial activities in current times, and in expanding the scope for female political participation. Without necessarily intending to do so, we shed light on the activism of that particular generation of women who remained in rural areas and sustained their agro-based livelihoods under policies that were not always favourable to agriculture. The women who took up factory work in rural areas as part-time employee-housewives during the 1960s and 1970s, as discussed in Chapter 8, are construed to be one generation younger. Further investigation should be carried out on the similarities and differences between the two generations of women, and on the impacts their different life experiences had on their consciousness. Not only for the sake of research but for learning from the lived experiences of the earlier generation of women, there is an urgent need to record their life trajectories, primarily on the basis of their narratives.

Throughout the research work, the lack of experience and opportunities for conducting fieldwork in Japan of most of our members has circumscribed our scope for analysis. Furthermore, our discussions are generally limited to factual analyses of specific gender issues and fall short of being theoretical re-examinations in the light of the dominant gender and development debate. Therefore, readers should examine the work with a critical eye to assess how successful we have been in achieving the objectives mentioned at the beginning of this chapter. Nevertheless, in a situation where there is such a paucity of literature in English on Japanese experiences of gender and development, we hope that our humble efforts will contribute to creating an increase in interest on this particular theme. We also expect that this type of research will be further pursued as joint efforts between people in developing countries and in Japan and other developed countries, creating opportunities for us to learn from our mutual experiences.[6]

Notes

1   The term 'developing countries' in this chapter is not based on a rigid definition; rather, it is used as functional term to imply countries and regions covered by the research activities of IDE-JETRO. The coverage of IDE extends over Asia, the Middle East, Africa, Latin America, Oceania and Eastern Europe.
2   The initiative focuses support for the three sectors of education, health and economic and social participation as a means of achieving the empowerment of women and gender equality in development assistance.
3   The report of the second research group on gender/WID made a critical review of gender mainstreaming in Japan after about ten years. It states at the policy level, WID/GAD, has not been given priority. In the ODA Charter of 1992, reference to WID/GAD was not in the sections such as 'Basic Philosophy', 'Principles' and 'Priority', but was inserted as the twelfth list of 'Measures for the Effective Implementation of Official Development Assistance'. There was some improvement in the revised Charter approved in 2003. The importance of the gender equality perspective was mentioned in relation to the assurance of fairness, which

was listed as one of the 'Basic Policies' comprising 'Philosophy'. However, it is not elaborated further in the following sections such as 'Priority Issues', 'Principle of ODA Implementation', and 'Formulation and Implementation of ODA Policy', thus lessening the visibility of the issue as a concrete task to be dealt with (JICA, 2003a).

4 NWEC was established in 1977 as a training-cum-research institution with the objective of the formation of a gender equal society.
5 Epistemology is the theory of knowledge. According to Fonow and Cook (1991) it means 'the study of assumptions about how to know the social and apprehend its meaning'.
6 Through literature surveys, I find studies of Japan (or comparative studies including Japan and other countries) conducted by foreign scholars extremely interesting – to learn their perspectives and identify their areas of interest (see, for example, Balatchandirane, 2004).

References

Balatchandirane, G. (2004) 'Gender Discrimination in Education and Economic Development: Lessons from East Asia', in Sushila Narsimhan and Balatchandirane G. (eds), *India and East Asia: Learning from Each Other* (New Delhi: Department of East Asian Studies, University of Delhi and Manak Publications).
Bourdieu, Pierre (1990) *The Logic of Practice* (Cambridge: Polity Press) (original French text, *Le Sens Practique*, published 1980).
Chung, Chin-Sung (1996) 'Kankoku ni okeru shakai seisaku no jenda baiasu to joseigaku, josei undo' (Gender bias in social policies and women's studies, women's movement in Korea), in Hiroko Hara, Mizue Maeda and Mari Osawa (eds), *Ajia Taiheiyo chiiki no josei seisaku to joseigaku* (Women and gender in Asia-Pacific: policy development and women's studies in eight countries) (Tokyo: Shinyosha) (in Japanese).
Friedan, Betty (1963) *The Feminine Mystique* (New York: W. W. Norton & Company).
Fonow, Mary Margaret and Judith A. Cook (eds) (1991) *Beyond Methodology: Feminist Scholarship as Lived Research* (Bloomington, Ind.: Indiana University Press).
Giddens, Anthony (1984) *The Constitution of Society: Outline of the Theory of Structuration* (Cambridge: Polity Press).
Hara, Hiroko, Mizue Maeda and Mari Osawa (eds) (1996). *Ajia taiheiyo chiiki no josei seisaku to joseigaku* (Women and gender in Asia-Pacific: policy development and women's studies in eight countries) (Tokyo: Shinyosha) (in Japanese).
Harding, Sandra (1987) 'Introduction: Is There a Feminist Method?', in Sandra Harding (ed.), *Feminism and Methodology: Social Science Issues* (Bloomington, Ind.: Indiana University Press).
Ito, Ruri and Yoko Fujikake (2003) 'Kaisetsu: "Jenda to Kaihatsu" ni kansuru nihongo bunken deta besu' (Notes on the database of Japanese literature on 'Gender and Development'), in Research Group on Globalization and Gender Norms *'Jenda to kaihatsu' ni kansuru nihongo bunken deta besu* (Database of Japanese literature on 'gender and development') (Tokyo: Ochanomizu University) (in Japanese).
Iwao, Sumiko and Hiroko Hara (1979) *Josei gaku koto hajime* (The birth of women's studies) (Tokyo: Kodansha) (in Japanese).
Jayaratne, Toby Epstein and Abigail J Stewart (1991) 'Quantitative and Qualitative Methods in the Social Sciences: Current Feminist Issues and Practical Strategies', in May Margaret Fobow and Judith A. Cook (eds), *Beyond Methodology: Feminist Scholarship as Lived Research* (Bloomington, Ind.: Indiana University Press).

JICA (Japan International Cooperation Agency) (2003a) *ODA no jenda shuryuka o mezashite* (Targeting gender mainstreaming in ODA) Report of the Second Sector-wise Research Group on Gender/WID (Tokyo: JICA) (in Japanese).

JICA (2003b) *Chiiki okoshi no keiken o sekai e: tojokoku ni tekiyo kano na chiiki katsudo* (Sharing the experiences of regional development with the world: Regional development activities applicable to developing countries) (Tokyo: JICA) (in Japanese).

JICA (2003c) *Nihon no kyoiku keiken: tojokoku no kyoiku kaihatsu o kangaeru* (Japan's educational experiences: thinking educational development in developing countries) (Tokyo: JICA) (in Japanese).

JICA (2003d) *Second Study on International Co-operation for Population and Development: New Insights from the Japanese Experience* (Tokyo: JICA).

Josei-gaku kenkyukai (The Women's Studies Society of Japan) (ed.) (1981) *Josei gaku o tsukuru* (The making of women's studies) (Tokyo: Keiso Shobo) (in Japanese).

Kabeer, Naila (1994) *Reversed Realities: Gender Hierarchies in Development Thought* (London/New York: Verso).

Miyake, Yoshiko (2001) 'Nihon no shakai kagagu to jenda' (Social sciences in Japan and gender: an analysis of the discourse on Joko aishi [The pitiful history of female factory workers]), in Yoshiko Miyake (ed.), *Nihon shakai to jenda* (Japanese society and gender) (Tokyo: Akashi Shoten) (in Japanese).

Sato, Hiroshi (eds.) (2003) 'Tokushu: hinkon sakugen to nihon no keiken' (Special issue on poverty reduction and Japanese experiences), *Ajiken warudo torendo* (Ajiken world trend), vol. 9, no. 12, Institute of Developing Economies (in Japanese).

Sechiyama, Kaku (1995) 'Jenda kenkyu no genjo to kadai' (Current situation and challenges of gender studies), in Shun Inoue, Chizuko Ueno, Masachi Osawa, Manesuke Mita and Shunya Yoshimi (eds), *Jenda no shakai gaku* (Sociology of gender) (Tokyo: Iwanami Shoten) (in Japanese).

Tinker, Irene (1990) 'The Making of a Field: Advocates, Practitioners, and Scholars', in Irene Tinker (ed.) *Persistent Inequalities: Women and World Development* (New York/Oxford: Oxford University Press).

UNDP (1995) *Human Development Report* (New York: UNDP)

UNDP (2003) *Human Development Report* (New York: UNDP)

Wolf, Diane L. (1996) 'Situating Feminist Dilemmas in Fieldwork', in Diane L Wolf (ed.), *Feminist Dilemmas in Fieldwork* (Boulder, Col.: Westview Press).

Young, Kate (1993) *Planning Development with Women: Making a World of Difference* (London: Macmillan).

Part I
Reviewing Japanese Experiences

1

Economic Development and Gender Disparities: The Japanese Experience

Hiroki Nogami

Introduction

This chapter examines the relationships between gender disparities and economic development, and attempts to identify links between economic development and women's well-being in Japan's experience of industrialization.

Recent studies regarding the development of gender disparities in economic development reveal several factors relating to women's well-being. As Boserup (1990, 1995) points out, gender disparities in labour markets have been influenced by the pace of technological progress, the division of labour in factories, and social attitudes about female labour participation. According to Boserup (1990 [1987] p. 180), in many developing countries, economic and social developments are causing changes in female labour force participation and birth rates which resemble those of earlier periods in industrialized countries, but in other developing countries these changes are not occurring, either because of the negligibility of economic change or because of the strength of male resistance to changes in the traditional status of women.

Labour-intensive technical changes require the mobilization of female labour, and this factor may increase burdens on women and lead to the deterioration of women's health. On the other hand, some women cannot take advantage of new employment opportunities because of handicaps or institutional barriers to participation in the labour market. The significance of gender disparities is influenced not only by stagnant or uneven economic development, but also by the resistance of traditional society to change. These factors suggest that there seems to be no automatic linkage between economic development and the well-being of women, and this means that a development indicator which includes social as well as economic aspects of human well-being is needed.[1]

The United Nations Development Programme (UNDP) publishes an annual *Human Development Report*, in which various methods of assessing human well-being in the developing world are proposed. The Human Development Index (HDI) is proposed to assess the achievement of a basic capability for human development. The 1995 issue of the *Human Development Report* proposes two indicators for the assessment of the realization of gender equality, the Gender Development Index (GDI), an index which reflects welfare loss caused by gender disparities, and the Gender Empowerment Measure (GEM), an index that measures women's opportunities for political and social activities.

However, the indicators proposed by the UNDP have several shortcomings. In a review of the 1991 issue of the *Human Development Report*, David Morris argues that the HDI does not allow for the creation of a meaningful time series, and this, he argues, is its most serious shortcoming (Morris, 1993, p. 868). The same argument holds for the GDI and GEM. In order to overcome these shortcomings, this chapter attempts to compute historical series of the GDI for pre-war Japan and reviews characteristics of economic development and women's well-being in the early phase of Japan's industrialization.

In the second section the literature regarding human development, gender disparities and economic development that is relevant for prewar Japan is reviewed. In the third section the statistical procedures used in the compilation of GDI for pre-war Japan are explained and their implications examined. In the final section, the main findings are summarized and issues for further study are proposed.

Survey of the literature

Assessment of the UNDP *Human Development Report*

Since the 1990s, various authors have studied the relationship between human development and economic growth. There are also a few examples of analyses of the Japanese historical experience from the human development perspective. For example, the 1995 issue of the *Human Development Report* (box 2.7: 'Addressing legal inequalities in a post-industrial society – Japan') argues that Japan's postwar constitution clearly stipulates equality under the law, and prohibits discrimination based on sex, but policy measures to overcome discriminatory practices have gained momentum only since the 1970s (UNDP, 1995, p. 44).

The 1996 issue of the *Human Development Report* (p. 53, esp. box 2.3), reviews the relevance of Japanese economic expansion for human development in developing countries today. The UNDP assessment lauds the achievement of universal primary education in the early period of prewar economic development, postwar democratic reforms, the holding down of defence expenditure and the expansion of social expenditure, industrial policies that stimulated employment, and the role of small and medium-sized firms. The Japanese experience is an example of a 'virtuous cycle', in

Table 1.1 Gender-related Development Index for Japan and other countries

1 Japan and other developed countries

	Japan	U.K.	USA	Norway
HDI (2001)	0.932 (9)	0.930 (13)	0.937 (7)	0.944 (1)
GDI	0.926 (13)	0.928 (11)	0.935 (5)	0.941 (1)
GEM	0.515 (44)	0.675 (17)	0.760 (10)	0.837 (2)

2 Japan and other Asian countries

	Japan	India	China	Republic of Korea	Thailand	Indonesia	The Philippines
HDI (2001)	0.932(9)	0.590(127)	0.721(104)	0.879(30)	0.768(74)	0.682(112)	0.751(85)
GDI	0.926(13)	0.574(103)	0.718(83)	0.873(30)	0.766(61)	0.677 (91)	0.748(66)
GEM	0.515(44)	–	–	0.363(63)	0.457(55)	–	0.539(35)

Notes: Figures in parentheses are the country's ranking. HDI rank is out of a total of 175 countries. GDI rank is out of a total of 144 countries, and the figures are based on data for 2000–01. GEM rank is out of a total of 70 countries. The GEM figures are based on data from the 1990s to 2003.

Source: UNDP (2003), pp. 237–40, 310–17.

which progress in human development has both been stimulated by economic growth and has contributed to it. However the UNDP argues that Japan's record is not perfect, and that challenges lie ahead (slowdown in growth, unemployment, increasing income disparities, and environmental degradation, to name a few). Furthermore, the report argues that Japan lags behind in gender equality, and that women's participation in decision-making outside the home remains low (1996, p. 53).

Table 1.1 shows the HDI, the GDI and the GEM values for Japan and other countries. GEM, which is regarded as an indicator of women's level of political participation, reveals a relatively low level of achievement, a fact that supports the description in Box 2.7 of UNDP (1995), and UNDP (1996).

Development and gender disparities in late industrialization

Traditional development economics often utilizes the concept of 'late industrialization' in analyses of economic development under globalization. The development pattern in late industrialization tends to be uneven and telescoped; in other words, the country's modern sector absorbs advanced technologies while the other sectors utilize traditional technologies. This uneven pattern of technological development widens the gap between the modern sector that enjoys the benefits of technology absorption and the other, traditional, sectors (for example, small and medium-sized firms and agriculture), which absorb a portion of the female labour force.

According to Maddison's estimates (1995), in the period from 1900 to 1910, Japanese real GDP per capita was about US$ 1,200 (see Table 1.2). These historical series are expressed in 1990 Geary–Khamis dollars (a way of estimating purchasing power parity index for international comparison).[2] This level was almost the same as the values for Asian countries such as South Korea, Taiwan and Thailand in the 1950s and 1960s. Thus it can be said that the historical experience of prewar Japan is relevant to understanding the early phase of development in developing countries at the start of the twenty-first-century.

According to Nakamura (1995, p. 177), before the Second World War, traditional industries carried the burden of the production and distribution of non-agricultural consumer goods, and handled exports, absorbing a portion of the population second only in size to agriculture. However as Tanimoto (1998, pp. 12–13 (see Notes 17 and 18 to the Introduction in Tanimoto's text) points out, the literature on Japanese female labour tends to focus on employed workers, such as workers in spinning mills, and other important aspects of female labour such as the non-agricultural economic activity of peasant families and small craft industries have not been studied sufficiently. Tanimoto (1998, pp. 12–13) also points out that female labour in agriculture, which absorbed a large proportion of the total female labour force, has not been studied systematically.

27

Table 1.2 Real GDP per capita (in 1990 Geary–Khamis dollars)

1 Japan and other developed countries

Year	Japan	UK	USA	Norway
1890	974	4099	3396	1617
1900	1135	4593	4096	1762
1910	1254	4715	4970	2052
1920	1631	4651	5559	2529
1930	1780	5195	6220	3377
1940	2765	6546	7018	3718

Source: The figures are from pp.297–9 and pp. 306–7 of the Japanese edition of Maddison (1995).

2 Japan and other Asian countries

Year	Japan	India	China	Republic of Korea	Taiwan	Thailand	Indonesia	The Philippines
1890	974	608	615				663	
1900	1135	625	652	850	759	812	745	1033
1910	1254	688	–		958		844	
1920	1631	629	–	1167	921		973	
1930	1780	654	786	1173	1112		1198	
1950	1873	597	614	876	922	848	874	1293
1960	3879	735	878	1302	1399	1029	1131	1488
1970	9448	878	1092	2208	2692	1596	1239	1766

Source: Maddison (1995), pp. 194–205. [Japanese translation by Hisao Kanamori [translation supervisor] and Institute of Political Economy, Toyo Keizai Shinposha, 2000). The figures are from pp. 297–9 and 306–7 of the Japanese edition of Maddison (1995).

If we can assume that the absorption and diffusion of modern technology are the most important driving forces of late industrialization, linkages
between human development and economic growth depend on the extent
of linkages between modern technology and improvements in the standard
of living in traditional and agricultural sectors. Ohkawa and Rosovsky
(1973, pp. 213–15) and Nishinarita (1985, pp. 7–8) identify the uneven and
telescoped pattern of development as one of the characteristics of Japanese
economic development. According to Nishinarita (1985, pp. 7–8), technological progress in prewar Japan provided benefits for employed labour in
modern sectors, but self-employed workers could not enjoy the benefits of
borrowed technology from abroad. Nishinarita (1985, p. 29) also points out
that in the postwar period, two factors (the abolition of the traditional
family system through democratic reforms, and labour-saving technological progress in the home because of the diffusion of consumer durables)
promoted the labour market participation of middle-aged and elderly
women.[3]

These findings suggest that improvements in various aspects of well-
being cannot be connected automatically with macroeconomic growth and
technological progress, and this is one reason why we require social indicators for various aspects of human development.

Relevance of the Japanese experience for development with gender equality

The UNDP (1996, p. 53) identifies the slow pace of improvement in gender
equality as one of the most important issues for Japan, a finding that the
historical evidence supports. For example, Table 1.3 shows the evolution of
male and female wage disparities (among factory, especially spinning-mill
workers) in the period between the two world wars. In order to reflect
gender disparities in economic opportunities in this period, we have to

Table 1.3   Average daily cash earnings of workers by sex (in yen)

	Factory workers			Spinning mill workers		
	Male (a)	Female (b)	Relative wage (b/a)	Male (a)	Female (b)	Relative wage (b/a)
1926	2.346	0.961	0.41	1.558	0.944	0.606
1930	2.551	0.913	0.358	1.584	0.845	0.533
1935	2.433	0.726	0.298	1.33	0.635	0.477
1940	2.781	1.046	0.376	1.81	0.885	0.489
1945	5.559	2.368	0.426	4.588	1.981	0.432

Source: Statistical Bureau, Management and Coordination Agency (ed.) (1988) *Historical Statistics
of Japan*, Japan Statistical Association, vol. 4, p.242.

Table 1.4   School enrolment ratios and population structure, 1873–1940

	School enrolment ratio			Population (thousands)		Population share (%)	
	Male	Female	Total	Male	Female	Male	Female
1873	39.9	15.14	34,985	17,755	17,230	50.8	49.2
1895	76.65	43.87	41,557	20,960	20,597	50.4	49.6
1900	90.35	71.73	43,847	22,051	21,796	50.3	49.7
1905	97.72	93.34	46,620	23,421	23,199	50.2	49.8
1926	99.47	99.39	60,741	30,521	30,220	50.2	49.8
1930	99.52	99.50	64,450	32,390	32,060	50.3	49.7
1935	99.59	99.59	69,254	34,734	34,520	50.2	49.8
1940	99.64	99.65	71,933	35,387	36,546	49.2	50.8

Table 1.5   Average number of years of schooling, 1890–1940

	Japan		USA	
	Male	Female	Male	Female
1890	1.9	0.6	6.7	6.3
1900	2.9	1.1	7.3	7.1
1910	4.1	2.0	7.8	7.7
1920	5.4	3.1	8.3	8.4
1930	6.8	4.4	9.0	9.1
1940	7.5	5.6	9.8	9.8

consider the wage disparities in the agriculture, transportation, and mining industries as well, but wage disparities among factory workers to some extent reflect economic gender disparities in the labour market as a whole.

Tables 1.4 to 1.7 show the achievements in education and life expectancy, respectively, of the population in prewar Japan. In these tables we can see persistent gender disparity in the achievement of well-being. For example, Hijikata (1994, pp. 9–20) examined historical statistics regarding primary school enrolment in prewar Japan from the 1890s to the 1930s. In this study she suggests that official figures tend to overestimate the rate of female school attendance, and that universal primary education for girls lagged behind that of boys. Hijikata concludes that it was only in the 1930s that universal primary education for girls was achieved in Japan (in other words, thirty years later than for boys). Utilizing a case study of Higashi-Matsuyama City (Saitama Prefecture), Hijikata (1994, pp. 14–18) argues that many girls enroled in primary school failed to graduate, and that their dropping out of school was a result of the migration of the labour force caused by industrialization. This suggests that, in order to evaluate the level

Table 1.6   Relative Japanese achievement of years of schooling to the United States

	Male	Female	Gender-disparity adjusted schooling years
1890	28.36	9.52	
1900	39.73	15.49	0.223
1910	52.56	25.97	
1920	65.06	36.90	
1930	75.56	48.35	0.590
1940	76.53	57.14	0.653

Sources: Average number of years of schooling is based on the statistics of Godo and Hayami (2002: p. 965) Table 1 which defines 'Average Schooling' as the average number of years of schooling per person in the working-age population (16–64 years old). Figures regarding Population are based on Statistical Bureau, Management and Coordination Agency (ed.) (1988). *Historical Statistics of Japan,* Japan Statistical Association, vol. 1, pp. 48–9. School enrollment ratios are based on Statistical Bureau, Management and Coordination Agency (ed.) (1988). *Historical Statistics of Japan,* Japan Statistical Association. vol. 5, pp. 212–31. Note: Japanese achievement relative to the USA is the percentage of Japanese achievement relative to US achievement. The calculation is as follows: (Years of schooling of Japanese male (or female) population/Years of schooling of US male (female) population) × 100.

Table 1.7   Life expectancy by sex and age, 1891–1947

	Life expectancy at birth		Life expectancy at age 5	
Year	Male	Female	Male	Female
1891–98	42.80	44.30	50.70	51.50
1899–1903	43.97	44.85	51.90	51.97
1909–13	44.25	44.73	52.57	52.16
1921–25	42.06	43.20	50.35	50.71
1926–30	44.82	46.54	51.85	53.00
1935–36	46.92	49.63	52.22	54.40
1947	50.06	53.96	53.61	57.45

Source: Figures in this table are based on the Statistics Bureau, Management and Coordination Agency (editorial supervision), 1987, *Historical Statistics of Japan,* vol. 1, Japan Statistical Association, pp. 270–1.

of educational attainment of a population properly, we should not rely solely on school enrolment ratios. Reflecting these considerations, Table 1.5 shows the average number of years of schooling estimated by Godo and Hayami (2002, p. 965). The Godo and Hayami figures refer to average number of years of schooling of the labour force – that is, the population between 16 to 64 years of age.

Table 1.7 shows the life expectancy of the male and female populations, and one interesting finding is that, in the 1920s, while GDP per capita reveals improvement, there is a deterioration in life expectancy for both the male and female populations.

GDI for pre-war Japan

Procedures for the computation of the GDI

In this chapter, GDI is utilized as a method of evaluation of the contribution of economic development to women's well-being in the Japanese historical experience. In order to overcome the shortcomings identified by Morris (1993), we attempt to compile time series of the GDI for prewar Japan. In computing the GDI, this chapter partly reflects revisions proposed by Bardhan and Klasen (1999). Most of the data are based on Statistical Bureau figures (1988).

Bardhan and Klasen criticized the procedure for the computation of the GDI proposed by the UNDP (1995) for its inclusion of non-agricultural wage disparities. According to them, this variable cannot reflect the gender disparities in overall economic opportunities in developing countries. This is because the concept of earned income excludes unremunerated work and reproductive labour, which is substantial in most parts of the developing world (Bardhan and Klasen 1999, p. 992). Furthermore, knowledge and health levels are influenced by the assets and lifestyle of the population, and wage disparities reflect gender inequality in cash income or economic flows. According to Saito (1991, p. 39), since the eighteenth century, labour-intensive innovations in Japanese agriculture induced the mobilization of the female labour force, and this factor was related to a deterioration in the health of rural women. Taking these factors into consideration, this chapter provides an alternative computation of the GDI (with and without wage disparities).

The UNDP (1995, pp. 125–35) proposes the following index of gender-related educational achievement (with the formula used by Basu and Foster 1998, pp. 1744–5. Note 16 with slight modification):

$$He = (S(F)F^{1-a} + S(M)M^{1-a})^{1/1-a} \qquad (1.1)$$

In Equation (1.1), $S(F)$ and $S(M)$ refer to the female and male shares of the population, respectively, F and M refer to the respective educational achievements of the female and male populations (such as adult literacy rates), and the parameter a reflects the social preference of inequality aversion. He is a gender-disparity-adjusted education achievement index. If we assume that the value of a is 0, the value of He equals the average value of the educational achievement of the total population. If the parameter a equals a positive value, the gender disparities tend to lower the index, and this factor reflects a social welfare loss from gender disparities. We can compute gender-related health and income-generation achievement indicators, and the GDI is an average of the education, health and income-generation achievement indicators. This procedure reflects an assumption that a 1 per cent improvement in one of the three indicators can compensate for a 1 per cent deterioration in one of the other indicators.

Table 1.8   Components of GDI for pre- war Japan

		GDI (I)	GDI (II)	GDI (III)	GDI (IV)
Education:	Enrolment	O			
Education:	Schooling years		O	O	O
Health:	Life expectancy at birth	O	O		
Income:	Gender adjusted income index			O	
Income:	(Gender adjusted Income Index) ×(Per capita Japanese GDP relative to the United States)				O

The components of GDI are summarized in Table 1.8. We cannot compile time series of education, health and income-appropriate indicators (indicators appropriate for education, health and income) for GDI because of data constraints, so have computed GDIs using two indicators. For the computation of GDI for prewar Japan, we utilize the assumption of UNDP (1995) that the inequality aversion parameter a is 2 as a benchmark. This assumption is based on the standard procedures utilized in UNDP (1995). In this chapter, taking the criticisms and suggestions of Bardhan and Klasen (1999. pp. 996–7) into consideration, we also compute the averages of health and education achievement indicators. The indexes (GDI (I) and GDI (II) in Tables 1.8 and Table 1.9) are the values computed with education and health indicators. GDI (III) is an average of the gender-disparity-adjusted income index and the schooling index. Original figures for the schooling index are converted into ratios relative to figures for the USA. In GDI (IV), the gender-disparity-adjusted income index is multiplied by the relative position of Japanese GDP per capita to that of the USA.

As health indicators, this chapter uses life expectancy at birth, and the original figures are standardized with the formula proposed by the UNDP (1995, pp. 130–3). Health achievement values are estimated by differences between the actual value and the minimum value (22.5 years for men and 27.5 years for women). And this value is standardized by taking the ratio to a maximum value of 60 years for both men and women. We also apply the same methodology with the UNDP (1995) method for educational achievements. Indicators for educational achievements are school enrolment ratios and average schooling years estimated by Godo and Hayami (2002). For averages of schooling years, original figures are converted into values relative to those for the USA, and these were summarized in Table 1.6.

Table 1.9 GDIs for pre-war Japan

Year	Gender-disparity adjusted school enrolment ratio (a)	Life expectancy index male/female	Gender-disparity adjusted life expectancy at birth index (b)	Japanese per capita GDP relative to the USA (c)	Income index (d)	Gender-disparity adjusted schooling years (e)
1895	0.559	0.34/0.28	0.3067			
1900	0.800	0.36/0.29	0.3201			0.223
1930	0.995	0.37/0.32	0.3426	0.29	0.340	0.590
1935	0.996	0.41/0.37	0.3870			
1940	0.996			0.39	0.356	0.653

	GDI(I) ((a)+(b))/2	GDI(II) ((b)+(e))/2	GDI(III) ((d)+(e))/2	GDI(IV) (((c)×(d))+(e))/2
1895	0.433			
1900	0.560	0.272		
1930	0.669	0.466	0.465	0.344
1935	0.691			
1940			0.5045	0.397

Notes: (a) is a gender disparities adjusted school enrollment ratio, and the adjustment is based on the formula proposed by UNDP (1995); (b) is a gender disparities adjusted life expectancy at age 0 index, and the adjustment is based on the formula proposed by UNDP (1995). The figures used for (c) are Japan relative GDP to United States. Gender disparity adjustment is based on UNDP (1995).
In the case of adjustment of life expectancy, the figures are value at age 0, and original figures are converted into indexes with an assumption that minimum life expectancy is 22.5 for men and 27.5 for women, and maximum value is assumed 60 for men and women (UNDP, 1995, p. 132) Japanese per capita GDP relative to the USA is based on estimates of Maddison (1995; p. 298 of Japanese translation) (see table 1–2 (1)); (e) is a gender disparity adjusted schooling years (relative to the value of United States) based on UNDP (1995)'s formula, and original figures are based on Godo and Hayami (2002, p. 965, Table 1). In case of GDI(I), the value of life expectancy in 1900 is the same as those for 1899–1903 and the value of 1930 are the same as those of 1926–1930 in the table 1.7 (The 16th Life Table by Ministry of Health). As for the Income Index (d), the figures are the same as those of Table 1.11, please see explanation of Table 1.11.

The most difficult issue is the computation of gender-disparity-adjusted income index. The UNDP (1995, pp. 130–3) derives the wage index using data related to non-agricultural wages and converts this factor into the income disparities index for the total population using labour participation ratios. However, since it is very difficult to derive representative wage values for the total female labour force, we utilize the daily wages of factory labour. The male share of wage income is computed as follows:

$$\frac{\text{male daily wage}}{\text{average wage}} \times \text{male share of labour force} \qquad (1.2)$$

In the case of UNDP (1995), these figures are deflated by the male population share and converted into male income share for the total population. This procedure is based on the assumption that the average female-to-male wage ratio in the non-agricultural sector is the same as the income share over the economy as a whole. The same procedures are applied to the female figures. Bardhan and Klasen (pp. 992–3) criticize this procedure because it assumes a great deal of intersectoral mobility, both male and female. They contend that this assumption of intersectoral mobility is hard to reconcile with the evidence of labour market rigidities of varying degrees across regions and sectors, and skill levels within the economy as a whole. Therefore, the procedure proposed by UNDP (1995) is not applied here, and the gender shares of gainfully employed population and labour income are used for the computations. For the variables in Equation (1.1), $S(F)$ is female labour share, $S(M)$ is male labour share, F is female labour income share, and M is male labour income share, and the income indices are computed according to Equation (1.1). This procedure implies that the income index reflects the magnitude of gender inequality in labour income for the gainfully employed population.

Using these figures, indices of gender-adjusted wage income are derived for prewar Japan. Tables 1.10 and 1.11 shows statistics for these wage indicators. This gender-disparity-adjusted income index is based on the income shares of the gainfully employed male and female populations and cannot reflect the impact of absolute improvement of income on the well-being of the population. For example, in an unequal phase of economic development, female wages may improve while the share of females in the labour force may decline. In this case, we have to evaluate the welfare significance of absolute wage improvement (in other words, economic development)

Table 1.10   Gainfully employed population 15 years and over by labour force status and sex, 1920–50

Year	*Gainfully employed workers*				
	Total	*Male*	*Female*	*Male share %*	*Female share %*
1920	25 866 195	16 349 914	9 516 281	0.63	0.37
1930	28 547 947	18 547 510	10 000 437	0.65	0.35
1940	32 661 308	20 450 340	12 210 968	0.63	0.37

Table 1.11   Average daily cash earnings of workers by sex (in yen)

Year	Average daily cash earnings of workers (in yen)		Average wages of total labour force	Relative wage to average wage		Wage share of labour force		income index
	Male	Female		Male	Female	Male	Female	
1930	2.551	0.913	1.98	1.29	0.46	0.84	0.16	0.340
1940	2.781	1.046	2.13	1.30	0.49	0.82	0.18	0.356

Notes: Gainful workers (*Yugyosha* in Japanese), a person with ordinary work or occupation was a concept utilized in population censuses in 1920, 1930 and 1940, and this concept is approximate to employed person (*Shugyosha* in Japanese). This explanation is based on the Statistics Bureau, Management and Coordination Agency (editorial supervision), 1987, *Historical Statistics of Japan*, vol. 1, Japan Statistical Association, pp. 352–3.

Source: Figures for gainfully employed population are from the Statistics Bureau, Management and Coordination Agency (editorial supervision), 1987, *Historical Statistics of Japan* vol. 1. Japan Statistical Association, pp. 366–7. Figures for wages are Statistical Bureau, Management and Coordination Agency (ed.) (1988), *Historical Statistics of Japan*, Japan Statistical Association, vol. 4, pp. 242.

and increases in gender disparity. Taking this into consideration, we compute GDP per capita in Japan relative to that in the USA (Japanese GDP per capita/US GDP per capita), and this GDP ratio is multiplied by the gender-disparity-adjusted income index. This procedure can at least consider the welfare significance of economic development and gender disparity at the same time, and GDI (IV) is the result of the computation.

Results and their implications

Table 1.9 shows preliminary GDI estimates for prewar Japan. The values are computed for the period from the beginning of the 1900s to the 1940s. The gender-adjusted health index shows the lowest achievement, and this fact reflects poor improvements in female labour, health conditions and nutrition. GDI (II) in Table 1.9, which is the average of gender-disparity-adjusted life expectancy and schooling years, reveals the lowest achievement of the various estimates of GDI.

In order to utilize the GDI for the assessment of performance of Japanese historical economic development in achieving women's well-being, it is useful to estimate the factor contribution to total GDI growth. We utilize the GDI (I) as a basis for such calculation, because it covers the longest periods, from 1895 to 1935. Table 1.12 shows the factor components of improvements in the GDI (GDI (I)) for prewar Japan. In the GDI (I) from 1895 to 1930 there were rapid increases in gender-disparity-adjusted school enrolment ratios, and this factor was responsible for the improvement in GDI (I). In general, statistics regarding education reveal rapid increases, and

Table 1.12   Levels and average annual growth rates of GDIs for pre-war Japan

1 Levels

	(1) Gender-disparity-adjusted school enrolment ratio	(2) Gender-disparity-adjusted expectancy index	(3) GDI (I) = (1) + (2)/2
1895	0.559	0.3067	0.433
1900	0.800	0.3201	0.560
1930	0.995	0.3426	0.669
1935	0.996	0.387	0.691

2 Average annual growth rates

	(4) Gender-disparity-adjusted school enrolment ratio (Growth Rate)	Gender-disparity-adjusted life expectancy index (Growth Rate) (5)	GDI (I) (Growth Rate, %) (6)
1895–1900	0.074	0.009	0.053
1900–30	0.007	0.002	0.006
1930–35	0.000	0.025	0.007

Source: (1), (2) and (3) are the results presented in Table 1.9.

this may be because school enrolment tends to be influenced by formal institutional change. Life expectancy indicators tend to reveal continuous improvement, and this may be because health indicators tend to be influenced by the long-term changes brought about by economic and social development. After 1930, continuous improvement in the life expectancy index is the main factor contributing to the improvement in GDI (I).

Summary and conclusion

Gaps between achievements in average human development and gender equalities are indicators reflecting basic social structures in rapidly and unevenly industrializing countries. This may be one of the reasons why composite well-being indicators, including GDI and GEM, are effective tools for the assessment of development patterns. Taking this into consideration, we examine improvements in women's well-being in prewar Japan. The analysis is based on GDI, a standard technique for the assessment of gender-related aspects of contemporary developing countries. Using the GDI, we attempted to identify the relevance of the prewar Japanese experience for contemporary developing counties. The pace and magnitude of achievement of gender equality in historical Japanese development can be evaluated quantitatively by the compilation of time series GDI.

The analysis shows that the achievement value in education, especially that of school enrolment, showed a relatively higher performance than other indicators. However, achievement in terms of schooling years for females tends to lag behind that for males, and this suggests a gap between the diffusion of the modern school system and the actual living conditions of the people, including social attitudes towards school enrolment of girls. These attitudes tend to reduce the successful completion of primary school attendance by girls. Improvement in life expectancy tends to lag behind other well-being indicators, and this suggests that an improvement in health conditions requires improvements in resource allocation for women in the home, and improvements in labour conditions (especially in the agricultural sector), and public health provision.

Hayami (1995, pp. 156–7, and 1997, pp. 142–3) suggest that, in the early phase of economic development, developing countries are likely to suffer from a scarcity of human capital, and this factor tends to promote labour-saving technological progress dependent on borrowed technology and specialization in standardized products. If the social benefits of investment in women's human capital are underestimated, families tend to neglect investment in girls' human capital and this factor promotes gender inequality in long-term economic development. In the Japanese case, gender gaps in education and health continued throughout the prewar period, and the postwar democratic reforms were necessary to enable women to share in the benefits of economic development. In order to overcome this unequal phase of development, the development policy authority must take care to ensure a favourable environment for investment in women's human capital. The development policy authority must also address the issue of improving labour and health conditions in rural areas, which absorb a large portion of the female population.

In this chapter we have provided a tentative GDI for the Japanese economy as a whole, but it is necessary to refine our indicators for the assessment of long-term achievements in the standard of living in Japan. In the first place, this is because there are serious regional disparities in health conditions, school enrolment and economic development. Taking this into consideration, further studies will be required for the compilation of regional GDIs for the assessment of the Japanese experience.

Second, the implications of an indicator at one stage of development can differ from its implications at another stage. For example, in an early phase of development, gains in life expectancy can be interpreted as an indicator of improvement in overall well-being. However, in advanced countries, gains in life expectancy do not provide automatic opportunities for a disability-free life. Taking this factor into consideration, indicators such as disability-adjusted life years – DALYs (World Bank, 1993, pp. 25–7) can be utilized for the assessment of long-term gains in well-being in Japan.

Third, in order to utilize GDI for evaluation of the historical performances of the Japanese economy, it is necessary to compile time series of HDI, because GDI can be, at least theoretically, interpreted as a gender-disparity-adjusted HDI. However, as Morris (1993, pp. 868–9) argues, the HDI does not allow for the creation of a meaningful time series. This is because the HDI scales are set by the worst and best performances by a country over a year, so that the HDI is really ranking countries only relationally. There is no fixed scale against which to measure performance over time because the scale for components (especially income) changes over time. In order to overcome these shortcomings, further study will be required for historical well-being indicators.

Notes

* An earlier version of this chapter was presented as a paper at the 4th Spring Study Meeting of the Japan Society for International Development (held on 14 June, 2003). The author thanks Professor Yasuo Uchida (Kobe University), Professor Kazunori Akaishi (of Towa University at the time of the meeting, now of Takushoku University), and Professor Etsuko Kita (Center for International Health & Humanitarian Studies, The Japanese Red Cross Kyushu International College of Nursing). The author also thanks three anonymous reviewers for their kind suggestions for improvements to the chapter. Of course, any errors are solely the responsibility of the author.
1 For example, Goldin's (1995, pp. 61–3) hypothesis that across the process of economic development the adult women's labour force participation rate is U-shaped.
2 For international comparison of gross domestic product (GDP) there are several options for converting national currencies into a common unit. The Geary–Khamis approach (initiated by R. S. Geary in 1958 and developed by S. H. Khamis in 1970 and after) is an ingenious method for multilaterizing the results which provides desirable properties, and is preferred by Maddison (1995) for multilateral measure. For a further explanation of the Geary–Khamis approach, see Appendix C of Maddison (1995, pp. 162–9).
3 On the interrelationships between economic, cultural and institutional factors, Boserup (1995, p. 60) concludes that a purely economic theory of the position of women in development is as misleading as one that neglects the micro- or macroeconomic factors, and she argues for the necessity of multidisciplinary co-operation.

References

In Japanese

Hayami, Yujiro (1995) *Kaihatsu keizaigaku: Shokokumin no hinkon to tomi* (Development economics: poverty and wealth of nations) (Tokyo: Sobunsha).
Hijikata, Sonoko (1994) *Kindai nihon no gakkou to chiiki shakai: Mura no kodomo wa dou ikitaka* (School and local communities in modern Japanese history: how village children lived) (Tokyo: University of Tokyo Press).

Nishinarita, Yutaka (1985) 'Joshi rodo no shoruikei to sono henyo: 1890s–1940s' (Types of female labour and their evolution: 1890s–1940s), in Masanori Nakamura (ed.), *Gijutsu kakushin to joshi rodo* (Technological innovation and female labour) (Tokyo: United Nations University and University of Tokyo Press), pp. 7–31.

Saito, Osamu (1991) 'Nogyo hatten to joshi rodo: Nihon no rekishiteki keiken (Agricultural development and female labour: Japanese historical experiences), *Keizai kenkyu* (Economic Review), vol. 42, no. 1, January, pp. 30–9.

Statistical Bureau, Management and Co-ordination Agency (ed.) (1988) *Nihon choki tokei soran* (Historical Statistics of Japan) (Tokyo: Japan Statistical Association).

Tanimoto, Masayuki (1998) *Nihon ni okeru zairaiteki keizaihatten to orimonogyo: Shijo keisei to kazoku keizai* (Traditional economic development in Japan and the textile industry: the market economy and the household economy) (Nagoya: University of Nagoya Press).

In English

Bardhan, Kaplana and Stephan Klasen (1999) 'UNDP's Gender-Related Indices: A Critical Review', *World Development*, vol. 27, no. 6, pp. 985–1010.

Basu, K. and J. E. Foster (1998) 'On Measuring Literacy', *Economic Journal*, vol. 198, no. 451, November, pp. 1733–49.

Boserup, Ester (1987) 'Inequality between the Sexes', in John Eatwell, Murray Milgate and Peter Newman (eds), *The New Palgrave: A Dictionary of Economics* (London: Macmillan and New York: Stockton Press) reprinted in Boserup (1990), pp. 175–80.

Boserup, Ester (1990) *Economic and Demographic Relationships in Development* (Baltimore: Johns Hopkins University Press).

Boserup, Ester (1995) 'Obstacles to Advancement of Women During Development', in T. P. Shultz (ed.) *Investment in Women's Human Capital* (Chicago: University of Chicago Press), pp. 51–60.

Godo, Yoshihisa and Yujiro Hayami (2002) 'Catching Up in Education in the Economic Catch-up of Japan with the United States, 1890–1990', *Economic Development and Cultural Change*, vol. 50, no. 4, July, pp. 961–78.

Goldin, Claudia (1995) 'The U-shaped Female Labor Force Function in Economic Development and Economic History', in T. P. Shultz (ed.), *Investment in Women's Human Capital* (Chicago: University of Chicago Press), pp. 61–90.

Hayami, Yujiro (1997) *Development Economics: From the Poverty to Wealth of Nations* (Oxford: Clarendon Press).

Maddison, Angus (1995) *Monitoring the World Economy 1920–1992* (Paris: OECD) (Japanese translation by Hisao Kanamori (translation supervisor) and Institute of Political Economy, Toyo Keizai Shimposha, 2000).

Morris, Morris David (1993) 'Reviews: UNDP Human Development Report 1991', *Economic Development and Cultural Change*, vol. 41, no. 4, July, pp. 865–70.

Nakamura, Takafusa (1995) *The Postwar Japanese Economy: Its Development and Structure, 1937–1994* (Tokyo: University of Tokyo Press).

Ohkawa, Kazushi and Henry Rosovsky (1973) *Japanese Economic Growth: Trend Acceleration in the Twentieth Century* (Stanford, Calif.: Stanford University Press).

UNDP (1995) *Human Development Report 1995* (New York: Oxford University Press).

UNDP (1996) *Human Development Report 1996* (New York: Oxford University Press).

UNDP (2003) *Human Development Report 2003: Millennium Development Goals: A Compact Among Nations to End Human Poverty* (New York: Oxford University Press).

World Bank (1993) *World Development Report 1993: Investing in Health* (New York: Oxford University Press).

2
Gender Perspectives in Family Planning: The Development of Family Planning in Postwar Japan and Policy Implications from the Japanese Experience

Yasuko Hayase

Introduction

Japan is now facing an ageing and declining population, a result of the demographic transition[1] that occurred in the 1960s. In prewar Japan, however, demographic interest centred mainly on overpopulation in relation to food shortages and unemployment, similar to the current status in developing countries. In the 1920s, 'neo-Malthusian' proponents of contraception – Keikichi Ishimoto, Isoo Abe and others (Fujime, 1999) – addressed such issues as the need for birth control and the promotion of emigration to foreign countries, and with birth-control advocate Margaret Sanger's visit to Japan in 1922, the birth control movement became more active. The need for birth control as a measure to ensure the health and welfare of women, and for their emancipation, came to be recognized as an important social issue during the 1920s. The movement was banned in 1935, when the government initiated policies favouring population expansion for military purposes. After the Second World War, Japan was faced with rapid population growth because of the repatriation of overseas Japanese and the resulting 'baby boom' from 1947 to 1949. This led to a fundamental pro-natalistic change in the government's attitude, from a pro-natalistic policy in the prewar period to fertility control in the postwar period (Ota, 1969; Kuroda, 1984; Muramatsu, 1984; Fujime, 1999; JICA, 2003).

During the early postwer years, people resorted to illegal and unsafe abortions and infanticide, which had been common since the late Tokugawa period (1603–1867), to limit family size because of food shortages as well as employment and housing problems. Contraceptive methods were not widely known to the people at that time. The Eugenic Protection Law, established in 1948, sanctioned induced abortions, resulted temporarily in the general use of induced abortion as the main method of birth control for married couples, increased the number of induced abortions, harmed maternal health, and caused maternal deaths. With the 'New Life Movement', which began in 1955, both the public and private sectors promoted family planning, and contraception replaced induced abortion as the primary method of birth control.

During the 15-year period from 1983 to 1998, the proportion of governments in developing countries that considered their rates of population growth to be too high increased from 47 per cent to 54 per cent, and the proportion having policies aimed at decreasing population growth increased from 33 per cent to 51 per cent (UN, 1999a; Hayase, 2004). Implementation of family planning programmes led to a substantial increase in contraceptive use in developing countries and has contributed considerably to the decline in average fertility rates. The full range of modern family planning methods, however, still remains unavailable to at least 350 million couples worldwide, many of whom say they want to space or prevent another pregnancy (UN, 1995). In developing countries in the late 1980s, it became clear, based on Demographic and Health Surveys,[2] that there was still a high level of unwanted births and mistimed childbearing as a result of unmet needs for family planning, which might be related to the low status of women and ineffective government efforts to lower population growth.

Gender issues have become central to politics and policy-making. The need to promote gender equity and equality was given special emphasis in the Programme of Action of the International Conference on Population and Development (ICPD) in 1994, and in the Platform for Action of the Fourth World Conference on Women in 1995. Gender norms and systems vary widely across cultures, but they shape people's lives and interactions in all societies. The social roles of men and women and the differential power associated with those roles influence their sexual behaviour, marriage and childbearing patterns, and reproductive health and rights in various ways. In general, as women's education improves, gender systems become more egalitarian, and an associated trend towards later marriage, fewer children and a reduction in unwanted pregnancies can be observed, although causality may run in both directions (UN, 2001, pp. 8, 20).

With the above as background, this chapter aims to review the development of family planning in postwar Japan, and to consider what implications or suggestions for developing countries can be drawn from Japan's experience. The structure of this chapter is as follows: in the second section, government views and policies on current fertility in developing countries are introduced, and the current status of family planning and its relationship to the status of women is analysed. The third section reviews the development of family planning policies after the Second World War in Japan and the implementation of the 'New Life Movement' programmes in industrial companies. The fourth section evaluates fertility and contraceptive methods in Japan as an outcome of the family planning programmes, and the fifth section summarizes the chapter and suggests some implications for developing countries from the Japanese experience in family planning.

Population policies, family planning and gender relations in developing countries

Government views and policies on population growth in developing countries

The world population in 2003 reached 6.3 billion and is growing at a rate of 1.2 per cent annually, according to the United Nations' world population prospects as at 2002. The population growth rate has slowed from 1.94 per cent in 1970–75 to 1.35 per cent in 1995–2000. Considerable differences in growth rates exist between the more developed and less developed regions, the growth rates in the more developed regions were 0.78 per cent in 1970–5 and 0.34 per cent in 1995–2000, while those for the less developed regions were 2.36 per cent and 1.61 per cent, respectively. The difference in growth rates between the two types of region is related to the difference in their current levels of fertility.

Since 1974, the United Nations has been monitoring government views and policies periodically concerning levels of population growth, fertility, mortality, spatial distribution, international migration and so on, in most countries in the world. Continued high rates of population growth remain an issue of policy concern for many developing countries. According to these periodical world population monitoring reports, the proportion of governments in developing countries that consider their rates of population growth to be satisfactory decreased from 44 per cent in 1974 to 34 per cent in 1998. In contrast, the proportion of governments in developing countries that consider their rates of population growth to be too high increased from 37 per cent in 1974 to 52 per cent in 1998. In parallel with this, the proportion of governments perceiving their growth rate to be too low declined from 25 per cent in 1974 to 14 per cent in 1998 (UN, 1999a; Hayase, 2004).

Regarding government policies in developing countries, the proportion of governments that have policies aimed at influencing population growth increased from 58 per cent of 129 countries in 1983 to 65 per cent of 135 countries in 1998. In contrast, the proportion of governments with policies of non-intervention in population growth rate decreased from 42 per cent to 35 per cent between 1983 and 1998. The proportion of governments that have policies intervening to decrease their rate rose from 33 per cent to 51 per cent between 1983 and 1998. In parallel with this, the proportion of governments with policies intervening to raise growth rates decreased from 16 per cent to 7 per cent, and those for maintaining the rate also decreased from 9 per cent to 7 per cent, between 1983 and 1998. It was found that a large proportion of the developing countries considered their

Table 2.1   Government views and policies on fertility rates in Asian countries, 2000

Government views policies/TFR	Too high		Satisfactory				Too low	
	Lower	No	Raise	Maintain	Lower	No	Raise	No
Under 2.0	Thailand		Armenia		China	Rep. of Korea	Singapore Georgia	Japan
2.0–2.4	Sri Lanka	Myanmar		Dem. People's Rep. of Korea			Cyprus	
2.5–2.9	Iran Indonesia Vietnam Turkey			Mongolia Kuwait	Bahrain	Brunei Lebanon	Israel	
3.0–3.4	Bangladesh India Malaysia Philippines					United Arab Emirates		
3.5–3.9				Qatar				
4.0–4.4	Nepal							
4.5–4.9	Cambodia Jordan					Syria		
5.0–5.4	Maldives Pakistan						Iraq	
5.5–5.9				Laos Oman Saudi Arabia			Bhutan	
Over 6.0	Yemen	Afghanistan						

Notes: TFR: total fertility rate, 1995–2000; Lower: intervene to lower; No: no intervention; Raise: intervene to raise; Maintain: intervene to maintain.
Source: United Nations (2001).

rate of population growth to be too high and intervened to lower growth rates.

   Next, we observe the case of Asian countries, to examine the relationship between government views and policies to their current fertility rates (see Table 2.1). Out of 41 Asian countries, 19 (46 per cent) perceived their fertility rates to be too high, while 16 (39 per cent) perceived them to be satisfactory, and the remaining 6 (15 per cent) considered them to be too low. Considering the level of total fertility rate (TFR, average number of children per woman) for 1995–2000, not all of the countries with high TFR of 3 and over viewed their fertility rates as being too high. Such cases are observed in the United Arab Emirates (UAE) (TFR 3.0–3.4), Laos (5.5–5.9), Saudi Arabia (5.5–5.9) and so on. Saudi Arabia views its fertility rate as satisfactory and has a policy to intervene to maintain the current rate. The current situation of labour shortage and high proportion of foreign workers (25 per cent of the total population in the year 2000) in Saudi Arabia influences this policy. In contrast, Thailand, which has a low fertility rate (TFR below 2.0) still views it as being as too high and has a policy in place to intervene to lower the current rate. China, which has fertility levels at below population replacement[3] level (TFR below 2.0) has views its fertility rate as being satisfactory; it maintains a policy to lower the current rate by continuing its one-child per family policy. Japan has viewed its fertility rate as being too low, but has a policy of non-intervention. Instead, it has strengthened various family policies, such as one-year parental leave, the expansion of public child care facilities and services, and increase in financial incentives for childbearing to assist in the mitigation of a declining and ageing population. From Table 2.1, it can be seen that both the views and policies of governments toward their respective fertility rates are not simply a direct consequence of the level of the fertility rate. We can also see that 31 countries have policies aimed at influencing population growth, while 9 countries have policies of non-intervention regardless of their views on the fertility rate.

The current status of family planning and gender relations in developing countries

The ability of women to control their fertility and choose the number of children they have is widely considered as a crucial factor in raising the status of women as well as improving the health of women and children along with their economic situation. Equality between men and women in access to family planning is stressed in the Programme of Action of the ICPD. Family planning is widely perceived as one of the success stories of development co-operation (Cassen, 1986), but, because of cultural factors and the way in which health-care services and family planning are organized, access to these services at present is far from assured on a basis of equality among men and women (UN, 1996a, p. 309).

Gender preferences for children are shaped by cultural traditions and community norms, and may have a significant influence on reproductive decisions (UN, 2001, p. 21). A strong preference for sons may be associated with reduced levels of contraceptive use, higher fertility (couples continue having children until they have the desired number of sons), infanticide, abortion and the distortion of sex ratio at birth. The introduction of ultrasound and portable ultrasound machines has enabled prenatal sex selection. If the sex of the unborn child is seen to be female, the pregnant woman chooses to undergo an abortion. High sex ratios in China and the Republic of Korea (110 in the year 2000 for both countries) might reflect the links between gender systems and fertility regimes under the declining fertility of the one-child policy in China or the rise of the 'opportunity cost' of the mother's time (the income a woman could earn if she were not at home caring for her children) of rearing children in Korea.

Since the 1970s, the availability of safer methods of modern contraception has been increasing, although it is still inadequate in some respects, because a big gap in availability exists across countries. In 1997 about 60 per cent of couples in developing regions use some method of family planning (see Table 2.2), and this figure represents almost a fivefold increase since the 1960s (UN, 1995, p. 32). Family planning programmes have contributed considerably to the decline in average fertility rates for developing countries, from about five or six children per woman in 1970–5 to around three or four children in 2000–5, as shown in Table 2.2. However, the full range of modern family planning methods still remains unavailable to at least 350 million couples worldwide, many of who want to space or prevent another pregnancy (UN, 1995, p. 32).

Women may seek to end a pregnancy resulting from a lack of contraceptive information and services, unsuccessful contraception and so on. Abortion is legal under some circumstances in nearly all the countries of the world: 98 per cent of countries recognize a threat to the mother's life as a legal basis for terminating a pregnancy. An estimated 25 million abortions are performed each year in countries where it is legal. Protection of women's health is a legal ground for abortion in 89 per cent of developed countries, but in only 52 per cent of developing countries (UNFPA, 1997, p. 22). In Asia, a large number of countries prohibit induced abortion even in such circumstances as protection of women's physical or mental health, rape and so on. Bangladesh, Iran, Nepal, Pakistan, Sri Lanka, Brunei, Cambodia, Indonesia, Malaysia, Myanmar, the Philippines, Kuwait, UAE, Yemen among others are in this group. In contrast, abortion is legal regardless of circumstances in China, Mongolia, Republic of Korea, Singapore, Turkey, Vietnam, among others (Hayase, 2004; UN, 1992, 1993, 2002a). It was stated in the Programme of Action of the ICPD that abortion should not be promoted as a method of family planning, but in reality it seems to

Table 2.2 Total fertility rate and world contraceptive use

Country or area	Number of married women aged 15–49 in 2000 (thousands)	Year	Contraceptive prevalence rate (%)									Need for family planning, percentage of women with unmet need	Total fertility rate	
			Any method	Modern method	Traditional method	Sterilization Female	Sterilization Male	Pill	Injectables	IUD	Condom		1970–5	2000–5
World	1,047,499	1997	61.9	55.6	6.3	20.1	4.1	7.8	2.6	14.9	5.1	–	4.48	2.69
More Developed Regions	170,277	1994	70.4	59.2	11.2	10.4	7.2	17.3	0.1	7.6	15.0	–	2.13	1.56
Less Developed Regions	877,223	1997	60.2	54.9	5.3	22.0	3.6	5.9	3.1	16.3	3.1	–	5.42	2.92
Africa	116,618	1997	25.2	19.8	5.4	2.2	0.1	7.1	4.2	4.9	1.1	–	6.71	4.91
Latin America and The Caribbean	83,665	1996	68.8	59.9	8.9	29.5	1.6	13.8	3.0	7.4	4.2	–	5.03	2.53
Asia	691,671	1997	65.6	60.6	5.0	24.1	4.3	4.7	2.9	19.0	4.7	–	5.06	2.55
Eastern Asia	292,664	1997	81.8	80.4	1.4	30.8	7.3	1.7	0.0	33.5	6.5	–	4.46	1.78
China	263,174	1997	83.8	83.3	0.5	33.5	7.7	1.7	0.0	36.4	3.4	–	4.86	1.83
China, Hong Kong	1,110	1992	86.2	79.7	6.5	18.9	0.9	17.1	1.7	5.1	34.5	–	2.89	1.00
Dem, People's Rep. of Korea	3,504	1990/92	61.8	53.0	8.8	4.1	0.3	0.1	0.0	48.5	0.0	–	3.87	2.02
Japan	15,946	1994	58.6	52.8	5.8	3.4	0.7	0.4	0.0	2.2	45.5	–	2.07	1.32
Mongolia	434	1998	59.9	45.7	14.2	2.4	–	4.2	3.1	32.2	3.5	–	7.33	2.42
Rep. of Korea	8,404	1997	80.5	66.9	13.6	24.1	12.7	1.8	–	13.2	15.1	–	4.28	1.41

Table 2.2 Total fertility rate and world contraceptive use   continued

Country or area	Number of married women aged 15–49 in 2000 (thousands)	Year	Contraceptive prevalence rate (%)									Need for family planning, percentage of women with unmet need	Total fertility rate	
			Any method	Modern method	Traditional method	Sterilization		Pill	Injectables	IUD	Condom		1970–5	2000–5
						Female	Male							
South-Central Asia	278,228	1998	48.0	40.9	7.1	23.3	1.6	5.3	3.5	3.7	3.2	–	5.59	3.25
Bangladesh	25,966	1999/00	53.8	43.4	10.4	6.7	0.5	23.0	7.2	1.2	4.3	15.3	6.15	3.46
India	198,151	1998/99	48.2	42.8	5.4	34.2	1.9	2.1	0.0	1.6	3.1	15.8	5.43	3.01
Iran	10,853	1997	72.9	56.0	16.9	15.5	1.9	20.9	–	8.3	5.4	–	6.40	2.33
Nepal	4,297	1996	28.5	26.0	2.5	12.1	5.4	1.4	4.9	0.3	1.9	31.4	5.79	4.26
Pakistan	21,631	1996/97	23.9	16.9	7.0	6.0	–	1.6	1.4	3.4	4.2	32.0	6.28	5.08
Sri Lanka	2,939	1993	66.1	43.6	22.5	23.5	3.7	5.5	4.6	3.0	3.3	–	4.08	2.01
South-Eastern Asia	90,730	1997	57.9	49.6	8.3	7.7	0.8	13.0	13.0	10.4	2.0	–	5.53	2.55
Cambodia	2,250	2000	23.8	18.5	5.3	1.5	0.2	7.2	7.4	1.3	0.9	–	5.54	4.77
Indonesia	40,181	1997	57.4	54.7	2.7	3.0	0.4	15.4	21.1	8.1	0.7	9.2	5.20	2.35
Laos	814	1993	18.6	15.0	3.6	5.1	0.0	6.4	2.2	1.2	0.1	–	6.15	4.78
Malaysia	3,482	1994	54.5	29.8	24.7	6.4		13.4	–	3.9	5.3	–	5.15	2.90
Myanmar	7,332	1997	32.7	28.4	4.3	5.5	2.2	7.4	11.7	1.3	0.1	–	5.75	2.86
Philippines	11,292	1998	46.0	28.2	17.8	10.3	0.1	9.9	2.4	3.7	1.6	19.8	6.00	3.18
Singapore	695	1982	74.2	73.0	1.2	22.3	0.6	11.6	–	–	24.3	–	2.62	1.36
Thailand	11,400	1996/97	72.2	69.8	2.4	22.0	2.0	23.1	16.4	3.2	1.8	–	4.97	1.93
Vietnam	13,140	1997	75.3	55.8	19.5	6.3	0.5	4.3	0.2	38.5	5.9	6.9	6.70	2.30

48

Table 2.2 Total fertility rate and world contraceptive use   *continued*

Country or area	Number of married women aged 15–49 in 2000 (thousands)	Year	Contraceptive prevalence rate (%)									Need for family planning, percentage of women with unmet need	Total fertility rate	
			Any method	Modern method	Traditional method	Sterilization		Pill	Injectables	IUD	Condom		1970–5	2000–5
						Female	Male							
Western Asia	30,049	1997	47.8	29.3	18.5	3.0	0.0	6.1	0.6	13.6	5.0	–	5.66	3.45
Iraq	3,306	1989	13.7	10.4	3.3	1.4	0.0	4.7	0.5	2.8	1.0	–	7.11	4.77
Jordan	612	1997	52.6	37.7	14.9	4.2	0.0	6.5	0.7	23.1	2.4	14.2	7.79	3.57
Syria	2,661	1993	36.1	28.3	7.8	2.2	0.0	9.9	0.0	15.7	0.3	–	7.50	3.32
Turkey	12,259	1998	63.9	37.7	26.2	4.2	0.0	4.4	0.5	19.8	8.2	10.1	5.15	2.43
Yemen	2,824	1997	20.8	9.8	11.0	1.4	0.1	3.8	1.2	3.0	0.3	38.6	8.40	7.01

Notes: Women with unmet needs are those who were fecund but not using contraception at the time of the survey, and yet wanted no more children or wanted the next child with a delay of two years or more. Data pertain to women in a marital or consensual union. Malaysian figures mean sterilization for both sexes.

Sources: United-Nations: www.un.org/esa/population/publications/contraceptive2001; United Nations (2001)

be used widely to control fertility, regardless of its legal basis. If better contraceptive services were given to all, abortion rates would be reduced.

Based on the Demographic and Health Surveys in developing countries in the late 1980s, it became clear that there was still a high level of unmet needs, which is defined as the percentage of women who do not desire pregnancy but who are not using contraception (JICA, 2003). The proportion of women with unmet family planning needs in selected Asian countries ranged from 39 per cent in Yemen to 7 per cent in Vietnam, as shown in Table 2.2. The contraceptive prevalence rate for any methods in countries with high unmet needs was less than 30 per cent; for example, 28.5 per cent for Nepal, 23.9 per cent for Pakistan and 20.8 per cent for Yemen, lower than the average for developing regions (60.2 per cent).

With regard to the type of contraception, the proportion of couples using modern methods in Asia accounts for 60 per cent, compared to only 5 per cent using traditional methods. There are, however, such countries as Turkey, Sri Lanka and Malaysia where the proportion of couples using traditional methods accounts for around 20 per cent. The differences in type of contraception use may be related to cultural factors and availability of the contraceptive devices or methods. The proportion of female sterilization is higher than that for male sterilization in both developed and less developed regions. The difference in proportion of sterilization between men and women is, however, much greater in less developed regions: 22.0 per cent for female sterilization, as compared to 3.6 per cent for male sterilization in less developed regions; while in developed regions it is 10.4 per cent for women and 7.2 per cent for men. Women's high sterilization rate also reflects the cultural norm that men are more valuable in the labour force than are women.

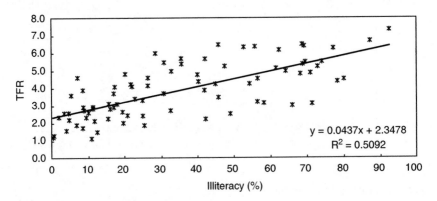

Note: Data for 82 developing countries.
Source: World Bank (2000).

Figure 2.1 Total fertility rate and women's illiteracy rate, 1998

Education is one of the most important means of empowering women with the knowledge, skills and self-confidence necessary to participate fully in the development process (UN, 1995). Figure 2.1 shows the relationship between total fertility rate and illiteracy rates for women aged 15 years old and over in 82 developing countries. Figure 2.1 shows the positive correlation between these two factors. This indicates that a country where women's status by education is low has very high fertility. In other words, a country where women's literacy is high has low fertility, which implies that these women are able to control their own fertility because of better access to family planning programmes, through improving their educational attainment and increasing their economic opportunities.

Figures 2.2 and 2.3 shows the positive correlation between TFR and The maternal mortality ratio (maternal deaths per 100,000 live births), and the positive correlation between TFR and the infant mortality rate (infants deaths per 1,000 live births) in developing countries, respectively. These correlations indicate that not only do mothers with many children have high health risks during their pregnancy and childbirth, but so do their infants. Many women resort to unsafe abortions to terminate unwanted pregnancies, and many men remain ignorant of, or indifferent to, their responsibilities towards the family and its reproductive health (UN, 1999b, pp. 1–2). In countries where abortion is against the law because of cultural or religious norms, abortions are unsafe. Such unsafe induced abortions harm maternal health and cause maternal deaths.

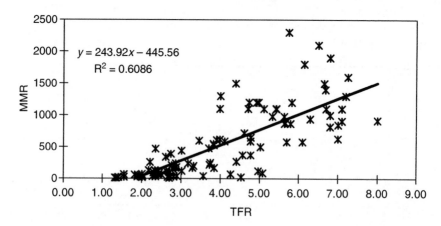

Source: United Nations (2002b).

Notes: Data for 102 developing countries. The maternal mortality ratio is maternal deaths per 100,000 live births.

Figure 2.2 Total fertilty rate and maternal mortality ratio, 2000–5

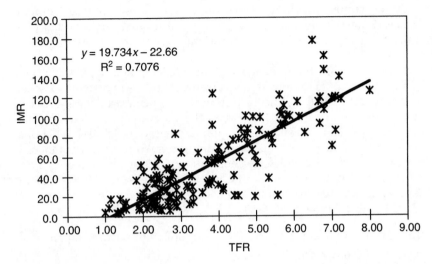

Note: Data for 150 developing countries. Infant mortality rate is infant deaths per 1,000 live births.
Source: United Nations (2002b).

Figure 2.3   Infant mortality rate and total fertility rate, 2000–5

The development of family planning policies and programmes in Japan

The dawn of family planning in Japan

In prewar Japan, demographic interest centred mainly on overpopulation in relation to food shortages and unemployment, much like the current status in developing countries. The annual rate of population growth was 1 per cent or more, combining increasing birth rates and decreasing death rates accelerated by a high economic growth rate (about 4 per cent per year in real terms) from the middle of the 1880s. The Meiji government issued a proclamation in December 1868 to prohibit abortion and infanticide, which had become widespread since the late Tokugawa period (early 1800s). The practice of limiting the number of births linked to changes in the economic situation was accepted by the people (Kuroda, 1984; Muramatsu, 1984).

It was around 1920 that family planning came to be recognized in Japan as an important social issue. The birth control movement was quite active during the 1920s, particularly with the influence of Margaret Sanger the American birth control advocate following her visit to Japan in 1922, though her activities were restricted by the Japanese government. Her ideas concerning birth control were based on women's liberation and opposed to traditional values restricting the role of women only to raising children to continue family lines (Ota, 1969; Muramatsu, 1984). Shizue Ishimoto assisted Sanger during her visit to Japan, and dedicated herself to disseminating Sanger's ideas of birth control and raising the status of women (Suzuki, 1997).

Since the 1920s, the basic ideologies supporting family planning have changed from time to time in tandem with changes in the political, social and economic situation. The birth control movement, which was active in the 1920s, was banned in 1935 when the government initiated policies favouring population expansion for military purposes. In 1941, a national pro-natalistic policy was adopted and strongly urged efforts toward increasing the birth rate and achieving a population target of 100 million by 1960. However, this policy was not so effective and did not reverse the downward fertility trend that economic and social development had encouraged (Kuroda, 1984; Muramatsu, 1984).

The historical background to population policy in postwar Japan

After the Second World War, the government changed its prewar pro-birth attitude towards fertility control, as a result of the rapid increase in population by a net immigration of about five million people after the repatriation of Japanese nationals from abroad, the return of Koreans and Chinese (Taiwanese) to their homeland, and the resulting baby boom between 1947 and 1949. About 2.7 million births were added each year during the period 1947–9, and the population of Japan rose from 72 million in 1945 to 83 million in 1950 (see Figure 2.4). Few people at the time had any accurate knowledge of contraception, and it was difficult to obtain contraceptives. As a result, there were many unwanted pregnancies, necessitating a dramatic increase in illegal 'unsafe abortions'. The Population Problems Advisory Council was set up in 1949 as an advisory organ of the government, and it submitted recommendations to reduce the rate of population growth through birth control and emigration (Kuroda, 1984; Muramatsu, 1984; JICA, 2003).

With regard to birth control, the council made some specific suggestions: (i) the improvement of health centres, the training of personnel, and the provision of nationwide education on population problems and family planning; (ii) efforts to diffuse knowledge of contraception among lower socioeconomic groups; and (iii) the establishment of a government office to address population issues, including guidance in family planning, and the strengthening of the Institute of Population Problems and the National Institute of Public Health. These recommendations formed the basis for the subsequent 1951 Cabinet decision on birth control that, in turn, resulted in the launching of a national family planning programme (Kato, 1978; Kuroda, 1984).

The Eugenic Protection Law[4] was enacted in 1948 through the efforts of the members of the Diet to protect mothers from unsafe abortions, and this

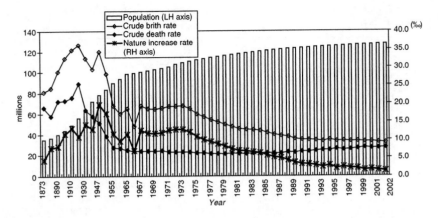

Source: National Institute of Population and Social Security Research (2003).

Figure 2.4 Population, crude birth rate, crude death rate, natural increase rate, Japan, 1873–2002

law permitted induced abortions for 'physical reasons by a mother with several children' and the sterilization of persons with hereditary diseases; it was amended partially in 1949 to permit any woman to undergo abortion 'for economic reasons', and this resulted in a more widespread use of abortion (Okazaki, 1955; JICA, 2003). The Allied Forces General Headquarters of the United States (GHQ) supported the enactment of the Eugenic Protection Law.

The sharp decline in the crude birth rate from 34 per thousand population in 1947 to 17 per thousand in 1957 was mainly a result of the increase in induced abortion (see Figure 2.4 and Table 2.3). The drastic increase in induced abortions harmed maternal health, and the maternal mortality ratio was as high as 178.8 per 100,000 live births in 1955. The government first formulated its national family planning programme in 1952 as part of its health and welfare policy, the purpose of which was to promote proper contraception in order to combat 'the marked increase of induced abortion' which was liable 'to endanger the life and health of mothers'. The government programme for the promotion of family planning was not intended to encourage small families; rather, it was launched primarily to assist the people in achieving their desired family size, but with increasing industrialization and modernization, the concept of small family size became an accepted norm (Muramatsu 1984; Ota 1969; Ogino 2001).

The programme included three kinds of education and technical guidance in contraception, namely (i) individual guidance (case work); (ii) collective guidance (group work); and (iii) general education (mass education). Individual guidance was given by a doctor or family planning worker – a

Table 2.3 Fertility, contraception, induced abortion and maternal mortality in
Japan 1949–2002

Year	Total population 1,000s	Total fertility rate	Contraceptive prevalence rate	Births 1,000,000s	Induced abortion			Maternal mortality ratio
					Number 1,000s	Rate (%)	Ratio births (%)	
1949	81,773	4.32	–	2,697	102	4.9	3.8	–
1950	83,200	3.65	19.5	2,338	320	15.1	13.7	176.1
1955	89,276	2.37	34.1	1,731	1,170	50.2	67.6	178.8
1960	93,419	2.00	42.7	1,606	1,063	42.0	66.2	130.6
1965	98,275	2.14	55.5	1,824	843	30.2	46.2	87.6
1970	103,720	2.13	52.1	1,934	732	24.8	37.8	52.1
1975	111,940	1.91	60.5	1,901	672	22.1	35.3	28.7
1980	117,060	1.75	62.2	1,577	598	19.5	37.9	20.5
2002	127,435	1.32	55.9	1,154	329	11.4	28.5	7.3

Notes: The data prior to 1972 do not include Okinawa Prefecture. Contraceptive prevalence rate is the proportion of married women aged 15–49 currently practising contraception; the data for 1960, 1970, 1980 and 2002 are data for 1959, 1969, 1979 and 2000, respectively. Induced abortion rate pertains to the population of women aged 15–49. The abortion–birth ratio is the ratio of the number of induced abortions to 100 live births. The maternal mortality ratio is maternal deaths per 100,000 live births.
Source: National Institute of Population and Social Security Research (2003).

midwife, public health nurse or clinical nurse trained for the purpose. Collective guidance was given by a medico-social worker, health educator, promoter of improved living, social worker or health control officer in the form of information and education in a lecture or group meeting (Kato, 1978; JICA, 2003).

At the national level, the National Institute of Public Health (under the Ministry of Health and Welfare) organized training courses for instructors of family planning workers. The ministry emphasized, in its notification to the prefectural governors, the need for co-operation with professional medical and paramedical associations at local and prefectural levels in organizing the training courses. For promoting contraception in the field, eugenic protection centres were established, mainly in public health centres, the national network of which was well developed during wartime. In addition, there were several private eugenic protection centres, usually established within hospitals or obstetric clinics (Kato, 1978; JICA, 2003).

The early stage of implementation of the government programme was unsatisfactory, as there was no sign of a decrease in induced abortions. While the dissemination of general and group education seemed to be successful, individual guidance conducted by the local centres proved to be unsuccessful. The reason for the failure was because the highly personal nature of contraception made many people too embarrassed to seek assistance, especially at a government-run health centre. This failure indicated the need for family planning workers to go out to see people in their homes. Other reasons for failure were the small budget for the implementation of the programme, and no payment for family planning workers by the government – the beneficiaries were expected to pay for their services (Kato, 1978).

In August 1954, the Council for Population Problems, which replaced the former council to become a permanent body, submitted to the government a 'recommendation on the quantitative adjustment of population size', to 'promote family planning from the standpoint of population problems' and made several suggestions: (i) making contraceptives available without charge or at a low price to poor and low-income families; (ii) encouraging family planning workers by paying for their services from public funds; and (iii) securing the co-operation of employers in promoting family planning for industrial workers. The recommendation was particularly important because the idea of family planning changed from merely the protection of mothers' health to the implementation of population policy; second, the idea of family planning in industry was suggested (Kato, 1978).

The widespread adoption of family planning practice during the postwar period was basically accomplished largely on a voluntary basis, and the demand for family planning services originated from the people themselves, since they were struggling with poverty, food shortages and housing problems. The practice of birth limitation was not a sudden or new phenomenon, but traditional behaviour since the Tokugawa period, a reaction of people to dire economic straits (Kuroda, 1984; Muramatsu, 1984). Some family planning activities were already in place among white-collar workers, in particular educated people in the cities, even in prewar days, and twenty private groups that promoted family planning were in existence immediately after the war. One of the leading organizations active in promoting family planning was the Foundation Institute for Research of Population Problems[5] (Kato, 1978; Shinozaki, 1978; Muramatsu, 1984). The Foundation Institute emphasized family planning in the context of its 'New Life Movement' campaign.[6] The New Life Movement then became a driving force in propagating and organizing family planning projects at the level of industrial companies see page 59 below (Kato, 1978; Shinozaki, 1978).

The year 1955 was a turning point with regard to family planning policy in Japan. First, a special scheme of family planning was introduced for low-income families. They were given not only free technical guidance by a trained family planning worker, but also contraceptives at no charge or at a reduced price (Kato, 1978). The key to the widespread use of family planning in the model villages for planned childbirth in the 1950s was that it first educated whole villages and gained the understanding and co-operation of the people living around the women who needed to practice family planning – the mothers and fathers, and in-laws, for example. The women of the villages actively participated in and highly valued this guidance, and the guidance bore fruit as shown in changes in contraceptive methods and a reduction in induced abortion (JICA, 2003, p. 21). A change in farmers' ideas about family size came about via an amendment in the civil law on inheritance by equal distribution, which could potentially divide parcels of land into tiny lots (Ogino, 2001).

Second, the New Life Movement, which began in 1955, when a voluntary organization called the New Life Movement Council was established, with state support in the form of annual subsidies. Though the objective of the movement was to enrich the private and social lives of individuals, it was understood that the first step would be to introduce family planning among industrial workers. Indeed, the term 'New Life Movement' soon came to mean family planning for industrial workers (Kato, 1978).

In 1958, the Ministry of Health and Welfare began to shift, stage by stage, the administration of the family planning programme from the public health centres, which had incorporated eugenic protection services, to the local community authorities – namely, city, town and village authorities. The maternal and child health centres, established in 1958 as a new project with construction costs being shared equally among the central, prefectural and municipal governments, was to function as the nucleus of health services for mothers and infants, as well as to provide prenatal assistance. That shift was intended to bring the services closer to the people, as the main emphasis of the programme was placed on practical consultation in preference to general education. This work was to be carried out largely through qualified midwives trained for this purpose (Muramatsu, 1965, p. 70; Kato, 1978). In the past, most births had taken place at home with the assistance of midwives, but from the late 1950s, deliveries in maternal and child health centres increased dramatically, and this change improved both maternal and child health (Nakayama, 2001).

In 1963, in view of the continued prevalence of induced abortions, the government introduced guidance for newly married couples to promote family planning through contraception, and to increase prenatal assistance. The concept of spacing children began, in fact, to constitute an integral element of family planning. Under the Maternal and Child Health Law enacted in 1965, family planning became an integral part of maternal and child health services.[7] The public funds provided for the contraceptive programme were not great. Since more than 80 per cent of these funds were spent on low-income families, the funds available for the general scheme were negligible. Public funds spent on family planning have declined year by year, since by the late 1960s people were already adequately motivated towards small family size norms in the high economic growth (Kato, 1978; Muramatsu, 1984).

Family planning programmes and the New Life Movement in private companies

The practice of family planning in Japan spread rapidly among the population in the late 1950s, and family planning in companies contributed to this in no small measure. Development of family planning in companies was aided by a voluntary movement to promote the new lifestyle for employees that was initiated by the Foundation Institute for Research of Population Problems. The main objective of the movement was the dissemination of family planning, and in order to achieve that objective, the following aims were set: to stabilize household finances; promote family health; emphasize children's education; and strive for educated and culturally enriched lives. Family planning guidance was easy for companies to provide to employees as a group, and as a result it spread quickly among the various industries – steel, shipbuilding, coal, electricity, chemical industries, paper manufacturing, the national and private railway companies and so on. By March 1958, 82 companies were involved, and each employer organized a family planning project for its employees[8] (Kato, 1978; JICA, 2003; Ogino, 2003). Below is a case study from one of the steel companies, as an illustration of the positive results of the New Life Movement.

The main reason why the steel company decided to organize a New Life Movement for its employees is that the employer understood that 'safety begins at home', from studies on the causes of industrial accidents that had occurred in the factory in the recent past. The company found that about 70 per cent of all such accidents could be attributable to reasons connected with employees' private lives outside the workplace. It launched a family planning project for the workers' welfare, with the participation of the labour union and the technical co-operation of the Foundation Institute for Research of Population Problems (Kato, 1978; Ogino, 2003).

The welfare section of the company conducted an enquiry among 803 families living in company accommodation for employees to obtain basic information for the New Life Movement. It was found that family planning was urgently needed by the women. Although 31 per cent of respondents were currently using various contraceptive methods, and a further 8 per cent of them had used them in the past, those with three or more children in particular had undergone induced abortions. Moreover, the majority of women with one child or more had suffered from the ill-effects of pregnancy or childbirth. For these reasons, it was decided that the New Life Movement should begin with family planning (IPP, 1958; Kato, 1978).

After guidance, the contraceptive prevalence rate in the steel company increased from 39 per cent to 56 per cent. The rate for women aged 40–44 years old was the highest – a 22 per cent increase, from 25 per cent to 47 per cent. These women would have had abortions had they become pregnant. The success in family planning promoted by the company was mainly due to the well-equipped and readily available company's health and medical services provided for employees. The Foundation Institute had prepared a booklet entitled 'Guide to the New Life Movement' to enable companies to disseminate family planning information to their employees. In formulating a family planning programme, the principle of gradual application was favoured, starting with a pilot project followed by phased expansion until the wives of all employees were covered at the final stage. In selecting the pilot areas for the project, families living in company accommodation were dealt with first, as this facilitated the organization of on-the-spot guidance work by family planning workers (IPP, 1958; Kato, 1978).

In the pilot areas, the women were asked to organize themselves into small units of five or ten. Members of each unit selected a leader, whose function was to arrange meetings and maintain liaison with the secretariat and the family planning worker. All women, irrespective of their age, were invited to participate, because the New Life Movement was not confined merely to controlling births, but also included health care for mothers and children. A woman was expected to contribute to the rise in productivity of the company through a stable family life. It is interesting to note that, in most cases, the necessary funds for the family planning project were provided by the employer and even by the labour union (Kato, 1978; Ogino, 2003).

The family planning projects in private companies had remarkable success in that the number of births decreased, induced abortions also decreased rapidly, and a stable family life contributed to a decrease in industrial accidents. The company also benefited from a reduction in costs for various family allowances as a result of the decrease in family size. The New Life Movement reached beyond the family-planning field to cover such aspects as health and welfare of children and mothers, and an improvement in family life, and it continued until the late 1960s (IPP, 1958; Kato, 1978; Ogino, 2003).

The outcome of family planning programmes and fertility decline in Japan

Family planning and fertility decline

The population, crude birth rates, crude death rates and natural increase rates during the period 1873–2001 are shown in Figure 2.4. It can be seen from Figure 2.4 that Japan has gone through a demographic transition from high fertility and mortality to low fertility and mortality. The period 1947–9, the 'baby boom', was a temporary phenomenon: the crude birth rate declined sharply from 34.3 per thousand population in 1947 to 28.1 per thousand in 1950. The sharp decline in crude birth rate was mainly a result of the equally sharp increase in induced abortion. According to Table 2.3, the number of abortions in 1955 was about 1.17 million, births numbered 1.73 million, and the abortion–birth ratio was 67.6 per cent. This indicates that contraceptive methods were not widely known, and people resorted to abortion as a contraceptive method.

Based on the Survey of Diffusion of Birth Control in 1952 conducted by the Institute of Population Problems, the contraceptive prevalence rate among couples with wives under 50 was 28.3 per cent for the whole of Japan, 36.9 per cent for urban areas, and 22.6 per cent in rural areas (Okazaki, 1994, p. 43) The rate rose drastically from 28.3 per cent in 1952 to 63 per cent in 1959. This sharp increase in the contraceptive prevalence rates in the 1950s resulted in a steady decrease in the number of registered induced abortions, as shown in Table 2.3. This remarkable success can be verified by the decrease in both crude birth rates and induced abortions. However, the fact that there was still a large number of abortions implies a failure on the part of some individuals to practise contraception (Ohbuchi, 1984). This also seems to suggest that there were people who did not practise any form of contraception.

The total fertility rate during the period of high economic growth in the 1960s stayed at the level of replacement of population (TFR is around 2.1) (see Table 2.3). The Mainichi Survey[9] showed that the ideal number of children stayed at two to three on average in this period (see Table 2.4). Few respondents desired one or no children, or more than four, and the two-child norm became common throughout the country, in rural as well as urban areas (Okazaki, 1994). The gap in the survey between the ideal number of children and the actual number of children increased over the years, as shown in Table 2.4. This meant that couples were facing difficulties in having their ideal number of children because of problems such as the increase in the cost of living, children's education, housing, and a rise in the 'opportunity cost' of the mother's time.

According to the Mainichi Survey, the most important factor contributing to the postwar decline in fertility was economic. Faced with serious economic pressure and facilitated by permissive legislation for fertility limitation, a large number of married couples opted to limit their family sizes. During the high economic growth period in the 1960s, the crude birth rate remained more or less stagnant at around 18 per thousand population. The period also witnessed an active nationwide promotion of family planning, its acceptance being prompted by the desire to provide a better education for children and better health for mothers. The unexpectedly low fertility in 1966 is attributed to the *Hinoeuma*, or Fire Horse, year of the Chinese lunar calendar, during which it is believed to be inauspicious to bear a daughter, and therefore many couples avoided having children during that year (Atoh, 1984; Muramatsu, 1984). The abortion-birth ratio in 1966 was a high 59 per cent, compared to 46 per cent in 1965 and 39 per cent in 1967.

The Mainichi Survey also asked respondents with children about their expectations of support from their children in their old age. The question asked was: 'Will you depend on your children in your old age?' – 67 per cent of respondents answered 'Yes', and 11 per cent 'No' in 1950. This answer reflects the traditional Japanese norm (Okazaki, 1994). However,

Table 2.4   Percentage distribution of married women by ideal number of children, actual number of children and total fertility rate, Japan in 1963–79

	1963	1965	1967	1969	1971	1975	1979
Married women by ideal number of children (%)							
No children	2.2	1.4	3.3	0.7	0.9	1.1	2.9
1 child	1.4	1.9	2.3	2.3	2.5	3.3	2.6
2 children	26.1	30.8	25.4	31.5	33.0	39.7	43.8
3 children	44.9	47.3	45.8	47.4	46.1	41.7	39.5
4 or more	8.6	7.8	10.8	14.3	13.3	10.2	8.5
No response	16.8	10.7	12.4	4.0	4.3	4.0	2.7
Ideal number of children							
Average	2.24	2.38	2.36	2.68	2.64	2.51	2.44
Actual number of children							
Average	2.33	2.24	2.08	2.06	2.04	1.96	1.91
Total fertility rate							
	2.00	2.14	2.23	2.13	2.16	1.91	1.77

Sources: Mainichi Shinbunsha Jinkou Mondai Chosakai (ed.) (2000); National Institute of Population and Social Security Research (2003).

this norm changed completely over the years: in the survey in 1963, 33 per cent of respondents thought they would depend on their children, but 48 per cent did not; and in 1975, the responses were 26 per cent and 50 per cent, respectively (Mainichi Newspapers, 1994). Based on the sixth National Fertility Survey conducted by the Institute of Population Problems of the Ministry of Health and Welfare in 1972, the perception of parents with regard to the value of their children was that most married couples thought of children as a source of psychological gratification in creating a happy home environment (Atoh, 1984). Changes in the perception of parents with regard to the value of children also affected fertility decline.

Methods of contraception

Compared to other countries, the pattern with regard to contraceptive methods used by Japanese couples presents certain unique features. First, Japan has the highest rate of condom use in the world (see Table 2.2). According to half a century of surveys on family planning conducted by the Mainichi Newspapers a uniform pattern of contraceptive methods has been observed (see Table 2.5). There are several reasons for the high rate of condom use: they are inexpensive, easy to use, and do not need individual examination or fitting. The rhythm method or safe period method introduced by Kyusaku Ogino, a Japanese doctor, is the most popular method after condoms. Most Japanese couples alternate condoms and the rhythm method. However, in terms of effectiveness, the rhythm method may pose problems, especially to lay women who cannot determine accurately the

Table 2.5   Methods of contraception among married women of reproductive age in Japan 1950–2000 (percentages)

	1950	1959	1967	1971	1977	1984	1990	1994	1998	2000
Condom	35.6	58.3	65.2	72.7	78.9	80.4	73.9	77.7	77.8	75.3
Ogino method	27.4	46.5	37.4	32.9	27.0	20.2	15.3	13.9	8.4	6.5
IUD/ contraceptive/ pill	–	–	6.1	9.6	12.4	8.5	5.7	4.3	4.2	4.2
Sterilization	–	6.3	3.6	3.9	5.3	10.5	9.8	7.0	5.8	6.4
Withdrawal/ spermicides, etc.	55.0	43.0	26.4	21.0	15.2	6.0	9.0	8.6	9.3	27.5
BBT method	–	–	–	–	–	8.4	8.0	6.8	8.2	9.8
Others/not stated	15.0	5.3	4.2	4.3	3.2	5.4	2.5	3.1	2.6	2.4

Note: BBT method is the basal body temperature method; it was included in the Ogino method until 1977.
Source: As Table 2.4.

safe dates to avoid pregnancy (Muramatsu, 1984). Only a few women use the contraceptive pill in Japan, though it is widely used in other countries (see Table 2.2 and 2.5). This is largely because the pill was only legally authorized for contraceptive use in 1999.

With regard to contraceptive methods, Coleman (1981, 1982) suggests that the extensive reliance of couples on condoms as the main device for fertility control stems largely from the unavailability of other methods in the cultural context of embarrassment and passivity towards contraception, which in turn is caused by the low status of Japanese women (Muramatsu, 1984; Tsuya, 1994). Although Japan has been considered traditionally as a male-dominated society, men participate widely in family planning, and the Mainichi Survey showed that 93 per cent of husbands co-operated in family planning in 1963.

Policy implications from the Japanese experience in family planning

Japan underwent a fertility transition from high to low fertility over a short period after the Second World War as a result of the government's maternal and child health programmes, the New Life Movement, and activities in the private sector (non-governmental organizations and independent midwives). Several factors can be pointed to as contributing to the dramatic development of family planning programmes. First, Japan had already established a potential foundation for this transition: widespread education,[10] social and human resources, and organizational competence prior to the Second World War. Second, the public health nurses and independent midwives played a key role in providing these services, because they were able to build strong relationships of trust, and their services were provided based on the actual needs of the people and were not forced on them (JICA, 2003). Third, the New Life Movement in both urban and rural areas contributed towards improved maternal and child health, and disseminated family planning concepts via the co-operation of private industries and the involvement of women's group and local leaders (JICA, 2003). Fourth, men's involvement in family planning was very important. In Japan, men's co-operation in family planning has been quite high since the early 1950s.

The socioeconomic environments of developing countries vary from country to country, but several suggestions could be made from Japan's experiences regarding the development of family planning in developing countries. First, education is universally recognized as the crucial key for economic and social progress, and individual well-being. The highest priority should be placed on the improvement of the educational status of women and the elimination of gender inequality within the family and in society. The empowerment of women by improving their educational attainment and increasing their economic opportunities contributes to the decrease in unwanted births because of better access to family planning programmes.

Second, the government and other organizations should construct a practical implementation system to make family planning advice, information, education, communication, counselling and contraceptive supplies and services affordable, acceptable, and accessible to all individuals in need. Since assistance in family planning is an extremely sensitive area that intrudes on the private lives of people, it is essential to build strong relationships of trust, as in the case of Japan, and therefore informal networking in the community to disseminate family planning should be carried out, and the attitudes and awareness of the service providers at the field level must be improved to meet the actual needs of people. It is important to involve women in the implementation (for example, midwives or community-based distributors), leadership, planning, decision-making, management, organization and evaluation of services for the spread of family planning. The objection by husbands to the use of contraception and a lack of communication between couples about family planning were the main reasons for the unmet needs of contraception. Therefore, increasing the participation of, and sharing of responsibility by, men in the practice of family planning is also indispensable (UN, 1995; JICA, 2003; Ogino, 2003).

Third, the decisions on whether to have children, and how many, vary according to the value of children in each society. The economic theory of fertility assumes that a couple's demand for children is determined by family preference for a certain number of surviving (usually male) children (that is, in regions with high mortality, parents may produce more children than they really want in the expectation that some will not survive, as we saw from the positive correlation between infant mortality rate and fertility in Figure 2.3), by the price or 'opportunity cost' of the mother's time spent rearing these children, and by the level of family income. Children in poor societies are seen partly as economic investment goods in that there is an expected return in the form of both child labour and the provision of financial and caring support for parents in old age. When the cost of children rises as a result of increased educational and employment opportunities for women and the cost of higher education for children, parents will want fewer additional children (Todaro, 1994, pp. 196–201; Nogami and Hayase, 2003, pp. 59–74).

If these conditions are still not met in a country where the people are willing to limit the number of births as a rational choice, the policy will result in failure, even if the government and non-governmental organizations support and promote family planning. In Japan, people had a strong incentive to limit family size because of shortages of food and employment, and housing problems. Government efforts to improve maternal and child health and to disseminate family planning under the New Life Movement with various projects for a better life for the people resulted in fertility transition within a short period. Governments in developing countries should also make efforts not only to implement family planning and maternal and child health programmes but also to formulate projects for improvement in the quality of life. The empowerment of women will raise women's opportunity cost and cost of education for children, and these will motivate people to limit family size.

Over the last few decades, many governments have experimented with such schemes as, including specific incentives and disincentives in order to raise or lower fertility. Examples include, in Singapore in 1984, women with higher educational attainment encouraged to have three children; in India, in 1975, forced family planning programmes (coercive sterilization); and 'the one-child policy' since 1979 in China. However, most such schemes have had only marginal impact on fertility and in some cases have been counter-productive, except in China (Ogino 2003; UN 1995).

In conclusion, in the case of Japan, the government first legalized induced abortion through the Eugenic Protection Law and then implemented family planning as part of its health and welfare policy, to promote proper contraception in order to combat 'the marked increase of induced abortion'. The government's programmes were not meant to induce the desire for a small family; rather, they were launched primarily to assist people to achieve their desired family size. Women's educational attainment in Japan is as high as men's, but inequality between the sexes still exists in political, social and economic areas, although fertility transition has occurred. Based on the Japanese experience, it is important to respond to people's (particularly women's) needs, desires and consent to the formulation and implementation of successful family planning programmes and policy. In order to ensure these conditions, the empowerment of women, and equality and equity of men and women are indispensable. Gender systems interact with family planning programmes to determine their success. Further studies will be required for a comprehensive understanding of gender relations and systems in society.

Notes

1 Demographic transition is a theory by which economic development brings about a shift from high to low birth and death rates.
2 The Demographic and Health Surveys (DHS) are a 13-year project to assist government and private agencies in developing countries to conduct national sample surveys on population and maternal and child health. Funded primarily by the US Agency for International Development (USAID), DHS is administered by Macro International Inc. in Calverton, Maryland, USA. The main objectives of the DHS programme are (1) to promote widespread dissemination and utilization of DHS data among policy makers, (2) to expand the international population and health database, (3) to advocate survey methodology, and (4) to develop in participating countries the skills and resources necessary to conduct high-quality demographic and health surveys.
3 The population replacement is concerned with the natural process through which a population replaces its numbers.
4 The purpose of the law in 1948 was to prevent an increase in eugenically inferior births and to protect the life and health of the mothers. The Law was amended as 'Mothers' Bodies Protection Law' in 1996 by excluding the clause on eugenically inferior births from the previous law.
5 The Foundation-Institute for Research of Population Problems (under the presidency of Dr Toru Nagai) was established in 1933 to contribute to the study of population policy (Kato, 1978, p. 17).
6 The Council for Population Problems, in its resolution of 20 August 1955, requested the government to co-operate with the New Life Movement centred around family planning (The Social Development Institute (ed.), *Sengo no shakai hosho* (Social security in the postwar period), Collection of Materials, vol. II, p. 687).
7 A typical centre is staffed by a full-time midwife, who is usually in charge of management, part-time midwives and public health nurses, together with one or two part-time doctors, and the necessary administrative personnel. In 1969, there were 567 centres throughout the country (Kato, 1978).
8 According to a JICA report (JICA, 2003, p. 25), at its peak, family planning projects under the New Life Movement involved the participation of 55 companies or groups, and 1.24 million individuals.
9 The Mainichi Survey, since its start in 1950 up to the year 2000, has been conducted by *Mainichi Newspapers* about once in every two years. The purpose of the survey is to collect national public opinion on family planning from about 4,000 women aged 16–49 years, selected by random sample in Japan.
10 Japan's educational system started in 1872, and the enrolment ratio for primary school was already as high as 98 per cent by 1908.

References

Atoh, Makoto (1984) 'Trends and Differentials in Fertility', in *Population of Japan*, Country Monograph Series No. 11 (New York: United Nations), pp. 23–42.

Cassen, Robert and Associates (1986) *Does Aid Work?* (Oxford: Clarendon Press; New York: Oxford University Press).

Coleman, Samuel (1981) 'The Cultural Context of Condom Use in Japan', *Studies in Family Planning*, vol. 12, pp. 28–39.

Coleman, Samuel (1982) *Family Planning in Japanese Society: Traditional Birth Control in a Modern Urban Culture* (Princeton, NJ: Princeton University Press).

Fujime, Yuki (1999) *Sei no rekishigaku* (History of sex) (Tokyo: Fuji Shuppan) (in Japanese).

Hayase, Yasuko (2004) *Ajia no jinko gurobaruka no nami no nakade* (Asia's population in the age of globalization) (Chiba: Institute of Developing Economies, JETRO) (in Japanese).

IPP (Institute of Population Problems, Ministry of Health and Welfare) (1958) *Kazoku keikaku o chushin to suru shinseikatsu taido no jitchi shido kenkyu kekka no gaiyo – Nihon Kokan ni okeru jitsurei* (An outline of research on practical guidance of family planning under the new life movement – Case study of Nihon Kokan Iron and Steel Company) Research material No. 129 (in Japanese).

JICA (Institute for International Cooperation, Japan International Cooperation Agency) (2003) *Second Study on International Cooperation for Population and Development, New Insights from the Japanese Experience, Executive Summary* Tokyo: JICA.

Kato, Toshinobu (1978) 'The Development of Family Planning in Japan with Industrial Involvement', *Population Studies Translation Series*, No. 2, ESCAP (Economic and Social Commission for Asia and the Pacific) (New York: United Nations), pp. 3–34.

Kuroda, Toshio (1984) 'Population Policy', in *Population of Japan*, Country Monograph Series No. 11 (New York: United Nations), pp. 269–79.

Mainichi Newspapers, The (The Population Problems Research Council) (ed.) (1994) *The Population and Society of Postwar Japan: Based on Half a Century of Surveys on Family Planning*, (Tokyo: Mainichi Newspapers.)

Mainichi Shinbunsha Jinkou Mondai Chosakai (The Population Problems Research Council, Mainichi Newspapers) (ed.) (2000) Nihon no Jinko-Sengo 50 nen no Kiseki-Mainichi Shinbunsha Zenkoku Kazokukeikaku Seron Chosa: Dai 1 kai – Dai 25 kai Chosa Kekka (The Population of Japan-Its Track Postwar 50 years: Based on National Opinion's Surveys on Family Planning, 1st to 25th) (Tokyo, Mainichi Shinbunsha)(in Japanese).

Mason, Karen Oppenheim (1984) *The Status of Women: A Review of Its Relationships to Fertility and Mortality* (New York: Rockefeller Foundation).

Muramatsu, Minoru (1965) 'Action Programs of Family Planning in Japan'. in Minoru Muramatsu and Paul A. Harper, (eds) *Population Dynamics: International Action and Training Programs: Proceedings of the International Conference on Population*. The Johns Hopkins School of Hygiene and Public Health, May 1964 (Baltimore, Md.: The Johns Hopkins University Press).

Muramatsu, Minoru (1984) 'Family Planning', in *Population of Japan*: Country Monograph Series No. 11 (New York: United Nations), pp. 280–94.

Nakayama, Makiko (2001) *Shintai o meguru seisaku to kojin* (Policy and individuals over the body) (Tokyo: Keiso Shobo) (in Japanese).

National Institute of Population and Social Security Research (2003) *Jinko tokei shiryoshu 2003* (Latest demographic statistics 2003) (Tokyo) (in Japanese).

Nogami, Hiroki and Yasuko Hayase (2003) '*Jinteki shigen*' (Human resources), in A. Kuchiki, H. Nogami and T. Yamagata (eds) *Tekisuto bukku kaihatsu keizaigaku shinpan* (Textbook economic development, new edition) (Tokyo: Yuhikaku) (in Japanese).

Ogino, Miho (2001) 'Kazoku-keikaku e no michi: haisen Nihon no saiken to jutai chosetsu' (The road to family planning: reconstruction and family planning in postwar Japan), *Shiso* (Thoughts), vol. 925, no. 2001–6, pp. 168–95 (in Japanese).

Ogino, Miho (2003) 'Hanten shita kokusaku: kazoku-keikaku undo no tenkai to kiketsu' (Reversed national policy: development and consequence of family planning programmes), *Shiso* (Thoughts), vol. 955, no. 2003–11, pp. 174–95 (in Japanese).

Ohbuchi, Hiroshi (1984) 'The Demographic Transition', in *Population of Japan*, Country Monograph Series No. 11 (New York: United Nations), pp. 8–22.

Okazaki, Ayanori (1955) 'Nihon ni okeru yusei seisaku to sono kekka ni tsuite' (Eugenic policy in Japan and its result), *Jinko mondai kenkyu* (Journal of Population Problems), vol. 61, pp. 1–8 (in Japanese).

Okazaki, Youichi (1994) 'Economic Development and Population Problems in Postwar Japan', in The Population Problems Research Council (ed.), *The Population and Society of Postwar Japan: Based on Half a Century of Surveys on Family Planning* Tokyo: The *Mainichi Newspapers*), pp. 29–47.

Ota, Tenrei (1969) *Nihon sanji chosetsu-shi* (History of birth control in Japan) (Tokyo: Japan Family Planning Association) (in Japanese).

Shinozaki, Nobuo (1978) 'Basic Guidelines for Propagating Family Planning in Business Organizations', in *Population Studies Translation Series*, No. 2. (Economic and Social Commission for Asia and the Pacific: ESCAP) (New York: United Nations), pp. 35–42.

Suzuki, Hiroko (ed.) (1997) *Nihon josei undo shiryo shusei* (Compilation of materials for Japanese women's movement), Vol. 7, *Seikatsu to rodo* (Life and labour) (Tokyo: Fuji Shuppan) (in Japanese).

Taeuber, Irene B. (1958) *The Population of Japan* (Princeton, NJ: Princeton University Press).

Todaro, Michael P. (1994) *Economic Development*, 5th edn (Singapore: Longman Singapore).

Tsuya, Noriko (1994) 'Proximate Determinants of Fertility Decline in Postwar Japan', in The Population Problems Research Council (ed.), *The Population and Society of Postwar Japan: Based on Half a Century of Surveys on Family Planning* (Tokyo: The Mainichi Newspapers), pp. 97–132.

Tsuya, O. Noriko and Larry L. Bumpass (2004) *Marriage, Work, and Family Life in Comparative Perspectives: Japan, South Korea, and the United States* (Honolulu: University of Hawaii Press).

United Nations (1992) *Abortion Policies: A Global Review. Vol. 1, Afghanistan to France*, (New York: United Nations).

United Nations (1993) *Abortion Policies: A Global Review. Vol. 2, Gabon to Norway* (New York: United Nations).

United Nations (1994) *International Conference on Population and Development* (New York: United Nations).

United Nations (1995) *Population and Development, Programme of Action Adopted at the International Conference on Population and Development, Cairo, 5–13 September 1994* (New York: United Nations).

United Nations (1996a) *Family Planning, Health and Family Well-Being* (New York: United Nations).

United Nations (1996b) *Population and Women* (New York: United Nations).

United Nations (1999a) *World Population Monitoring, 1999: Population Growth, Structure and Distribution* (New York: United Nations).

United Nations (1999b) *Review and Appraisal of the Progress Made in Achieving the Goals and Objectives of the Programme of Action of the International Conference on Population and Development, 1999 Report* (New York: United Nations).

United Nations (2001) *World Population Monitoring 2000: Population, Gender and Development* (New York: United Nations).

United Nations (2002a) *Abortion Policies: A Global Review*, Vol. 3, *Oman to Zimbabwe* (New York: United Nations).

United Nations (2002b) *World Population Prospects: The 2002 Revision* (New York: United Nations)

United Nations Population Fund (UNFPA) (1995) *The State of World Population 1995, Decisions for Development: Women, Empowerment and Reproductive Health* (New York: United Nations Population Fund).

United Nations Population Fund (UNFPA) (1997) *The State of World Population 1997, The Right to Choose: Reproductive Rights and Reproductive Health* (New York: United Nations Population Fund).

World Bank (2000) *World Development Report 2000* (New York: Oxford University Press).

3

'Livelihood Improvement' in Postwar Japan: Its Relevance for Rural Development Today

Hiroshi Kan Sato

Introduction

In this chapter, we shall describe the features of Rural Livelihood Improvement in Japan during the post-Second World War period (1945–64). During the years immediately after the war, rural and urban areas in Japan were plagued by severe poverty. People suffered from food shortages and starvation, poor sanitary conditions, outbreaks of communicable diseases, and a lack of sufficient income. At that time, Japan's development goal was poverty alleviation. In addition to poverty alleviation, the USA, as an occupation power, ordered Japan to be 'democratized'. Consequently, the government and people of Japan were given two main development goals; poverty alleviation and democratization.

Poverty alleviation and democratization are two common goals for today's developing countries. Democratization is usually given as a goal by outside actors such as the World Bank or other international donors. On these points, postwar Japan faced the same difficulties as most of the developing countries do at the time of writing.

In the face of these challenges, Japan's Ministry of Agriculture formulated the Livelihood Improvement Programme (LIP) in accordance with instructions from the GHQ (General Headquarters of the Allied Forces.)[1] It was a woman-focused (though not exclusively for women) development programme. It was successful in both alleviating poverty and uplifting the social and economic status of rural women, and thus contributed to rural democratization to a certain extent. Based on this understanding, we presume the LIP experience may provide some lessons for today's developing countries in both poverty alleviation and rural democratization. Therefore, it is worthwhile reviewing Japan's rural development experience from the 1940s and 1950s.

When attempting to compare Japan with the developing countries, we expect strong objections. People may wonder whether studies of livelihood improvement in postwar Japan have any practical applications, especially for the rural development of the developing countries of today. There is validity in these critiques. First, the world of the 1940s and 1950s was very different from the current globalizing world. Second, the economic potential of Japan at that time did not resemble the potential in the developing countries today. Third, and most important, Japan has a unique sociocultural environment, including the strong norm of mutual help in community activities, a sense of responsibility among government officials, and a high literacy rate even among rural women; if these social conditions were the key to success, it will be impossible to transplant Japan's experiences to other cultures. These challenges are indeed very difficult to refute.

The purpose of this chapter is to survey the process and extract features of the LIP as groundwork for this discussion. In the following sections, we shall first review preceding studies, and then deal with the concept of livelihood improvement. In the fourth and fifth sections, we shall observe closely detailed facts and examples of the LIP in postwar Japan. In the sixth section, a hypothesis will be put forward on a relationship between rapid economic growth and the LIP. Finally, in the seventh and eighth sections we shall take some lessons from LIP experiences for rural development today.

Preceding studies and their impasse

There is an abundant accumulation of studies on the LIP (sometime the term 'Home Living Improvement Extension Service Program' is used as a translation of the same programme)[2] in Japanese, mostly by rural sociologists, home economists and administrative historians. But none consider the LIP to be a rural 'development' programme equivalent to those in the developing world of today. Consequently, there are few preceding studies on the LIP in the contexts of rural development. Important exceptions are the achievements of the study group on 'Home Living Improvement Extension Service Program (HLIESP)[3] in the early 1990s, Ichida (1995) and Amano (2001).

Some quotations from the literature are as follows:

Recently an analysis of Japanese women's experience in postwar rural development is needed in the International Development world as a model for women's roles in the modernization process in the Asian cultural context. (Taniguchi *et al.*, 1993, p.15 in English abstract)

The Home Living Improvement Extension Service Program, starting with the support of the GHQ in postwar Japan, has been highly evaluated by international development circles as a desirable rural development project from the WID (Women in Development) perspective. (Yamasaki *et al.*, 1994, p.7 in English abstract)

The program itself had two main objectives from the outset: improving the quality of life through the rationalization of traditional lifestyles and the raising of Japanese women's social status through the democratization of rural patriarchal society. (Yamasaki *et al.*, 1994, p.7 in English abstract)

We share most of these authors' points of concern, although we do not think the importance of the LIP (HLIESP in their terminology) is confined only to WID but involves a wider rural development perspective, including males. We totally agree with their analysis of the features of this programme as mentioned below:

The following aspects of the program demonstrate the well-balanced harmony and complementarities of top-down and bottom-up policy approaches. (1) Priority was given to the improvement of living conditions, (2) Participatory development was based on local initiatives, and (3) Proposals were appropriate to local cultural contexts through the intensive commitment of extension workers. They provided feedback information to policymakers. (Taniguchi *et al.*, 1993, pp. 15–16 in English abstract)

Some arguments have been put forward on how we should evaluate the 'gender perspective' of the LIP:

These aims (improvement of quality of life and raising of women's social status) are not necessarily compatible, as they are quite different. We can assume the existence of a modern-family ideology which was originally from the US as the background for the co-existence of the two objectives. (Yamasaki *et al.*, 1994, p.7 in English abstract)

The analysis of the LIP from the gender perspective leads a slightly different evaluation from that of the poverty alleviation point of view:

However, the social status of rural Japanese women has not been raised very much in spite of the eagerness for reform of the social structure. This is because during the first stage, the modern-family ideology was acculturated into the Japanese social structure. (Yamasaki *et al.*, 1994, p.8 in English abstract)

They conclude that the LIP did not contribute much to changing gender relations. This evaluation of the LIP's limited impact on gender relations is identical to Amano's conclusion (Amano, 2001, pp. 12–13). Also, Ichida (1995) points out a very interesting feature of LIP. She characterizes the first two decades of the LIP as concentrating on private/domestic concerns, and writes that practical/technical improvements were believed to be entry points for livelihood improvements, including in the social status of rural women. Living techniques are perceived as a tool for rural democratization (Ichida, 1995, p. 111). Since we do not have adequate information about the change (or lack thereof) in gender relations in rural Japan, we shall withhold judgement on this matter for the time being. But at the same time, Yamasaki and Taniguchi observe:

> It can be said that rural Japanese women have achieved empowerment through these (home living improvement) activities. (Yamasaki *et al.*, 1994, p. 8 in English abstract)

They intended to move forward based on these findings:

> Topics such as a desirable triangular structure linking donor agencies, recipient government and local people, gender analysis accompanying a dynamic theory of social movement will be explored hereafter in relation to the Home Living Improvement Extension Service Program. (Taniguchi *et al.*, 1993, p. 16 in English abstract)

Our concern in this article is mainly for the synergetic relationship among frontline officials, local governments (town and village governments) and the community under the broader Livelihood Improvement Movement (LIM), which included LIP. This synergetic relationship seems to be one of the key lessons that Japan can offer to today's developing countries. In contrast, it seems rather difficult to analyse the LIP from a gender perspective and draw some lessons from it although this is necessary. We have been carrying out fact-finding exercises through interviews with ex-Livelihood Improvement extension workers and ex-LIP group women.[4] We hope that this accumulation of knowledge may lead to a breakthrough for gender analysis of the LIP.

Rural development and the concept of 'livelihood'

If we place the LIP experience successfully in the context of development studies, the Japanese experiences can be utilized in developing countries. Along with 'participatory development', the concept of livelihood is the most important keyword for understanding the LIP experience.

In debates on development aid, many donor organizations, including JICA (Japan International Cooperation Agency) and JBIC (Japan Bank for International Cooperation) proclaim that the biggest challenge for development is to 'alleviate poverty'. Rural development is an efficient strategy for poverty alleviation because the majority of the poor live in rural areas. 'Participatory development', on the other hand, represents an essential tactic and tool for poverty alleviation. The idea of participatory develop-ment is based on the understanding that traditional development assist-ance, which focuses exclusively on the transfer of economic and physical resources, has not necessarily succeeded in the alleviation of poverty.

When the LIP began, food security, especially increasing rice production, was the first priority for the entire nation. Thus the necessity of agricultural improvement extension workers, the colleagues of LIP workers, was obvi-ous. But agricultural improvement extension workers – all of them men – tended to ignore the importance of improvements in everyday home life. In such a circumstance, the Division of Livelihood Improvement in the Ministry of Agriculture, which acted as the controller of all LIP workers in Japan (with director Matsuyo Yamamoto from 1947 to 1965) claimed that if workers' home lives were not healthy and democratic, production increases would never be sustainable. Consequently, their slogan became 'production and home life are a pair of wheels in rural development'.

This slogan represents the concept of livelihood in LIP. Livelihood is not only an issue of production, domestic work or income, and it is not a matter of females alone. Livelihood is a basis for life as a whole, including production, income, family, health, nutrition and happiness.

Therefore, improving livelihood does not simply mean increasing income, as daily life may be improved even without an income increase. For example, a saving of money, energy or time can also lead to more com-fortable living conditions. In other words, any improvement in livelihood contributes to enriching survival strategies for the poor. Another feature of the concept of livelihood is the balance between agricultural (fishery in fishing villages, forestry in forest villages) production and home life. Even if production and income increase, livelihood improvement is not automatic-ally attained if people still suffer long working hours or unhealthy living conditions.

The Livelihood Improvement Programme

Beginning of the LIP

The LIP was an extension programme introduced by the GHQ, which occu-pied Japan for seven years (from 1945 to 1952). The core motivators of the programme were the extension workers (livelihood improvement/agricul-tural improvement) under the Ministry of Agriculture. Livelihood improve-ment activities were not confined to this programme, but expanded from agriculture to other sectors such as health and education. As a result, liveli-hood improvement grew into a nationwide movement, the LIM.

The GHQ made strong demands for the democratization of Japan, think-ing that, once democratized, the country would never again make war against the USA, and as one of the essential efforts for democratization, the GHQ ordered rural reform. There were three successive reform laws introduced under pressure from the GHQ just after the war: the Land Reform Law in 1946 (and again in 1949); the Agricultural Co-operative Law in 1947; and the Agricultural Improvement Promotion Law introduced in 1948. With these three laws, tenant farmers became independent farmers and the government worked hard to build a supportive environment for the newly-independent farming households. Under the Agricultural Improvement Promotion Law, two kinds of extension workers emerged. One was agricultural improvement extension workers, whose agricultural techniques were transmitted to the farmers. Almost all the agricultural extension workers (who were sometimes called Farm Advisers) were men, and their target clients were also men, because agricultural production was perceived as a male domain. The others were Livelihood Improvement extension workers (hereafter, LIP workers). The LIP workers (sometimes called Home Advisers) were expected to encourage rural women to improve their livelihoods. Almost all of these were women. Both the agricultural extension workers and the LIP workers contributed to rural reforms and improving livelihood, but in this chapter we shall concentrate on the achievements of the LIP workers, because their activities have more relevance to today's social development workers on development projects.

These extension services were totally foreign to rural communities in Japan. In fact, 'working women' were very rare in rural areas. Therefore, the LIP workers faced difficulties when they began to move around rural villages, as no such activities had been observed previously.

Achievements of the LIP/LIM

A decade after the LIP started, the achievements of this nationwide Livelihood Improvement Movement (LIM) were, first and foremost, an escape from poverty and the recovery of food security. Other achievements included substantial improvements in health, nutrition and sanitation in rural areas. Furthermore, LIP workers tried to nurture 'self-governing/thinking farmers'. The 'self-governing farmer' or 'thinking farmer' is considered to be the foundation of a democratic rural society. To construct a democratic society, each individual farmer (male and female alike) needed to become aware, self-conscious and independent, and to have sufficient knowledge to make day-to-day decisions.

Finally, the two decades of the LIM laid the foundation for economic development, and created the momentum for the rapid economic growth that started in the 1960s.

The role of LIP workers

Who became LIP workers?

The first batch of extension workers under the LIP was recruited in 1949. Copying the US extension system, people with some knowledge of home economics were recruited as extension workers. For the first few years, the

LIP workers were dominated by ex-teachers and war widows. The LIP workers were all women, and their main target group was also women. Their primary activities were improving rural home life and empowering rural women. Several years after the programme started, new graduates from women's high schools (and women's colleges) began to predominate among LIP workers. Most of them were local women (from within the same prefecture), but with a slightly higher education than ordinary rural women. Because of this difference in social background, rural women called LIP workers *sensei* (teacher), showing some degree of respect.

Methodology and technique of LIP workers

Now, let us turn our attention to the skills of extension workers. What roles did they assume, and what techniques did they possess? First, they possessed so-called livelihood techniques (home-life techniques). They underwent training in cooking, sewing and keeping household accounts, among other things. Indeed, the training for LIP workers even included plastering. We believe it is very significant that Japanese extension workers literally 'dirtied their hands' in helping the rural population.

Apart from practical livelihood techniques, in the process of accumulating their experiences they acquired sophisticated extension theory (with the co-operation of prominent sociologists, psychologists and educational scientists) and an extension methodology of their own; here we call it the LIP extension technique. LIP workers received training to serve as facilitators or catalysts – listening to the hitherto unheard voices of rural women, encouraging them to identify problems, and working together to find a solution to the problems and giving advice on how to reach the solution.

The LIP approach to rural women

Listening to voiceless women

The primary objective of the LIP was to nurture 'self-governing farmers' by motivating rural women to make spontaneous improvements rather than providing them with technical guidance.

Since LIP workers did not have a manual to refer to, they started by going into the villages and listening to the voices of rural women. Then they encouraged rural women to identify their own daily problems. LIP workers did not use their professional insights to assert, 'these are your problems'. Rather, they helped the farmers and women identify their problems, and worked with them to find solutions. Under instructions from Mrs Yamamoto (director of LIP at the Ministry), LIP workers were advised not simply to instruct people as to how to solve the problems. They just considered the issues together. It was only when the people really wanted improvements that the LIP workers suggested possible ways for solutions. This philosophy of 'don't teach' was the first and most important feature of what we call the 'LIP approach'. We believe that this philosophy is very similar to the participatory development approach that is widely adopted in developing countries today.

Frequent visits and face-to-face contact

Agricultural extension workers (including LIP workers) were equipped with green bicycles, and the LIP workers rode these bicycles to every corner of their rural communities. In rural Japan at that time there were only three types of women who moved around on bicycles: primary school teachers, public health nurses and LIP workers. Without doubt, farmers viewed those three types of women as messengers of modernization.

The LIP workers were encouraged to do their utmost to make contact with farmers – by addressing community meetings, giving lectures in women's classes held in community halls, or providing cooking lessons as requested by village women's associations. Thus they took every opportunity to convey a range of messages and worked on rural women's awareness, rather than mobilizing people to conduct fixed programmes planned by the Ministry. This was the second feature of the LIP approach.

Approach to the social environment surrounding women

Husbands and mothers-in-law

The third important feature of LIP workers' activities was that they facilitated changes in the social environment that surrounded rural women. Although they usually worked with women, the LIP Division at the Ministry of Agriculture, headed by Mrs Yamamoto, believed that the advancement of women would be impossible if they worked exclusively with women. Thus, the LIP workers tried to stimulate changes in men, mothers-in-law, local authorities, village leaders and others. For example, exhibitions of improved meals and improved working clothes were held in an extension office during the agricultural off-season to win over the villagers, including men, to the necessity of livelihood improvement.

Co-operation with other sectors and the utilization of outside resources

The fourth feature of the LIP approach was that it involved co-operation with other sectors. Public health nurses and LIP workers had a common field of activities – rural communities – but they gathered different sorts of information. Public health nurses collected health care information, whereas LIP workers knew the structure of each family and its current level of poverty. Therefore, these two kinds of frontline officers often exchanged relevant information to find suitable approaches.

A fifth feature of the LIP was the mobilization of external resources. One example is the use of a Kitchen Car, designed for nutrition improvement promotion activities. Dieticians travelled in the car, providing cookery lessons in various rural communities. LIP workers also travelled about in these cars. The Kitchen Cars were donated by the USA to the Ministry of

Public Health. The LIP workers utilized mechanisms developed by other donors or administrative departments to promote livelihood improvement with a minimum input of their own resources.

Group activities

LIP groups

The sixth feature of the LIP approach was the promotion of group activities. Why did LIP workers choose the group approach? They did so because the number of LIP workers was limited (they amounted to just a tenth of agricultural extension workers at the beginning, and only a fifth even in the peak years, with a total of approximately 2,000 in all of Japan's forty-seven prefectures in 1975), and individual guidance would thus not have been very effective. It was hoped that a ripple effect could be generated from group guidance. Also, individual housewives, particularly young wives, who were not allowed to do anything on their own initiative, could only express their opinions in gatherings with their equals. Thus, LIP groups were essential for allowing rural women to let their voices be heard. The LIP groups were designed to promote mutual aid for the improvement of fellow members' livelihoods. We may say that the group activities aimed at the empowerment of rural women.

In the course of these group activities, the LIP workers focused on finding and nurturing group leaders. LIP group leaders were required to attend training classes designed for them by the extension office. After returning to their groups, the leaders then shared what they had learnt with other group members. This 'second-hand' diffusion of knowledge was an ethical obligation in Japanese society. This stands in sharp contrast to many developing countries, where the knowledge given in seminars is retained by individuals, who try to use it only for their own benefit. We may call it social capital for the development of rural Japan. The LIP used this social capital to its advantage.

Communal cooking and communal nurseries

Let us look at a few examples of group-based livelihood improvement practices. LIP workers started to identify the problems in rural area. The first problem they identified was the issue of overwork and fatigue during the busy farming season. Agricultural mechanization did not begin until the mid-1950s, so the planting and harvesting of rice was arduous work. During busy times (approximately two weeks each for planting and harvesting), agricultural extension workers emphasized maximizing production, whereas LIP workers concerned themselves with the health conditions of farmers.

Based on surveys conducted by LIP workers together with rural women, LIP workers demonstrated that farmers were losing weight during the busy farming seasons. In most cases, these surveys involved participatory action research done by group members themselves, to show them that they were actually losing weight for no other reason than the heavy workload.

Also in the busy seasons, to make up for the extra labour demand, farmhouses had to hire outside helpers or seek co-operation from neighbours in the form of mutual labour exchanges.[5] In both cases, it was housewives who had to prepare meals for the workers. Thus rural housewives had the burden of preparing more meals than usual in addition to the heavy agricultural workload during the busy season. In addition, the lack of infant care and child care led to accidents or to grave consequences when parents were unaware that their children were unwell, perhaps with a fever.

In observations and consultations with women, LIP workers suggested solutions through communal cooking and nurseries. Usually, women from non-farming households in the villages did the cooking for the farmers. The women in farming households only had to bring their foodstuffs and collect their prepared meals at a given time, thus allowing them to concentrate on agricultural work. In this way, farming housewives could reduce their cooking tasks and at the same time eat more nutritious meals than usual, because they were prepared with the guidance of LIP workers or dieticians.

A similar mechanism worked for communal nurseries. Children were gathered in one place such as a Shinto shrine or Buddhist temple, and taken care of, allowing rural women to dedicate themselves to farmwork. LIP workers played a substantial role as co-ordinators between local authorities or women in non-farming households and groups of rural women, who could not assume this responsibility on their own.

Improved cooking stoves

Another example of a livelihood improvement practice is improved cooking stoves. In nearly all the films and photo slides recording the LIM during the 1940s and 1950s, improved cooking stoves appeared as a highlight of LIP activities. Indeed, the improved cooking stove represented a symbol of livelihood improvement at that time. However, LIP workers never looked at the improvement of cooking stoves as their ultimate goal, as they were instructed that their ultimate goal was the improvement of overall livelihood, including the empowerment of rural women.

The improvement of cooking stoves was also begun after listening to the voices of rural women, who became aware of the inconvenience of traditional cooking stoves, along with long working hours and harsh working conditions in the kitchen. Traditional cooking stoves did not have chimneys to let out smoke, and their open structure resulted in low heat efficiency and the use of a great deal of firewood. Since women carried the firewood, this doubled their workload. The smoke often caused eye diseases such as trachoma, and frequent crouching led to back pain. The accumulation of these problems finally led to a desire for improvements in cooking stoves.

Consideration was given to the improvement not only of stoves, but also of the kitchen as a whole. During the preparation process, 'time and motion surveys' were frequently used to persuade family members who were reluctant to invest in improvements. A LIP worker measured the distance that a rural housewife would walked when cooking, between the preparation place, stove, sink, stock room, water jar and so on in order to prepare a meal. The result showed that she walked about 217 metres over a period of 55 minutes, 30 seconds. After showing this to the housewife, the LIP worker suggested the possibility of improving her kitchen, including the improvement of the cooking stove.

The preparation process for kitchen improvement involved tailored improvements. The LIP worker advised housewives that if they wanted to improve the physical kitchen environment, they would need to develop scientific and rational ways of thinking. Since housewives are of different heights, the height of the sink and cooking stove should be adjusted accordingly. Thus there was never any standardized improved cooking stove kit or standard improved sink. In most cases, the improvements were carried out by the farmers themselves. In some cases, LIP workers went so far as to design hand-made and tailor-made cooking stoves to reduce the workload and expense for individual households.

Fund-raising

Although LIP workers tried to reduce the cost, the improved cooking stoves were not free of expense. Even small improvements in kitchens, lavatories, bedrooms or other places sometimes required expenditure. Financing this became a crucial issue in some cases. Basically, the LIP workers had no funds to distribute as subsidies for their target population. There were no international NGOs involving themselves in the rural development affairs of Japanese villages. Moreover, the Japanese government in the 1950s could not afford to hand out subsidies. Livelihood improvement groups were therefore mobilized to finance their own projects. There are several examples where LIP groups raised their own funds for improvements.

Collecting firewood – in the hamlet of Isshiki in Aichi Prefecture, one of the model hamlets for livelihood improvement, group members carried firewood and pooled the proceeds into a group fund to finance the improvement of cooking stoves. A traditional rotating credit system called *kou* was also utilized for improving cooking stoves. Another scheme was 'egg savings'. Under this, one group raised chickens, and the eggs were sold in the market, with the proceeds being pooled in a group fund. There was also a goat savings scheme.

'Imaginative Savings' was a unique scheme. The members imagined that they had been paid 10 yen for something, and imagined they were satisfied. They placed the 10 yen into a savings fund. This kind of saving is very difficult for individuals because it requires continuous encouragement by others; competition with other group members maintains the motivation for saving. Sometimes, a mother made a snack for her children with whatever ingredients she had on hand, and imagined that she had paid 20 yen at the grocery store for it. The money thus saved was pooled in the group fund and used for livelihood improvement. If available, an agricultural co-operative savings account was used for the group fund. The financial resources of LIP groups were generated in this way.

Economic growth and the LIP

By the time the era of rapid economic growth or the 'Japanese miracle' arrived in the 1960s, the LIP workers and groups had accumulated many achievements. The cash incomes of farmers had increased, both through agricultural production and other jobs such as construction work. Mechanization had reduced the workload of farmers. In due course, rural living conditions improved dramatically. For example, the improved cooking stoves disappeared, to be replaced by gas ranges. Ready-made clothes chased out hand-made work clothes, which had involved strenuous effort to produce. As for nutrition, various cookery ingredients appeared on the market at affordable prices. It was during the 1960s that Japan made a decisive departure from poverty.

Seeing these changes, one might be tempted to say: 'Well, the LIP merely filled the gap before the advent of rapid economic growth. All those baby-step efforts for livelihood improvements were rendered irrelevant by the overwhelming economic growth.' So, was livelihood improvement meaningless after all? We believe that it was not.

The economic growth certainly had a significant impact. The 'Japanese miracle' had a miraculous impact on Japan's socioeconomic situation. But while recognizing this impact, our hypothesis is that the LIP set the stage for economic growth by encouraging social development in rural areas, and that the rapid and fairly equitable distribution of the fruits of economic growth was only made possible by those earlier efforts. If this hypothesis is correct, the Japanese experiences provide a strong argument for the necessity of *improvement* preceding *growth*; and *social* development preceding *economic* development. We believe the Japanese example stands out when compared to the experiences of the current developing countries, particularly in South East Asia, where rapid economic growth in the 1980s has not helped to close the gap between rich and poor.

After Japan escaped from poverty, the LIP changed its approach to follow the changes in rural communities. Since the 1960s, younger people have tended to choose to be non-agricultural paid workers and moved into urban areas. The Japanese government broke from the traditional LIP approach in the 1960s, when the accumulation of financial resources allowed the introduction of subsidies as the primary means for livelihood improvements in agricultural and rural areas. From that point on, the LIP began to follow the old-fashioned 'economic development leads social development' theory.

Prior to the time of rapid economic growth, social development preceded economic growth. We believe that this is the most important lesson to be learnt from the LIP.

Lessons from the LIP as a rural development experience

A multi-sector approach and the spirit of *kaizen*

It is true that postwar Japan had several advantageous conditions for poverty alleviation, and several favourable sociocultural conditions for rural development. Still, there are some lessons that today's developing countries can learn from Japan's rural development experiences, regardless of sociocultural differences.

Livelihood improvement can be seen as a set of strategies for rural development, in that it brought improvements in every aspect, including environmental, sanitation, health and awareness, through direct contact with rural women. A multi-sector and participatory approach is one of the main lessons to be learnt from the LIP experience.

It employed a multi-sector approach in that many actors, under different ministries and agencies – including extension workers, public health nurses and dieticians, supervisors of social education and local authorities – participated in the livelihood improvement movement as necessary.

Second, the importance of the concept of *kaizen* in LIP should be elaborated. *Kaizen* is a Japanese term which refers to improvement or betterment through innovative thinking. The concept is well known in the field of industrial management such as the car manufacturing factories of the Toyota Motor Company.[6] But we think this spirit of *kaizen* also represents the Japanese idea of rural development at its best, mobilizing the maximum amount of local resources while minimizing inputs of external resources.

The LIP as a GAD approach

The LIP aimed at raising the standing of women (*fujin no chii kojo* in Japanese), but the main emphasis was on daily, domestic, women-specific matters such as cooking, clothing, nutrition and sanitation. Therefore, some researchers conclude that it concentrated only on the strategic needs of women, and failed to touch upon a wide range of gender relations. Others may conclude that it was based on the second wave of feminism, or liberal feminism. Therefore, it is usually categorized as a WID approach.

It is true, as mentioned by Ichida (1995, p. 111), that the LIP cast light on 'private' life or domestic matters that had been neglected under the government's service and official community meetings before the Second World

War. The LIP's strategy for raising the social and economical status of rural women was through capacity development and the extraction of spontaneous motivation for self-reliant improvement. It also contributed to the democratization of rural communities. For Mrs Yamamoto, shedding light on private home life did not mean accepting the existing division of labour. On the contrary, the prioritization of private home life meant attracting the attention of everyone (including husbands, older family members, and children) to daily life, uncovering illogical, inconvenient and unhealthy customs, and starting to think of ways of improving them. This may help not only to reduce the current burden of women's chores, but also can lead in the long run to the modernization and democratization of home life. Thus, we can state that the LIP included within its scope the transformation of gender relations, and that in fact LIP workers exerted great effort to empower young wives. From this point, we can categorize the LIP as a GAD (Gender and Development) approach, which can provide many lessons for today's GAD approach in developing countries.

Synergetic relations and the model area approach

The LIP approach pays great attention to the co-ordination between local administration and community-based groups. In the Japanese experience, we can find synergetic relations between local populations and the grassroots government apparatus. This synergy reduces the burden on the government and adds to the sustainability of the development process at community level.

Similarly, the 'concentrated model area' approach is a unique way of disseminating the development process. There were never enough extension workers to cover the entire region that an extension office was supposed to cover. Therefore, model areas were designated for intensive guidance, and most of the activities of extension workers were concentrated into those areas. Members of neighbouring communities visited model communities, and this was supposed to generate a ripple effect. The model areas (villages, hamlets and groups) were also used for experiments with innovative methods and techniques. In fact, the model areas were indispensable for accumulating the experiences of trial and error, and contributed to developing an LIP extension methodology. The experiences from the model areas were reported at the post-harvest agricultural festivals at the district extension centre level. Prominent groups proceeded to competitions at the prefecture level, and the winners from the prefectures gathered at a national annual LIP conference in Tokyo. Every year, LIP workers representing each prefecture gathered for a national conference, escorting rural women from prominent LIP groups in the prefectures. They travelled from their rural villages to Tokyo by train to make presentations at the national event. In this way, experiences in remote areas were fed back on a regular basis to the centre, the Ministry of Agriculture. This was another feature of the concentrated model area approach adopted in postwar Japan.[7]

There was also tacit knowledge concerning ways of finding suitable model areas. In the words of the LIP workers, it was important to find the seeds of improvement in community groups. Activities never worked where these seeds did not seem to exist. Thus, LIP workers said that the crux of the matter was finding seeds rather than sowing seeds themselves in sterile fields. We think this idea constitutes a method or concept of development assistance in its own right.

Conclusion

The occupation forces ordered the democratization of Japan, and democracy at that time was something alien to almost the whole of the rural population and society. However, what emerged was a distinctive form of democracy, different from Western-style democracy. This was because the relationship between the Japanese government and population was never the same as the Western-style relationship between the state and citizens or civil society.

If we can learn some lessons from the Japanese experience of rural development, the first would be the importance of synergetic relations between local administration, frontline officers and local people. Currently, there are several Japanese rural development aid projects emphasizing mutual correspondence between the local administration and local people, and those projects try to formulate social capital among the stakeholders at the local level.

The second lesson to be learnt from the Japanese experiences is that LIP extension methodology (the LIP approach) can be an efficient tool for rural development workers. It is true that the LIP approach is very similar to a 'participatory development approach', but this approach emerged through the accumulation of practical experiences of local activities. This means that it was fine-tuned to the local sociocultural environment in rural Japan, including the above-mentioned synergetic relations at the grassroots level.

Therefore, attempting to transplant this approach to other developing countries would be fruitless. The crucial point is the process through which Japanese people, officers and rural population alike, interpreted and domesticated the induced concept of 'democratization' and modernization. Further study will be needed to describe this domestication process

The current Sustainable Livelihood Approach (SLA) adopted by some Western donors is one of the most refined strategies for alleviating poverty, and emerged from the rich experiences of development aid. The LIP also aimed at alleviating poverty and raising the social status of postwar

Japanese rural women, based on trial and error. The two approaches have different origins, but similar strategies were adapted as a means of alleviating poverty. What we can do now is to identify clearly the similarities and differences between the two concepts. This issue should be discussed further by scholars in various fields of development studies in order to extract practical lessons for rural development policies for rural societies drowning in the waves of democratization and modernization today.

Notes

1 Japan was occupied by the Allied Forces (in practice, the USA) from 1945 to 1951. GHQ is also called SCAP (Supreme Commander of the Allied Powers).

2 In Japanese, the term is 'Seikatsu kaizen fukyu jigyo' (*Seikatsu* means livelihood, *kaizen* means improvement, *fukyu* is extension, and *jigyo* is programme). This programme had its roots in the 1948 Agricultural Improvement Promotion law. Based on this law, a US model of an agricultural extension system was introduced to Japan. LIP activities were placed under the umbrella of the Agricultural Improvement Extension Program, together with agricultural extension activities.

3 This study group was under the 'Development and Women' study division of the Japan Society for International Development (JASID), and was active in the early 1990s. The core members were Keiko Taniguchi, Yoshie Yamasaki, Akira Namae, Kumiko Nose, Yoko Fujinaga and Reiko Murayama.

4 Interviews took place between 2000 and 2003. The interviewees were ex-LIP workers (approximately 50), ex-public health nurses (approximately 15), resettlement area public health nurses (approximately 10), LIP group members (approximately 100) and some other related people and members of communities where LIP group activities had taken place. We conducted interviews in the prefectures of Ehime and Niigata (2000), Yamaguchi, Yamagata and Iwate (2001), Hiroshima, Fukuoka, Kumamoto and Okinawa (2002), and Hokkaido and Nagasaki (2003). We visited some of these prefectures repeatedly. We also conducted interviews in Tokyo with related officials.

5 In many agricultural communities, such forms of mutual labour exchanges are well known as *yui*, and there are other variant names such as *moai*. Traditional mutual help covers most of the community life such as funerals, fires, and so on. Labour contributions increasingly became cash payments during the 1970s and after.

6 The spirit of *kaizen* is applied to TQC (total quality control) and other factory management methodologies. The emphasis is on a group-orientated, participatory form of communication.

7 We are very interested in the fact that Japanese technical cooperation, particularly that conducted by JICA (Japan International Cooperation Agency), adopts a model area approach that is very similar to the LIP approach. However, there is a major difference between the domestic application and international application of the model area approach. On the one hand, the LIP model does not require much financial input from LIP workers and agricultural extension offices, which are trying to utilize the minimum of outside resources. On the other hand, in the international replica of JICA's projects, there is no limit to the amount of resources to be invested. I think this represents a substantial difference for the sustainability of development projects.

84 'Livelihood Improvement' in Postwar Japan

References

In Japanese

Amano, Hiroko (2001) *Sengo Nihon no josei nogyo sha no chii* (Status of female farmers in postwar Japan) (Tokyo: Domesu Shuppan).

Ichida, Tomaoko Iwata (1995) Seikatsu kaizen fukyu jigyo ni miru jenda-kan' (Gender views in the Livelihood improvement Programm), *Noson-shakai Kenkyu* (Studies on rural society), vol. 31.

Meguro, Yoriko, (1998) 'Jenda mondai to enpawamento' (Gender issues and empowerment), *Gendai no esupuri* (Gender and Spirit), no. 376, pp. 35–43.

Nishi, Kiyoko (1985) *Senryo-ka no Nihon fujin seisaku* (Japanese women's policy under the occupation) (Tokyo: Domesu).

Tanaka, Yumiko (2002) 'Kaihatsu ni okeru Jenda' (Gender in the context of development), in (eds), *Kaihatsu to jenda* (Development and gender) (eds), Yumiko Tanaka, Mari Osawa, and Ito Ruri (Tokyo: Kokusai Kyoryoku Shuppan Kai).

In English

Brown, Muriel W. (1957) 'Home Economics Around the World', *Journal of Home Economics*, vol. 49, no. 7, pp. 521–6.

Lewis, Dora S. (1949) 'Education for Family Living in Japan', *Journal of Home Economics*, vol. 41, no. 3, pp. 117–20.

Roelofs, Garritt E. (1951) 'Japan's Extension Service – Some Problems and Progress', *Foreign Agriculture*, vol. xv, no. 11, pp. 243–5.

Rokahr, Mary (1951) 'Home Economists the World Around', *Journal of Home Economics*, vol. 43, no. 2, pp. 93–4.

Taniguchi, Yoshiko, Akira Namae, Kumiko Nose, Yoko Fujinaga, Reiko Murayama and Yoshie Yamazaki (1993) 'The Historical and Structural Analysis of the Experience of Japanese Women in Rural Development – A Case Study of the Home Living Improvement Extension Service Program' (in English abstract), *Journal of International Development Studies*, vol. 3, pp. 1–8.

Thompson, Todd S. (2002) *A History of Extension at USAID*, (Washington DC: USAID and the World Bank).

Yamasaki, Yoshie, Yoshiko Taniguchi, Akira Namae, Kumiko Nose, Yoko Fujinaga and Reiko Murayama (1994) 'Rethinking the Home Living Improvement Movement of the Rural Women in Postwar Japan' (in English abstract), *Journal of International Development Studies*, vol. 4, pp. 9–16.

Ward, Gordon H. (1952). 'Japan's Agricultural Cooperative Program', *Foreign Agriculture*, vol. xvi, no. 6, pp. 115–19.

4
Entrepreneurship and Rural Women's Empowerment: Some Japanese and Thai Cases

Kazuko Kano

Introduction

Objectives

The feminization of agriculture' has become a commonly used term, indicating the ever-increasing importance of the role that women play in agriculture. In Africa, it is estimated that women produce about 80 per cent of the food people consume, while in Asia the figure is about 50 per cent.[1] Despite this fact, however, women rarely receive the recognition they deserve for their work. In developing countries, it is crucially important to shed light on the considerable contribution that rural women are making and to assess it properly. Only then will the social status of women there improve. And if the significance of women's role in agriculture was clarified, it would be possible, for example, to make support for rural women in Asia, Africa and Latin America a priority issue in Japan's development assistance programmes.

In Japan, women account for about 60 per cent of the total agricultural workforce, but it is only recently that their substantial contribution to agriculture has received attention. Now, however, various measures are being taken, and with some positive results, to promote women's role in agriculture. Entrepreneurial activities by rural women represent a breakthrough in the process of making it a little easier for women to gain the recognition they are due for their work. According to a survey conducted in 2004, there are 8,186 rural women's entrepreneurial activities throughout the country.[2] What is behind this surge in rural women's entrepreneurship?

Among the conclusions of a survey on 'food supply' that was conducted by the International Food Policy Research Institute (part of the 'Issues for Development Assistance in the 21st Century' research series commissioned by the International Finance Research Institute of the Japan Bank for International Cooperation), was the suggestion that Japanese experiences in agriculture and rural life could usefully be shared by developing countries. The reasons given were the fact that most Japanese farming is small-scale and family-orientated,[3] and that the government has played an important role in agriculture.[4] Also mentioned were the importance of environmentally sustainable agriculture and women's role in agriculture, both areas in which Japan has a long and rich experience.

In many developing countries, international organizations and governments support income-generating activities for women. These activities are considered to play a vital role in the empowerment of rural women, and empowerment of women lies at the heart of gender issues.

The purpose of this study is to clarify the process of empowerment of rural women that takes place through entrepreneurial activities. Several cases from Japan and Thailand will be discussed.

In the introductory section I shall touch on the topics, 'What is empowerment?' and 'Empowerment and gender'. In the second section, 'Women's role in agriculture', the topics discussed are 'The feminization of agriculture', 'Women's role in agriculture in Japan', and 'Problems female farmers face, and how they cope'. In the third section, entitled 'Entrepreneurial activities and rural women's empowerment', the topics discussed are: 'What are rural women's entrepreneurial activities?', 'Rural women's entrepreneurial activities today', 'Reasons for the increase in rural women's entrepreneurial activities', 'Providing rural women with a market: *michi-no-eki* (roadside stations)', 'The functions of rural women's entrepreneurial activities', and 'The processes of rural women's empowerment through entrepreneurial activities'. In the last section, four cases of rural women's entrepreneurial activities from Japan and Thailand will be analysed, followed by the concluding remarks.

What is empowerment?

The term 'empowerment' is an important word and is widely used by many people. It is, however, very difficult to define what the word means, and no single definition fits every case. The definition varies with the situation and field of study in which the word is used. The meaning and usage has also changed over time. This section introduces several viewpoints in order to better understand 'empowerment', especially as it relates to the field of development and women's empowerment. These viewpoints include: (i) the situations in which the word is used; (ii) its meaning; and (iii) the fields of study in which it has been used.

The English word 'empowerment' is said to have first been used in the seventeenth century as a legal term meaning 'to give someone the right or authority to do something'. It was not until the radical social movements that followed the Second World War, such as the civil rights movement in the USA, the counselling movement and the feminist movement, that the term became widely used in social situations. In recent years it has become increasingly popular in a number of fields including social welfare, development in the Third World, medicine, education and gender issues. There is always a common factor in situations in which 'empowerment' is used. In these situations one finds a group of people who, because of social discrimination or exploitation, are to some extent unable to control their own lives. Used by these people, 'empowerment' means the process of reclaiming one's rights, or taking the control of one's life back into one's own hands (Kukita and Watanabe, 1998)

In the 1980s, 'empowerment' began to appear in the field of business administration. In this area it can refer to either the delegation of power or to psychological motivation. It is the latter of the two senses that has attracted particular attention. For example, it is used to refer to 'the desire for self-realization' in Abraham Maslow's well-known 'Hierarchy of Needs' (Yonekawa, 2002). In order to see how the word is understood in Japan, it is helpful to take a look at the Japanese words for 'empowerment' which were recently introduced by the National Language Research Institute in Japan. The term 'empowerment' in Japanese would be translated as 'development of ability' or 'conferring of authority', meaning 'to bring out the inherent abilities in the individual or to confer social authority on him/her'.

- 'development of ability' is used with an emphasis on the aspect of bringing out the abilities of the individual; and
- 'conferring of authority' is used with an emphasis on the aspect of conferring authority on someone. In the case of a higher-ranking position giving authority to a lower-ranking one, the word 'delegation of authority' may be used.

The word 'empowerment' is formed by putting the word 'power' between the prefix 'em', and the suffix 'ment'. The prefix refers to 'inside', while the suffix merely functions to make the verb a nominative. Thus, the word connotes two important meanings: 'power' and 'inside'. These two connotations are the keys to understanding 'empowerment'. There are two kinds of power, positive and negative. The former includes knowledge, experience, skill, self-determination, freedom of choice, self-respect and so on. Empowerment means to activate these factors of positive power (Morita, 1998).

Empowerment implies an active, independent attitude with which women at the grass-roots level 'empower' themselves, create a sense of solidarity, and take action, as a way of bringing about positive change in their situation and social status (Muramatsu and Muramatsu, 1998).

Empowerment and gender[5]

Empowerment is often referred to in discussions of gender issues. Women typically are embedded in a social structure of discrimination and unable to make full use of their inherent capabilities. More often than not, in domestic matters and socially, women's roles are constrained and their access to various resources and services limited. There are also constraints on their political and economic activities, and they are subject to low-status treatment and heavy workloads and at risk of malnutrition and poor health. The 4th World Conference on Women was convened in Beijing in 1995 in order to improve this situation. The Conference designated twelve major areas, for which five-year action plans were adopted in a *Platform for Action*.[6] The idea underlying this document is 'empowerment', as it stated: 'The *Platform for Action* is an agenda for women's empowerment.' Women's empowerment is indispensable in the solution of gender problems (The Prime Minister's Office, 1996).

Women's role in agriculture

The feminization of agriculture

Women play a greater role in agriculture throughout the world than is generally imagined, and, according to FAO data,[7] women play a particularly important role in Africa. For every 100 men working in agriculture in Mozambique, there are 150 women; in Zimbabwe, the comparable number of women is almost 130, and in Bangladesh, more than 100. This phenomenon is called 'the feminization of agriculture'. According to data from one research institute,[8] in Africa as a whole, about 70 per cent of the female labour force is engaged in agriculture, while in East Africa, the figure is close to 90 per cent.

In Asia, women contribute to about one half of food production in the region as a whole, though the figures vary from country to country. In Indonesia, the figure is 54 per cent and in the Philippines, 46 per cent.

Women's role in agriculture in Japan

In 2001, primary industry accounted for 5 per cent of Japan's labour force, and secondary and tertiary industries, 30 per cent and 65 per cent, respectively. In terms of GDP, in the year 2000, primary industry accounted for 2 per cent, compared to 29 per cent and 70 per cent for the secondary and the tertiary industries, respectively. However agriculture weighs in more heavily when it is measured in relation to environmental issues, reflecting its multifaceted role.[9] The focus in recent years on food security has also highlighted once again the importance of agriculture.

Sixty per cent of agricultural workers in Japan are women, the highest figure among industrialized countries. By age, 55 per cent of those engaged in agriculture are 65 years of age or older. It is often said that today Japanese agriculture depends on the work of women and the aged.[10]

Recently, there has been a renewed interest in agriculture, and the number of people who are entering agriculture is increasing. The total number of people newly entering agriculture under 39 years of age tripled, from

6,000 in 1990 to 18,100 in 2000. The number of women newly engaged in farming who are under 39 years old also tripled, from 1,100 in 1990 to 3,000 in 2000 (Norinsuisan-sho, 2004). More female students are enrolling in agricultural colleges, and some of them are even from non-farming families. In the past, most women became farmers by marrying one, but today more women make the independent decision to choose agriculture as a profession.

Problems female farmers face, and how they cope

Female farmers in Japan face problems similar to those of their counterparts abroad. Farming in Japan usually involves all the family members. Women take part in many aspects of farming, but their contribution is often under-valued. For example, the income from the produce they have helped to grow, harvest and market usually goes into the bank account of the head of the household (usually the husband or father-in-law).

This invisibility of women's contributions can result in a lack of recognition by family members and communities. And there are few opportunities for women to participate in training programmes to boost their skills and self-confidence. Women farmers also tend to be overworked. For farmers in general it is difficult to draw the line between agricultural work and domestic work. In addition to farming, women are responsible for household work, child rearing and care of elderly family members, as well as community activities. They suffer from the hard work of what in gender studies is called 'triple roles', which means work in production, reproduction and community. Recently, however, the situation has begun to change for the better.

Since the mid-1980s, and especially from the beginning of the 1990s, efforts have been made to improve the status of female farmers facing the problems mentioned above. And in 1999, two basic laws of great importance were enacted. These were the Basic Law for a Gender-equal Society, and the Basic Law on Food, Agriculture and Rural Areas. A gender-equal society is defined as a society where both women and men are given equal opportunities to participate in activities in all fields as equal partners, are able to enjoy political, economic, social and cultural benefits equally, and share responsibilities equally. The Basic Plan for Gender Equality was formulated in compliance with the gender equality law. The plan states eleven priorities, one of which is the establishment of gender equality in rural areas. In order to achieve this goal, the plan calls for an improvement of the status of women and the promotion of a better working environment for them.

The previous Agricultural Basic Law that came into effect in 1961 aimed mainly to increase agricultural productivity and thereby raise farmers' income to the level of workers in other industries. The new law of 1999 reflects the considerable changes that have taken place in Japan over the thirty-eight intervening years. The new law is called the Basic Law on Food, Agriculture and Rural Areas, and it indicates social recognition of the importance of these three elements. The recognition and promotion of women's contribution to agriculture is stated as one of the policies of sustainable agricultural development:

> In consideration of the importance of securing opportunities for both men and women to participate in all kinds of activities as equal members of society, the State shall promote the creation of an environment in which women's roles in farming are fairly assessed and women can be provided with opportunities to become involved in farm management and other relevant activities on a voluntary basis. (Article 26)

Women have played an extremely valuable role in both farming and community activities, but their status has not reflected this. Article 26 clearly states a basic policy of action to remedy this. Some of the notable actions to be taken in order to implement the intent of the article are: (i) the dissemination of a 'family management agreement', a written contract describing conditions in family farming, such as responsibilities, holidays, salaries and who takes care of various household tasks – these agreements are considered to have made a significant contribution to promoting women's status in faming households, and the number of households that have concluded such agreements is increasing;[11] (ii) the promotion of women to senior positions, such as 'local agricultural adviser' and 'executive member' in agricultural co-operatives; and (iii) the promotion of women's entrepreneurial activities, referred to as 'other relevant activities' in Article 26.

With the enactment of the two basic laws, and building on the already existing efforts of many women, there has been steady progress in raising the status of female farmers, progress which inevitably varies from family to family, and from community to community, depending largely on the level of awareness. An important step in raising the level of awareness was the establishment in 1988 of a 'day for women in rural areas of agriculture, forestry and fisheries'. In explaining the background of the day, an editorial in a leading farmers' newspaper that appeared on the eve of this rural women's day referred to the importance of international efforts for the advancement of rural women:

> The designation of a special day was influenced by the activities of the United Nations. In 1979 the United Nations adopted the Convention for the Elimination of All Forms of Discrimination Against Women, and Japan ratified the convention in 1985. Japan has been working on related legislation, and public awareness of the issue has also been increasing. The improvement of the status of women in rural areas is

undoubtedly an important part of the issue, and this women's day was established to take concrete action to achieve it. It is hoped that March 10th, along with March 8th, International Women's Day, will be an occasion for people to think about the improvement of rural women's status.[12]

Japan Agricultural Co-operatives (JA) is also making efforts to promote women in its organization. An agricultural co-operative is an organization owned and controlled by member farmers, and its activities cover almost all aspects of farmers' lives. At the time of writing, there are 903 agricultural co-operatives in Japan.

According to the editorial quoted above, JA now has 276 female board members and 255 female senior advisers.[13] Also, 15 per cent of JA's total membership are women. The organization has set goals of having at least two women on the boards at branch offices, and having women comprise at least 10 per cent of executive bodies and at least 25 per cent of its total membership. Some prefectures and individual JA branches have reached one of these goals, but there is no prefecture that has as yet achieved all three goals.

Increasing numbers of women are getting public recognition by being acknowledged by official organizations. For example, in 2002, there were 3,402 registered female farmers; 602 female farming advisers; and 176 female farming advisers for youth. Similarly, more female farmers have earned such titles as 'certified female farmer' and 'life improvement adviser'. The number of such women totalled 7,219 in 2002.[14] Also, 2,261 women have joined agricultural committees, a development that is of particular significance, because one of the main tasks of an agricultural committee, whose members are elected by farmers, is to take decisions on applications for approval to sell farmland.[15]

While these facts show that women's involvement in farm management is progressing in many ways, and that noticeable improvements have been made, much more effort is necessary to bridge the awareness gap between men and women, and to enhance further organizational efforts to advance the status of female farmers.

Entrepreneurial activities and rural women's empowerment

What are rural women's entrepreneurial activities?

The expression 'rural women's entrepreneurial activities' made its first official appearance in a 1992 report entitled 'A fresh view of women in rural areas of farming, forestry and fishery: toward the year 2001', prepared by the Ministry of Agriculture, Forestry and Fisheries (Iwasaki and Miyagi, 2001). A basic definition of 'entrepreneur' is 'an individual who creates and operates a business with imagination and volition as a leader of innovation'.[16] In

Japan, there is a movement in which women living in rural areas start up independent economic activities, and 'women's entrepreneurial activity' is used to refer to such activities. Processing locally grown agricultural products into speciality goods, selling locally grown agricultural products in farmers' markets, and eco-tourism are examples (Norin suisan-sha, 2003).

In developing countries, various organizations, including many UN organizations, have been supporting income-generating activities for rural women, activities that have proved to be popular among women (Kano, 2001). Activities of this kind are considered similar to women's entrepreneurial activities in rural areas in terms of the ideas behind them.

Rural women's entrepreneurial activities today

Since 1997, the Ministry of Agriculture, Forestry and Fisheries has conducted annual survey on women's entrepreneurial activities in rural areas (see Figure 4.1).[17] Entrepreneurial activities had been increasing gradually from the mid-1980s, and this trend accelerated in the 1990s. The number of activities rose from 4,040 in 1997 to 6,039 in 1998. This rise of nearly 50 per cent in one year indicates the interest of many women in rural areas in entrepreneurial activities. The figure has been increasing every year, and reached 8,186 in 2003. While most are group activities, it is interesting to note the increasing number of activities begun by individuals in recent years – up to 1997 these accounted for only 10 per cent of the total, but in 2003 they

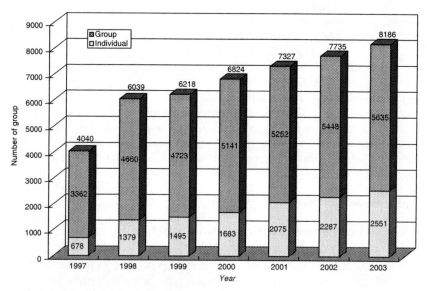

Source: Norinsuisan-sho (2004b).

Figure 4.1   Rural women's entrepreneurial activities

reached 31 per cent. This indicates that women have become empowered to the point where they can start up activities as individual entrepreneurs.

Entrepreneurial activities are usually divided into six categories:[18]

Type I: Agricultural production;

Type II: Food-processing;

Type III: Processing of non-food items;

Type IV: Sales and distribution, including farmers' markets and farm restaurants;

Type V: Rural–urban exchanges; and

Type VI: Service sector activities, including care of the elderly and meal delivery services.

Many activities use locally grown agricultural products, and 72 per cent of them are in the food processing sector, while 44 per cent are in the sales and distribution sector.[19] Activities in the service sector, such as care of the elderly, meal delivery service, and eco-tourism, account for only 0.7 per cent of all activities, but with the rapidly ageing population, and particularly acute in rural areas, this sector is expected to grow.

Many of the activities are small in size. However, 13 per cent of entrepreneurial groups have annual sales of more than 10 million yen (about US$ 94,000), and more entrepreneurs are seeking to be in this category in the future.

Reasons for the increase in rural women's entrepreneurial activities

There are various reasons behind this increase. One reason is that in Japan there is a long history of promoting the production of local products. Before Japan modernized, in the Meiji period (1868–1911) (that is, during the Edo period) (1603–1867) the country was divided into fiefdoms, and feudal lords encouraged the production of local products in their domains. In Kagoshima Prefecture, at the southern tip of Japan, for example, the lords of the Satsuma fiefdom encouraged the production of sweet potatoes and *the manufacture of* cut glass. In Ehime Prefecture, Iyo lords encouraged the production of mandarin oranges and fish paste. Many other fiefdoms promoted local speciality products in a similar way.

In 1979, a new movement to revitalize local communities called 'One Village, One Product' was launched in Oita Prefecture.[20] This initiative was received enthusiastically by many other prefecture and the One Village, One Product movement spread throughout the country.[21] The One Village, One Product movement is now spreading through Asian countries such as Thailand, China, Cambodia, Indonesia, Malaysia and the Philippines.[22]

Another movement that provided a spawning ground for rural women's entrepreneurial activities was the movement to improve living conditions that started after the end of the Second World War and lasted for more than forty years. In its heyday in the mid-1950s, 1960s and 1970s, there were more than 15,000 Livelihood Improvement Programmes (LIP), with a total membership of more than 300,000.[23] As discussed in Chapter 3, in many places, early activities aimed at improving health conditions through campaigns to eliminate fleas and mosquitoes, and to improve kitchen stoves to cut down on smoke and protect women's health. The programme soon expanded into other areas, including cooking classes focusing on the preparation of nutritious, low-budget meals, collective cooking at busy times, and workshops to make more practical work clothes for farm women. Members also studied household bookkeeping and family planning. When the Japanese economy entered its high-growth period, these group activities changed, as many of the initial objectives had been achieved. Building on their experience and accumulated know-how, some groups started entrepreneurial activities utilizing local products.

Another factor has been globalization. With economic growth and greater access to information, Japan imported increasing numbers of food products from all over the world, and information on these products was relayed to consumers. This brought about a significant change in the Japanese diet. A decrease in rice consumption, for example, led to chronic rice surpluses, and since 1970 a policy of limiting rice production has been in place[24] (see Figure 4.2). Per capita rice consumption at the time of writing is now half of what it was in 1960. As some farmers shifted from rice production to vegetables and soya beans, overproduction of vegetables became a problem. Faced with this situation, women responded by processing vegetables into pickles

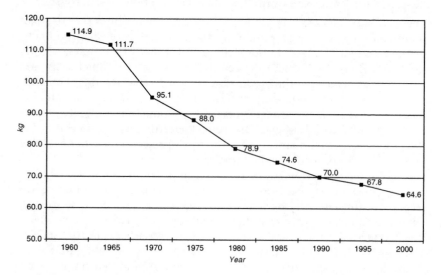

Source: Norinsuisan-sho (2002)

Figure 4.2   Decrease in rice consumption (kg/person/year)

and soya bean paste for sale. These products had hitherto been made by farm households for their own consumption. As the products of what had previously been invisible work, or shadow work, were now being sold and were generating cash income, this kind of women's labour now became visible work.[25]

Providing rural women with a market: *michi-no-eki* (roadside stations)

A special mention should be made of the program of *michi-no-eki*, or road stations, as the programme has provided very much needed markets for the entrepreneurial activities of rural women. The programme was launched by the Ministry of Land, Infrastructure and Transport in 1993, encouraged by a suggestion raised during a citizen's group discussion on roads in the Chugoku region a few years earlier. *Michi-no-eki* are facilities that provide, through the creative ingenuity of the local community, a comfortable place for road users to rest. They provide rural women with a market, encourage the inventiveness and efforts of local people, and have the potential to function as centres for community development. These facilities, which currently number 785 nationwide, have three basic functions:

(i) *As rest stops and relaxation facilities.* In addition to providing a safe parking space and sanitary toilets for motorists, *Michi-no-eki* are equipped with various facilities, such as farmers' restaurants managed by local women, farmers' markets with food-processing facilities, meeting spaces, biotopes offering environmental education for local children, and agricultural experiment space for visitors from the city.

(ii) *As information centres for motorists and local residents.* Information on traffic conditions, the weather, tourism and emergency medical services are available. Some *michi-no-eki* also conduct traffic safety campaigns, the success of which has been proved in lower numbers of accidents.[26]

(iii) *As bases for networking and community development.* Michi-no-eki can be bases for promoting co-operation between the local community and motorists as well as for strengthening ties within local communities. The inter-community cultural exchanges and volunteer activities held there usually contribute to activating communities.

Having visited nearly 100 *mich-ino-eki*, the author discovered several ways in which they can contribute to the empowerment of rural women. One way is by providing employment, and thus generating income, for women. For example, in Ehime Prefecture in the Shikoku region, where there are 21 *michi-no-eki*, 252 employees, or 72 per cent of a total of 349, are women[27] (see Table 4.1). In Gifu Prefecture there are 36 *michi-no-eki*, and women comprise 458 out of a total of 620 employees (74 per cent).[28] And in Niigata Prefecture, where there are 29 *michi-no-eki*, 514 of the 703 employees (73 per cent) are women.[29] It can be assumed that in most *michi-no-eki* the

Table 4.1 Employment in the *Michi-no-eki* in Ehime Prefecture

Workplace	No. of employees		Kind of work performed by female employees					
	Total	Female	Administration	Planning	Business	Customer service	Light work	Other
Seto Town Agricultural Park	6	5	1			4		
Minetopia Bessi	58	35	3		1	16	12	3
Hiyoshi Village (Yume-sonchi)	22	16	1			9	6	
Hirota	3	1			1			
Futami Seaside Park	5	3				3		
Uchiko Refresh Park 'Karari'	40	29	2			23	4	
Ikata 'Kirara' House	3	3				3		
Kinahaiya Shirokawa	14	10	2			6		2
Misho MIC	5	4				4		
Imabari Yunoura Spa	12	11	1			10		
Rainbow Forest Park Matsuno	33	17	2			8	4	3
Hiromi Forest Tricorn Hat	20	17	2	3		11	1	
Hakata S.C. Park	7	5				5		
Kamiura Town Tatara Shimanami Park	22	18	1			14	3	
Shimanami-no-eki, Mishima	5	3				3		
Komatsu Oasis	21	16	3			3	10	
Mikawa	9	7				4	3	
Home of Pure Streams† Hijikawa	29	23	1			16	6	
Fuwari	10	10	1	1		8		
Yoshiumi 'Iki-iki' House	19	15	1			8	6	
Mima	6	4				3	1	
Total (21 eki)	349	252						

Source: Data collected by the Road Section of the Ehime Prefectural Office in 2004.

majority of people who work there are women. In other words, *michi-no-eki* could not function without rural women's contributions. Another important feature of *michi-no-eki* is the fact that all the profits remain within the community and do not go to further enrich regional capital or Tokyo.

The author believes that the concept of the *michi-no-eki* has great potential to contribute to the empowerment of rural women in developing countries,[30] in addition to its contribution to narrow the economic gap between urban and rural areas. In February 2004, joint workshops on *michi-no-eki* were held in Ehime and Tokyo by the Japan Bank for International Cooperation (JBIC), the World Bank, and the Ministry of Land, Infrastructure and Transportation.[31] At the time of writing, with the assistance of JBIC, two *michi-no-eki* are being planned in Gansu Province in China, with the prime object of furthering rural women's empowerment. Similar plans are under way in Fubei Province. In the state of Uttar Pradesh in India, a similar activity is under consideration in conjunction with a tourism promotion project.[32] The World Bank is also considering assisting the plans for *michi-no-eki* in China and some African countries. Many women sell their agricultural products, processed food, and non-food merchandise at *michi-no-eki*. These roadside stations thus provide markets for rural women and senior citizens whose volume of merchandise is usually small. Also, there are no middlemen involved, so farmers make a larger profit.

Michi-no-eki provides capacity-building opportunities for rural women, opportunities to develop and show leadership. For example, there are currently about twenty women 'stationmasters'. Ms Shoda, the stationmaster of 'Taima' in Nara Prefecture, presented a report on their station's activities at a seminar in Lucknow, India, in June 2004. Ms Kurokawa, stationmaster of 'Asago' in Hyogo Prefecture, participated, together with the town mayor, and presented her experience at a seminar on participatory rural development in Bangkok organized by JBIC and the Thai government in January 2003. The third participant, from 'Asago', was Mrs Tsubakino, the 75-year-old leader of an entrepreneurial group that produces a popular soya-bean paste. The audience was impressed by her presentation and by her great vigour and innovativeness.

The themes of *michi-no-eki*, like 'women and agriculture', the theme of 'Menuma' in Saitama Prefecture, also contribute to women's empowerment. And the name of a *michi-no-eki* in Omi town, Shiga Prefecture '*Omi haha no sato*' (maternal homeland) is a reflection of the pride that Omi town takes in its history of producing women of superior capabilities.[33]

The functions of rural women's entrepreneurial activities

As we have seen, there has been a remarkable increase in women's entrepreneurial activities in rural areas in Japan. What functions do these activities have? These activities can be analysed in the light of their economic living and local community dimensions and their function in raising

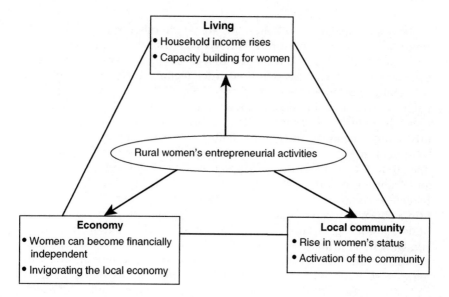

Source: prepared by author, based on the concept of triple roles.

Figure 4.3   Functions of entrepreneurial activities

women's status (see Figure 4.3). Economically, entrepreneurial activities generate employment and income, enabling women to financially contribute to their households or even become financially independent. This in turn stimulates the local economy. And as household income rises, basic family needs are met and the family's standard of living rises. The financial contribution a woman is able to make to the household through her entrepreneurial activities also raises the woman's status, in the eyes of both her family and the community.

Entrepreneurial activities are often carried out in groups at village festivals, school athletic competitions, youth and women's group meetings, and other events. Women often sell homemade cakes, lunches, buckwheat noodles and other local products, activities that breathe fresh life into the local community. Over time, women's groups often acquire their own centres from which they can pursue their activities. Several cases of entrepreneurial activities will be presented and analysed in the fourth section of this chapter.

The processes of rural women's empowerment through entrepreneurial activities

The author worked at the United Nations Population Fund (UNFPA) from the mid-1970s to the beginning of the 1990s, a time when the UNFPA was supporting income-generating activities for women in rural areas in many countries, including Malaysia, Indonesia and Thailand. At that time, these projects were so popular that many other UN agencies, such as UNICEF and UNDP, were also supporting such activities. In Japan, activities like this are called 'entrepreneurial activities'.[34] In many of the places the author has visited in Japan, women have indeed empowered themselves through their entrepreneurial activities. How has this come about?

Empowerment is not a static condition, but a process, a process that is both individual and collective, since it is through involvement in groups that individuals most often begin to develop their awareness and the ability to organize to take action and bring about change (Karl, 1995). The author's observations in several Asian countries, including above-mentioned countries and activities of various Japanese rural women's groups, lead her to view the process of empowerment through rural women's entrepreneurial activities as occurring, in general, in the following four stages.

In the first stage, that of awareness-building and participation, women become aware of the situation in their locality where improvement is needed and take steps, or participate in action, to further gender equality. The second stage is capacity building. Women need skills to start entrepreneurial activities to empower themselves. If they intend to make sweets, for example, they have to know what ingredients to use and the method of making the sweets, and they also have to have knowledge about things like hygiene, expiration dates, storage, wrapping, management and accounting. The third stage is that of carrying out the activity and getting responses from those around them, including their family and neighbours. In the fourth stage, transformation, various changes occur as the result of recognition from the family members and the local community.

The changes that take place are, first, in the women themselves: various interviews with the rural women engaged in entrepreneurial activities tell us that numerous positive changes occur in women, including gaining confidence, developing a broader point of view, finding something to live for, achieving self-realization, and getting satisfaction and pleasure out of farming and entrepreneurial activities. Second, changes in spousal and family relationships are seen, and these changed relationships contribute to gender equality. The cases of Mrs W in Tochigi Prefecture and Mr and Mrs S in Akita Prefecture are two good examples that will be discussed below. Third, there are changes in the community: in some communities, it is difficult to gain local acceptance for entrepreneurial activities, especially in the beginning. In many cases, however, men gradually recognize women's activities and even offer to help. The case of Mrs K and her group in Shizuoka Prefecture, which will be analysed below, is a typical example.

Empowerment may be economical, social or political. Women's entrepreneurial activities fall chiefly into the economical empowerment category. But as the three types are interrelated, after economical empowerment is achieved, social and/or political empowerment will often follow. An example is Ms Fumiko Noda, the chairperson of a 260-member farmers' association that sends their products to the 'Uchiko' *michi-no-eki* in Ehime Prefecture. In July 2003, at the request of JBIC, she presented her case of entrepreneurial activities at a seminar on industrial villages, a project financed by JBIC in Thailand. In February 2004 she was chosen as a 'charismatic woman in tourism' by the Prime Minister's Office in Japan. In May 2004 she published a book, *'Karari' which makes women happy* ('Karari' is the name of the *michi-no-eki* in Uchiko town in which Ms Noda works). Another example is Ms Goto of 'Agri-women Nakatsugawa', a farmers' market in Nakatsugawa, Gifu Prefecture. She went on to become a member of a local agricultural committee after her experience in entrepreneurial activities. There are many similar cases which show that economical empowerment through entrepreneurial activities can lead to the social and political empowerment of women as well.

Case studies of rural women's entrepreneurial activities

In this section we shall present three Japanese and one Thai case of rural women being empowered through entrepreneurial activities. Cases 1 and 4 are cases where the woman herself has been empowered; Case 2 is a case of fundamental changes in spousal and family relationships brought about by a change in the woman herself; and Case 3 is a case of changed relationships with the community. In all four cases we can see the processes of

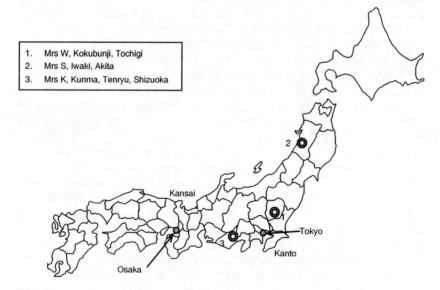

1. Mrs W, Kokubunji, Tochigi
2. Mrs S, Iwaki, Akita
3. Mrs K, Kunma, Tenryu, Shizuoka

Figure 4.4 Location of case studies, Japan

empowerment clearly. The three Japanese cases come from the central, north and the southern parts of eastern Japan (see Figure 4.4) – Tochigi, Akita and Shizuoka. The second of these cases is from Akita Prefecture, which has 376 rural women's entrepreneurial activities, the largest number among the country's 47 prefectures, according to the 2003 survey.[35] As the author assumes entrepreneurial activities can empower rural women regardless of locality, the cases were chosen primarily for the nature of the activities and the women's willingness to answer questions. The author hopes to be able to present more systematic case studies in the future.

Case 1: Mrs W, managing director of the W. Orchid growing company and a member of the Kokubunji rural life study group, Tochigi[36]

Personal profile: Mrs W lives in Kokubunji, Tochigi Prefecture. She was a kindergarten teacher when she married and is now engaged in flower cultivation with her farmer husband and family. She is active in a rural life study group and is also the chairperson of the All-Tochigi Rural Life Study Groups Association.

Family: There are six family members: Mrs W (in her fifties), her husband, parents-in-law, daughter and son.

Community: Kokubunji is located in the southern part of Tochigi Prefecture, about 85 kilometres north of the Japanese capital, Tokyo. The population is 16,000, and there are 550 farming households. The main agricultural products are rice, wheat, aubergine and spinach. Many households also raise cattle.

The processes of empowerment:

(i) *Awareness building and participation*. The W family used to grow mainly the traditional crops of rice and gourds. They had to work long hours from early morning to late evening, and their work seemed to be endless. In order to improve their situation, the family discussed ways in which they could earn an income commensurate with their labour and also how they could draw a line between work time and private time.

(ii) *Capacity building*. In order to improve the management of the farm, Mrs W's husband took a one-year course in flower cultivation at a farm in Nagoya. Mrs W learnt flower cultivation from her husband by working with him and then started trying out her ideas.

(iii) *Practice and effect*. In 1974 the couple built a 300-*tsubo*[37] greenhouse and started cultivating potted chrysanthemums. The W family was extremely busy at that time; the parents-in-law grew the rice, and the Ws, who were also busy with their young children, attended the young cultivated flowers. They had to be on a truck by two o'clock in the morning three times a week to ship their produce to a Tokyo market.

The couple continued to improve their understanding of the business by visiting other flower cultivators in the Kanto and Kansai areas, anxious to learn how they could increase profitability without expanding their facilities. They then switched from chrysanthemums to begonias and bougainvilleas, resulting in a boost in income. Mrs W became more interested in her work and became self-confident as she acquired knowledge and skills raising and marketing flowers, and as a result found farming to be challenging.

In 1982, they expanded their business by adding a 600-*tsubo* greenhouse to their facilities and switched from begonias and bougainvilleas to orchids. They also incorporated the business in 1988. In 1996 they put up another 300-*tsubo* greenhouse. The following year their son started working with them. They also employ seven part-time workers throughout the year.

After becoming incorporated they clarified each of their respective roles and responsibilities in the business as well as in the home. The husband looks after the overall management and is in charge of the marketing of orchids and of their care when they are in full bloom. Mrs W participates in various aspects of the business. She is responsible for bookkeeping and the marketing of the flowers. She is also expected to observe market trends and come up with sales ideas. For example, she must decide, from watching market trends, what kinds and colours of orchids to grow and sell each year. Moreover, she supervises the employees' well-being, making sure that they are not overworked. Their son is in charge of raising the orchid seedlings and the overall management of the growing plants. He is a member of the Tochigi Orchid Association and takes part in the association study group. The parents and their son hold weekly meetings to discuss ideas and problems, such as the style and colour of the orchids that are selling well, price-setting and so on.

(iv) *Transformation.* The transformation in Mrs W herself, who learned flower cultivation at the same time as she was responsible for household work, consisted in her becoming interested in growing flowers, gaining confidence and finding farming challenging. Through her active participation in the local study group's activities she became well known and was featured in an article in *Marronnier Living* on 8 September 2001.[38]

A transformation in spousal/family relationship is seen in the fact that now all the family members share the household work, as well as carrying out their own responsibilities in the cultivation and marketing of the orchids. Since the business was incorporated in 1988, Mr and Mrs W and their son have become equal partners, and the division of responsibilities has become clearer. The relationship between wife and husband has become egalitarian.

The transformation in Mrs W's relations with the community owes much to the rural life study group that she joined in 1987. The group studies ways of improving farmers' lives and then puts these ideas into practice. The study group consists of 8 sub-groups with a total of 54 members whose average age is 48. Among the group members, 37 per cent are full-time farmers, 48 per cent part-time, and 15 per cent non-farmers. In 1990, they concentrated their efforts on the economical and psychological independence of each member, and on participating in building a community network. As part of their efforts, members opened their own bank accounts, and they also started an open-air market that enabled them to sell locally grown vegetables directly to consumers. This was a wonderful opportunity for the members to realize that they were able to achieve things together that they could not have done alone. Moreover, the experience encouraged them to be more active and join in a variety of activities. In 1996, the study group compiled a report on their activities and accomplishments and entered it in the 45th National Agriculture Contest for the Life Improvement Award. They took first place at the regional level.[39]

Here, expected changes were observed, in which all the family members share the workload both at home and at work, which resulted from the recognition of Mrs W's contribution to the flower cultivation, as well as to the household work, by other family members. Based on those entrepreneurial activities, Mrs W has become more active in the rural life study group's activities. She opened a farmers' market with 45 neighbouring farmers in the year 2000, and it is successful. Such activities were recognized in the local community, and she was chosen to be the chairperson of the Association of All Tochigi Rural Life Study Groups in 2002. We realize from Mrs W's case that the relationship between husband and wife can become more equal as a result of entrepreneurial activities. And when a woman is recognized for her contribution by the community, an even more equal relationship between husband and wife can be achieved.[40]

Case 2: Mrs S of Iwaki, Akita Prefecture[41]

Personal profile: Mrs S lives with her husband in Iwaki Town, Akita Prefecture. They have three grown-up children who are now living on their own. Mrs S is in her early fifties. She produces thirty kinds of processed food including rice cakes dipped in soy-sauce, steamed red rice and cooked vegetables and sends them to the 'Iwaki' *michi-no-eki*. Her husband worked for a local branch office of the Japan Agricultural Cooperatives (JA) until his retirement. He is now a farmer and grows rice, flowers (chrysanthemums), as well as fruits such as apples, plums and pears. He sends the rice and flowers to JA and the fruits to the *michi-no-eki*.

Background: Mrs S first worked in the Forestry Co-operative office. She started working as a farmer, with her parents-in-law, after her marriage.
The processes of empowerment:

(i)   *Awareness building and participation*: Mrs S and her parents-in-law produced mainly rice and some vegetables, which they sent to the JA market. As not all of their vegetables matched the strict JA standards for length, size and colour, Mrs S came up with the idea of selling the 'rejects' at an unattended service stand. This provided another source of income for the family, which was used to help meet the educational expenses of the three children.

(ii) *Capacity building*: When the place where her vegetable stand was became a tourist spot, she had to give up selling there and started working at a school lunch kitchen. After five years, she became eligible to take a test to become a licensed cook, which she took and passed.

(iii) *Practice and effect*: She began selling vegetables with five other female farmers from the neighbourhood. They remodelled the back of a small truck into a vegetable stand from which they sold their produce once a week for several years. Because there were few fresh vegetables to sell from winter to spring, they explored the possibility of selling prepared food, like dishes made with cooked rice, and consulted with the agricultural extension workers and the staff of the health centre. Mrs S obtained advice and also got permission from the health office to sell prepared foods. She obtained permission not only to process food, but also to deliver cooked foods such as lunches to people in their homes.

When remodelling her house, she turned a shed into a food-processing unit. The expenses for this were covered by the vegetable sales and her savings from working for the Forestry Co-operative. Permission to process food at the new unit was obtained in November 1999. When the 'Iwaki' *michi-no-eki* was opened in April 2000, she began selling her products there.

(iv) *Transformation*: Mrs S has undergone a change herself. She has gradually gained confidence since starting the food-processing activities and feels satisfied with what she is doing. Mrs S's contribution to the family income is significant, and this has brought about a change in her spousal relationships. Mr S's income pays for the utility bills and her income covers the rest of the household expenses. Her husband, now shares domestic work such as cleaning, doing the laundry and washing the dishes. Such support is very helpful for Mrs S, especially during the busy morning period before the shipment of foods to the *michi-no-eki*. Their children were also helpful.

Mr S recognizes the transformation his wife's activities have brought about. 'Since she started her food-processing work, she has become more cheerful and has confidence in herself. Before, when she needed to call the town office, she asked me to do it. Now she does everything by herself.' He continues: 'During the summer, I earn more than her from my agricultural produce, but during the winter, she earns more than me from her prepared food. The power shifts from me to her'.[42]

This is an interesting case where a woman's entrepreneurial activity has resulted in a shift in decision-making and access to resources, and contributed towards a more equal relationship between wife and husband.

People in the community also appreciate Mrs S's activities, which makes her happy and gives her confidence. They also place orders for her red rice, rice cakes and other items. The transformation in relations with the community doubtless extends to other members of the group as well. According to Mr S, at the 'Iwaki' *michi-no-eki* general meeting held on 10 March 2004, it was revealed that eight out of forty members of the station's producers each had total sales of two to three million yen (about US$ 28,000). It is quite an accomplishment considering that those who sell their products to JA do not usually make that much. The 'Iwaki' roadside station attracts many customers because of the freshness of the products and its proximity to Akita City. An expansion of the sales section will be completed in May 2004, and the group is looking for new members to contribute their produce.

Case 3: Mrs K, stationmaster, *'Kunma-suisya-no-sato' michi-no-eki*, Kunma, Tenryu City, Shizuoka Prefecture[43]

Personal profile: Mrs K lives in Tenryu City, Shizuoka Prefecture. She is in her sixties, has two children and several grandchildren. She is the stationmaster of a *michi-no-eki* called 'Kunma-suisha-no-sato' and is concurrently the vice-president of a non-profit organization (NPO) called *'Yume-mirai kunma'*. She used to work in the timber industry with her husband.

Background: Kunma is a remote mountain village with a population of 1,000. Although it is administratively part of Tenryu City, it is largely covered with forests. Some Kunma women decided to make the most of their local resources by going into business in a country-style restaurant called *'Kaasan no ie'* (Mum's place). They also hold events such as 'The Firefly Festival', which, together with other activities, draws 70,000 to 80,000 people into the area annually.

The Kunma women contribute to the resolution of local problems with the funds they earn from their entrepreneurial activities. For example, they respond to the needs of elderly people who live alone by delivering meals and helping them to participate in recreational activities. There are quite a few elderly people living alone in the Kunma area and the women's activities are very much appreciated. These activities in turn inspired the local men to help the women and contribute to the revitalization of the community. This is a good example of entrepreneurial activities bringing about changes in the relationships between women and men, and women and

the community, changes that reflect a recognition of the significance of the
women's role there, and respect for it.
Processes of empowerment:

(i)   *Awareness building and participation*: Kunma is a small mountain village
      suffering from a triple dilemma: depopulation, an ageing population
      and a slump in the forestry industry, the main industry of the area.
      People 65 years old and over make up 40 per cent of the total popula-
      tion. The size of households is shrinking, and more people are living
      alone or with only their spouse. To seek ways to help the small moun-
      tain village of Kunma to survive, local women got together and sought
      to revitalize the village by taking advantage of its own food culture.
(ii) *Capacity building*: Through the activities of an LIP group, those women
      learnt a number of skills including cooking and managing household
      finances. In addition, they learned *soba* (buckwheat noodle)-making
      from a *soba* master in nearby Hamamatsu City, who was originally
      from the Kunma area, before starting their own restaurant, 'Mum's
      place', in 1996. They also learnt how to make sweets by utilizing local
      products.
(iii) *Pre-practice activities, practices and effects*: In 1976, fifty-three women
      founded the LIP group, of which Mrs K was a member. In 1983, the LIP
      Centre was built, providing the group with a place for their activities.
          In 1985, they formed a group to process agricultural products and
      started producing preserved foods like soya-bean paste and pickles.
          In 1986, the Association for the Promotion of Kunma Revitalization
      was founded, and all the households in Kunma joined. Kunma people
      started planting buckwheat on fallow land.
          In 1987, a core group of thirty-one women formed another group to
      set up the '*Kunma-suisha-no-sato*,' which included a shop. The facility
      was built primarily to process and sell agricultural products as part of a
      project for rural-area revitalization.
          In 1988, '*Kunma-suisha-no-sato*' began operation and 'The Firefly
      Festival' also started in that year.
          In 1989, the group received the Emperor's Award at the 28th Festival
      for Agriculture, Forestry, and Fisheries for its contribution to the re-
      vitalization of the village.
          In 1995, '*Kunma-suisha-no-sato*' was certified as a *michi-no-eki*, one of
      the 103 roadside stations in the first group.
          In 1996, the group opened a restaurant, 'Mum's place'. Annual sales,
      together with income from other activities, currently totals 80 million
      yen (about US$ 750,000), serving 75,000 customers annually.
(iv) *Transformation*: Realizing the serious problems the community faces,
      Mrs K is determined to make a contribution to the community, and not
      to simply pursue the group's financial interest. 'Many people,' she says,
      'tell me that more people in the community appreciate and respect

women now.' It is obvious that such responses have brought about a personal transformation in the women, giving them confidence.

A transformation has been seen in spousal/family relations as well. Kunma is a conservative area, so traditionally wives were expected to stay at home. When the group's activities began attracting increasing numbers of people to the area, NHK, a national TV network, featured it on a TV programme as an example of rural-area revitalization by women, which in turn encouraged more people to visit. Also, as they began bringing in income and spending it for the sake of their families, it gradually became easier for group members to gain their families' understanding. And when the people of the area realized that they could sell products at the shop, more of them were motivated to grow agricultural produce.

The women's group started to provide support for the community by utilizing profits from the shop to solve local problems, as stated above. This is also an expression of their gratitude for the financial support they received from the community at the outset of their activities. The community funded part of the group's start-up costs by selling cedar trees from the communally owned forest.

Once a month the group members deliver nutritionally well-balanced lunches to elderly people living alone and take time to chat with them. Mrs Okuwa, a beneficiary of the programme who lives in a remote area, said in a TV programme (see below), 'I rarely have the chance to talk with anyone, so I really look forward to having a chat with the person who brings my lunch.'

The Kunma area is divided into eight neighbourhood groups. The women hold monthly get-togethers for the elderly people in each group for recreation and exercise. The group members also support the child-care centre by taking care of children from two to four o'clock in the afternoon, after the centre's regular service hours, a very-much-needed service. These activities cost them in total three million yen (about US$ 28,000) annually, and this comes out of the profits of their entrepreneurial activities.

In July 2003, the group's activities were publicized by the NHK station in a programme entitled 'Rural women's entrepreneurial activities change villages'.[44] The TV programme showed a local man, Mr Oishi, getting ready for 'The Firefly Festival' in mid-June and commenting that 'women have brought us this far. From now on, I think it's also our turn to really think about what we, as men, can do to revitalize the community'. Women have brought about changes in men, and the community has moved closer to gender equality.

Professor Kumano of Kumamoto University said in the programme: 'Their actions are not based on an abstract plan. Rather, they are acting according to a concrete plan based on the people's needs. Their approach is tailored to each individual.'

Case 4: Examples of rural women's entrepreneurial activities in Thailand

Background: The population of Thailand is 63 million, 63 per cent of whom live in farming areas. Thus, farming lies at the very heart of Thai society. Although Thailand has for the most part established its basic social infrastructure – such things as a highway network, water supply, irrigation systems, communication network and power supply network – the income disparities between the urban areas and the rural areas are still great, and the government has made improvement of income and living standards in rural areas its top priority.[45]

There are a number of issues still to be solved with regard to the status of women in Thailand, although Thai women are better off than many of their Asian sisters in terms of access to education, health services and the like. Moreover, women in Thailand play an important role within their families and in society. A quarter of Thai families have a woman as head of the household and this makes it all the more important to provide opportunities for rural women to increase their income and to empower themselves.

The Thai government established the 'village fund' in January 2001 as an urgent measure. The system is intended to be a revolving fund for the purpose of encouraging people in rural areas to become independent. A village fund committee is in charge of managing the system. The committee consists of nine to fifteen people, half of whom must be women. Each village is allowed to use up to one million baht (us$ 25,000) as a revolving fund.

The Community Development Bureau of the Ministry of the Interior has encouraged farm people to form small groups with the aim of saving money together. At the time of writing there are 30,000 such groups saving money and lending it to members. Some of these groups, especially ones formed by women, have been engaged in income-generating activities.

Under the leadership of Prime Minister Taksin Shinawatra, the Thai government has been trying systematically to promote 'One Tambon (village), One Product' (OTOP), adopted from the One Village, One Product movement that began in Oita Prefecture in Japan in 1979. There is an OTOP committee chaired by the deputy prime minister.[46] The governors of all the seventy-five provinces in Thailand visited Oita Prefecture in September 2001 to study the activities of One Village, One Product.[47]

The Bank for Agriculture and Agricultural Co-operatives (BAAC) of Thailand has set up a lending programme for rural entrepreneurs in order to improve living standards in rural areas by creating employment and increasing income, which eventually, it hopes, will have a positive impact on the country's economy. The money-saving groups led by women mentioned above are its major clients.

Durian processing group, Chanthaburi Province, Eastern Thailand

The author visited a durian processing group in Chanthaburi Province in eastern Thailand in mid-September 2003 and interviewed Mrs WA, the leader. Durian products processed by this group are certified as OTOP products. In order to be certified, a product must pass the OTOP product standard prepared by the OTOP committee under the management of the Prime Minister's Office.[48]

In keeping with the four-stage empowerment process described above, Mrs WA's case is analysed as follows.

The processes of empowerment:

(i) *Awareness building and participation*: In Chanthaburi, agricultural products such as durians are cheap, and Mrs WA wondered how they could make better use of them. She got together with ten other women in the community who shared similar ideas and discussed possible solutions.

(ii) *Capacity building*: The women decided to collect 100 baht each and had a three-day training session at Mrs WA's home to learn how to process agricultural products. At first they utilized the traditional methods they had learned from their mothers to process local products such as durians and rose apples, but gradually they improved the product quality by adding their own ideas. They also improved the product packaging.

(iii) *Practice and effects*: The initial markets for their products were festivals and special events. Their products gained a good reputation, which led them to start selling in a large grocery store, 'Newport'. The store gave the group its own space where the products could be sold on a regular basis. The products started to sell well and were certified by the OTOP committee. Now the group is allowed to use the OTOP product logo.

(iv) *Transformation*: The group attracted the attention of the media and was featured on a local TV programme. They were chosen as one of the four best groups by the OTOP committee. Mrs WA was invited to visit Bangkok and was photographed with the prime minister. Then the group took another step forward and built a shop of their own next to the processing unit, where Mrs WA's husband now helps to sell their products.

She said that the income from the business accounted for more than a third of her family's total household income.

The women's initiative of going into business and making a success of it resulted in a change in Mrs WA's relationship with her husband. From gaining his understanding of her activities, she went on to gain his co-operation in the group activities. She said her children were also co-operative and helped her. The group also gained recognition in the community.

We also interviewed three other women who were working in the food-processing unit. They said that their earnings there provided them with about a quarter of their total household income. They all agreed that the income from the activities helps their families' finances substantially.

Mrs WA was observed to have reached the fourth stage of the empowerment processes mentioned above, after going through stages 1, 2 and 3. Stage 4 is the stage of transformation of individuals, families and communities. Specifically, some changes were noticeable in her relationship with her husband – a relationship of equal partnership. It is obvious that Mrs WA has improved her abilities in, and knowledge about, processing various fruits, and gained more confidence. The women's activities have been recognized by the local community, They are all now more confident, and by contributing to the family income have improved the standard of living of their households. From what we observed, it was clear that they had been empowered through their entrepreneurial activities.

Conclusions

We have observed the processes of empowerment of rural women through entrepreneurial activities. The first case is one in which the subject, through entrepreneurial activities, empowered and transformed herself. This led to more egalitarian relationships with her husband and other family members. Her role in the local group's entrepreneurial activities and study group activities gained her recognition by the community as well, which is reflected in her being elected chairperson of the prefecture-wide rural life study group organization.

The second case is a typical case of transformed relations between wife and husband through entrepreneurial activities. The husband's comment: 'During the summer, my income from agricultural work is larger, and during the winter, my wife's income from the food-processing activities is larger. Therefore the power relation is being reversed' explains clearly this important transformation. The power referred to has not only a monetary implication but psychological and social implications as well. The relationship became one of mutual respect, a relationship of equals. The wife is happy and seemed proud of herself when she described the recognition her activities had received from people in the community. It can be assumed that the many other women engaged in similar activities in Iwaki Town have also made gains in terms of community recognition.

When women are given opportunities and encouragement, they can improve their situation and accomplish the goals they set for themselves. The Iwaki *michi-no-eki*, for instance, provided a base for Mrs S's activities. It seems that one of the reasons for the Iwaki roadside station's success was the planning that took place with various groups in the town such as women's groups, the youth group, various farmers groups and the Chamber of Commerce.[49] It was done in a participatory way.

In the third case, the women's relationship with the community was transformed greatly through their entrepreneurial activities and contributions to the community. Using their business profits, women perform much-needed services for the elderly and for children, and these activities have stimulated men to think seriously about how *they* can work to activate their community. Mrs K's pleasure in seeing the community start to respect its women is surely shared by all the women in the remote, mountainous Kunma community.

The Japanese cases show that entrepreneurial activities are an effective and realistic means of bringing about the empowerment of rural women.

Although more study is needed in the case of Thailand, it is obvious that rural women are being empowered through entrepreneurial activities there as well. But while many income-generating activities have been carried out and various gains made, there are also many activities that cannot be sustained, mainly because of a lack of markets. The One Village, One Product programme and the *michi-no-eki* system can contribute to local communities if they can are introduced in ways that maximize women's participation and are based on the needs of local communities.

If women change, then men also change, and female–male relationships become more egalitarian. And if women and men change, rural communities can change, be invigorated and become more democratic.[50] Rural women's entrepreneurial activities can be a realistic option for such a transformation. This study is one step towards understanding the processes of empowerment of rural women through entrepreneurial activities. We hope to be able to continue the search for a better understanding of the processes of rural women's empowerment through entrepreneurial activities in Japan as well as in Thailand. If the processes involved can become clearer, more support for such activities in Asia and other developing areas could appear.

Notes

1 The data are based on FAO and UN publications.
2 Norinsuisan-sho (2004b).
3 Average area of cultivated land per household in Japan is 1.6 ha (as at 2001). The figure for China is 0.5 ha (as at 2000), while for the USA is 176 ha (as at 2001) (Zenkoku nogyo kumiai rengokai, 2004).
4 JBIC (2002).
5 Gender refers to social and cultural distinction between the sexes and differs from a biological distinction.
6 The twelve areas are: (1) women and poverty; (2) education and training of women; (3) women and health; (4) violence against women; (5) women and armed conflict; (6) women and the economy; (7) women in power and decision-making; (8) institutional mechanisms for the advancement of women; (9)

human rights of women; (10) women and the media; (11) women and the environment; and (12) the girl child.

7   FAO (2001), pp. 14–16.
8   Popyureshon refarensu byuro (1998).
9   According to an estimate by the Japan Academic Council in 2001, the value of the multiple functions of agriculture is equivalent to 8,220 billion yen (about US$ 77 billion). (Zenkoku nogyu kumiai rengokai, 2004, p. 93)
10 Zenkoku nogyo kumiai rengokai, 2004, p. 20.
11 There were 28,734 such agreements as of March 2004, according to the survey by the Ministry of Agriculture.
12 *Nihon nogkyo shinbun* (The Japan Agricultural News), 9 March 2004, p. 2.
13 The numbers of female board members are as at 1 September 2003. The total board members, as at 31 March 2001, is 22,981, *Nihon nogyo shinbun*, 9 March 2004.
14 Each prefecture has a system of its own to promote and encourage female farmers, and each has a different name.
15 Although the numbers and the ratio of female members are still small, they have increased noticeably recently. With 2,261 members, female ratio is 3.6% of the total committee members.
16 Shogakkan Random House (1993).
17 Norinsuisan-sho 2004b.
18 Noson chiiki keikaku senta (1994), p. 21.
19 Multiple answers were given in this questionnaire.
20 The movement is based on three major themes: 'Think globally and act locally', 'Independence and creativity', and 'Fostering human resources'.
21 These activities are similar in nature, even if some regions did not call them after the 'One Village, One Product' movement.
22 The Asian Productivity Organization organized a seminar on 'One Village, One Product' for Community Development', 17–23 August 2004, in Thailand, and thirteen countries from Asia participated.
23 Amano (2001), p. 225.
24 Whereas, an average Japanese person consumed 120 kilograms of rice per year in 1970, he/she ate only half that amount, about 60-plus kilograms, in 2000.
25 Higuchi and Adachi (1995).
26 *Michi-no-eki*, Asago in Hyogo Prefecture is a good example.
27 At the request of the author, the Roads Section of the Ehime Prefectural Government conducted the survey in January 2004, based on the scheme provided by the author. The construction of the framework was originally helped by Mr Kanja, of Gifu Prefectural Government.
28 As of April 2003, the data was provided by the Road Section of Gifu Prefecture.
29 As of February 2002, by the Roads Section, Niigata Prefecture.
30 Kano (2001).
31 *Japan Economic Review*, 15 March, 2004.
32 *Asahi Shinbun*, 23 July, 2004.
33 A more comprehensive analysis on the potentials of *michi-no-eki* for women's empowerment will be prepared separately.
34 We can say that income generating activities for rural women and rural women's entrepreneurial activities can mean almost the same thing. In Iwasaki and Miyagi (2001), they explain women's entrepreneurial activities as follows: economic activities of rural women have been done for many years and this is nothing new. 'Entrepreneurial activities' is recent nomenclature. Women's entrepreneurial activities are activities to be done on women's initiative. They

proposed a few qualifications to be called as women's entrepreneurial activities, namely (i) women are the main figure of activities, and they decide policies and planning and (ii) it should provide some income for women.

35 The survey by the Ministry of Agriculture, Forestry and Fisheries.

36 Interviews with her took place on 24 February, 2004 at the Kokubunji town office and on February 29 at Mrs W's unit.

37 A unit of land: 1 *tsubo* equals 3.3 square metres.

38 The *Marronnier Living* is published every Saturday by 'Tochigi Living' in Utsunomiya.

39 The contest was sponsored by the Mainichi Newpaper Co., Ltd.

40 The second interview was held on 29 February 2994 at the *'Yume-kobo'* (dream studio), a lovely building next to her house. It was built by the W's company with Mrs W's personal financial support. It is used for part-time female workers to take a break and get dressed for work. Women in the study group can also use it for meetings without bothering family members. Young female farmers visit *'Yume-kobo'* when seeking advice.

41 Interviews with her took place on three occasions in 2004–5 and 13 February, and 11 March (by telephone). Her husband was with her on 13 February and 11 March.

42 The author is planning to conduct further interviews on this point.

43 Interviews with Mrs K were held in May 2002 in Tokyo and 13 March 2004 by telephone. Previous visits were made in November 1999 and May 2002.

44 'Close-up Gendai,' a TV programme transmitted at 7:30 in the evening, which features current topical issues.

45 According to the Household Survey by the Statistical Bureau of the Ministry of Information in 2002, the average monthly household income in the north-east is 9,279 bahts, compared to 28,239 bahts in Bangkok and its neighbouring three prefectures, *JP Jiji News*, 17 April 2003.

46 The National Committee of One Village, One Product (2001) 'Policy Guidance of One Village, One Product,' and 'The Summary of Implementation of One Village, One Product,' 30 April 2001.

47 *Oita Godo* newspaper, 27 September 2003.

48 According to the OTOP product criteria, products and activities are divided into two groups: (1) commercial goods and (2) culture, tourism and services. In each group, products or activities are evaluated in terms of both product quality and management. Those two aspects have the following evaluation criteria: (i) product quality (product ingredients; the quantity of local specialities included in commercial goods); (ii) manufacturing (product quality and the effects on the environment); (iii) marketing (the ability to find new markets); (iv) accounting; and (v) availability of registration documents and the also availability of a network.

49 Association of Agricultural & Fisheries Experiments, 'The Report of Activities of Establishing Bases for Agriculture in Iwaki', 1998 and 2001.

50 Mr Shoichi Yamashita, farmer writer, made similar remarks in his recent book after his visit to JA Kinan representatives' meeting. He was impressed with the proportion of women representatives, which was 102 out of 500 – roughly 20%. The target is 30%. What changed after the increase of women representatives are: (i) men's opinion became more constructive; (ii) topics such as old people's care and living-related matters was now on the table for discussion; (iii) men's perceptions about women have been changed and have become more positive; and (iv) generally, women are taking their duties more seriously than men colleagues and are hard-working (Yamashita, 2004).

References

Amano, Hiroko (2001) *Sengo Nihon no josei nogyosha no chii* (*Status of female farmers in post-war Japan*) (Tokyo: Domesu Shuppan) (in Japanese).

Brown, Lester B. (2003) *Plan B: eko ekonomi o mezashite* (Plan B: rescuing a planet under stress and a civilization in trouble), translated into Japanese by Rakutaro Kitaoji (Tokyo: World Watch, Japan).

Craig, Gary and Marjorie Mayo (1995) *Community Empowerment* (London: Zed Books).

Datta, Rekha and Judith Kornberg (2002) *Women in Developing Countries* (London: Lynne Rienner).

Ebara, Yumiko (2002) *Jiko-ketteiken to jenda* (Self-determination and gender) (Tokyo: Iwanami Shoten) (in Japanese).

FAO (2001) *Sekaino syokuryo kakuho to noson jyosei* (Securing food and rural women) (Tokyo: Kokusai syokuryo Nogyo Kyokai) (in Japanese).

Fujii, Ayako (2004) *Nanohana eko Kakumei* (Nanohana eco-revolution) (Tokyo: Sorinsha) (in Japanese).

Fuijimori, Fumie (1999) *Shoku-gyo okoshi funtoki* (Striving for the development of food professions) (Tokyo: Nobunkyo) (in Japanese).

Fujitani, Atsuko (2001) *Nihon nogyo no joseigaku* (Japanese agriculture – women's studies) (Tokyo: Domesu Shuppan) (in Japanese).

Futatsugi, Sueo (2000) *Seiko-suru famazu maketto* (Successful farmers' markets) (Tokyo: Ie-no-hikari Kyokai) (in Japanese).

Godai, Mitsuru and Nobuko Kobayashi (1996) *Josei kigyoka monogatari* (Stories of women entreprenuers) (Nagoya: Aichi Shobo) (in Japanese).

Gojo, Yoshimi (2003) *Kazoku keiei kyotei no tenkai* (Development of the family management agreement) (Tokyo: Tsukuba Shobo) (in Japanese).

Hara, Hiroko and Mari Osawa (1997) *Henyo-suru dansei shakai* (A changing male-dominated society) (Tokyo: Shinyosha) (in Japanese).

Higuchi, Keiko and Adachi, Yukiko (eds.) (1995) *Ganbare josei no shokugyo okoshi* (Women's entrepreneurial activities in the food business), (Tokyo: Nobunkyo) (in Japanese).

Hiramatsu, Morihiko (1996) *Chiho karano hasso* (Ideas from local regions) (Tokyo: Iwanami Shoten) (in Japanese).

Hobo, Takehiko (1996) *Naihatsuteki hattenron to nihon no nosanson* (Endogenous development theory and Japan's rural districts) (Tokyo: Iwanami Shoten) (in Japanese).

Ikeuchi, Yasuko (ed.) (2002) *Niju-ichi-seiki no jenda ron* (Gender issues for the twenty-first century) (Tokyo: Koyo Shobo) (in Japanese).

Inakano Hiroin Wakuwaku Nettowaku (2003) *Anata e: no de hataraku josei karano messeiji* (For you: a message from women farmers) (Saitama: Inakano Hiroin Wakuwaku Nettowaku) (in Japanese).

Ito, Tatsuo and Sachiko Ito (2003) *Sankagata noson kaihatsu to enu-ji-o purojekuto* (Participatory rural development and NGO projects) (Tokyo: Akashi Shoten) (in Japanese).

Iwasaki, Yumiko and Michiko Miyagi (eds) (2001) *Seiko suru noson josei kigyo* (Successful rural women's entrepreneurial activities) (Tokyo: Ienohikari Kyokai) (in Japanese).

JBIC (2002) *Development Assistance Strategies in the 21st Century: Global and Regional Issues Volume 1*, Research Paper No 16–1, Tokyo: JBIC Institute, Japan Bank for International Cooperation.

James, V. and J. Etim (eds) (1999) *The Feminization of Development Processes in Africa: Current and Future Perspectives* (Westport, Conn.: Praeger).

Josei Seikatsu Katsudo Shien Kyokai (2003) *Nosangyoson no josei kigyo* (Women's entrepreneurial activities in rural areas) (Tokyo: Josei Seikatsu Katsudo Shien Kyokai) (in Japanese).

Kanemaru, Hiromi (2002) *Tadaima funto-chu* (Now, fighting) (Tokyo: NPA) (in Japanese).

Kano, Kazuko (2001) 'Tai-de ikiru gifu-ken no michi-no-eki no keiken' (Gifu's road stations' experiences utilized in Thailand), in *Development and Co-operation*, no. 10, August, JBIC (in Japanese).

Karl, Marilee (1995) *Women and Empowerment* (London: Zed Books).

Kawasaki, Kenko and Yoichi Nakamura (eds) (2000) *Anpeido waku towa nanika* (What is unpaid work?) (Tokyo: Fujiwara Shoten) (in Japanese).

Kokusai Koryu Kikin (Japan Foundation) (1998) *Onna-no kigyo ga sekai o kaeru* (Women's entrepreneurial activities will change the world) (Tokyo: Keibunsha) (in Japanese).

Kono, Hiroshi (2002) *Yutakana kokudo zukuri* (Rich nation-building) (Miyazaki: Komyakusha) (in Japanese).

Kukita, Jyun and Fumio Watanabe (1998) 'Enpawamento (empowerment)', *Modern Esprit*, November (Tokyo: Shibundo) (in Japanese).

Masukata, Toshiko and Kazunori Matsumura (2002) *Shoku to karada no shakaigaku* (Sociology of food, agriculture and the body) (Tokyo: Shinyosha) (in Japanese).

Matsuo, Yasunori (2003) *Isan no hyakusho tachi* (Farmers in Isan) (Tokyo: Mekon) (in Japanese).

Miyaguchi, Toshimichi (2001) *Chiiki o ikasu* (Revitalizing communities) (Tokyo: Taimeido) (in Japanese).

Miyake, Yoshiko (2001) *Nihon shakai to jenda* (Japanese society and gender) (Tokyo: Akashi Shoten) (in Japanese).

Morita, Yuri (1998) *Enpawamento to jinken* (Empowerment and human rights) (Chiba: Kaiho Shuppansha) (in Japanese).

Muramatsu, Yasuko and Yasuko Muramatsu (eds) (1998). *Enpawamento no jyoseigaku*, (Women's Studies of Empowerment) (Tokyo: Yuhikaku) (in Japanese).

Murthy, Ranjani and Lakshami Sankaran (2003) *Denial and Distress* (London: Zed Books).

Mushakoji, Kinhide (2002) *Atarashii Nihon no katachi* (New shape of Japan) (Tokyo: Fujwara Shoten) (in Japanese).

Nihon Nogyo Shinbun (The Japan Agricultural News).

Nishikawa, Jun (2001) *Ajia no naihatsuteki hatten* (Endogenous development in Asian countries) (Tokyo: Fujiwara Shoten) (in Japanese).

Nitta, Hitoshi (2002) *Mori e iko, sanson e iko* (Let's go to the forests and villages) (Tokyo: Shunjusya) (in Japanese).

Norinsuisan-sho (Ministry of Agriculture, Forestry and Fisheries) (2002) *Heisei 14 nen shokuryo jukyu hyo* (Food supply and demand table 2002), (Tokyo: Norinsuisan-sho) (in Japanese).

Norinsuisan-sho (Ministry of Agriculture, Forestry and Fisheries) (2003) *Nosansong-goson ni okeru josei o torimaku jokyo* (The conditions surrounding village women), (Tokyo: Norinsuisan-sho) (in Japanese).

Norinsuisan-sho (Ministry of Agriculture, Forestry and Fisheries) (2004a) *Heisei 16 nen nogyo kozo doutai chosa hokokusho* (Survey on structural dynamics in agriculture 2004), (Tokyo: Norinsuisan-sho) (in Japanese).

Norinsuisan-sho (Ministry of Agriculture, Forestry and Fisheries) (2004b) *Heisei 15 nen noson josei ni yoru kigyo katsudo jittai chosa* (Studies on women's entrepreneurial activities in rural areas), (Tokyo: Norinsuisan-sho) (in Japanese).

Noson chiiki keikaku senta (Regional Social Planning Centre) (1994).

Noson no jyosei kigyokatachi (women entrepreneurs in rural areas) (Tokyo: Ienohikari kyokai) (in Japanese).

Okabe, Mamoru (2000) *Noson josei ni yoru kigyo to hojinka* (Entrepreneurial activities and incorporatization by rural women) (Tokyo: Tsukuba Shobo) (in Japanese).

Okane, Yoshiaki (2001) *No to onna to kyodokumiai* (Agriculture, women and co-operatives) (Tokyo: Zenkoku Kyodo Shuppan) (in Japanese).

Popyureshon refarensu byuro (Population referece bureau) (1998).

Saito, Chihiro (1997) *Indo: NGO taikoku* (India: big NGO country) (Tokyo: Akashi Shoten) (in Japanese).

Sekai no jyosei deta shito (women of our world: data sheet) (2005) (Tokyo: Tokutei hieiri katsudo hojin nisengoju) (in Japanese).

Seki, Keiko and Kimiko Kimoto (eds) (1996) *Jenda kara sekai o yomu* (Reading the world from gender perspectives) (Tokyo: Akashi Shoten) (in Japanese).

Shioda, Sakiko (2000) *Nihon no shakai Seisaku to Jenda* (Japanese social policies and gender). (Tokyo: Nihon Hyoronsha) (in Japanese).

Shogakkan Random House (1993) *New Shogakkan Random House English–Japanese Dictionary* (Tokyo: Shogakkan).

Shokuryo nogyo noson kihonseisaku Kenkyukai (2000) *Shokuryo nogyo noson kihonho kaisetsu* (Commentary on the basic law on food, agriculture, and rural areas) (Tokyo: Taisei Shuppansha) (in Japanese).

Takahashi, Masayasu, Yoshiaki Yamaguchi and Hajime Ushimaru (2002) *Soshiki to Jenda* (Organizations and gender) (Tokyo: Dobunkan Shuppan) (in Japanese).

Tamura, Keiko and Masami Shinozaki (1999) *Ajia no shakaihendo to Jenda* (Social change and gender in Asia) (Tokyo: Akashi Shoten) (in Japanese).

Tamura, Mariko (1995) *Josei kigyoka-tachi* (Women entrepreneurs) (Tokyo: Nihon Keizai Shinbun) (in Japanese).

The Prime Minister's Office (1996). *Nairobi kara Pekin e* (From Nairobi to Beijing) (Tokyo: The Prime Minister's Office) (in Japanese).

Umezawa, Shotaro (1997) *Za tekisuto: nogyo maketingu* (The textbook: agricultural marketing) (Tokyo: Japan Agricultural Development and Extension Association) (in Japanese).

Wakatsuki, Toshikazu (2003) *Mura de byoki to tatakau* (Fighting off illness in the hamlets, by Saku Central Hospital) (Iwanami Shoten) (Tokyo: Iwanam; Shoten) (in Japanese).

Yamamoto, Masayuki (2004) *Kachinokoru famazu maketto* (Successful farmers markets). (Tokyo: Ienohikari Kyokai) (in Japanese).

Yamamoto, Tsutomu, Kazunori Kaku, Sadao Tokuno, and Kazuyoshi Takano (1999) *Gendai nosanson no shakaibunseki* (Social analysis of contemporary rural society) (Tokyo: Gakubunsha) (in Japanese).

Yamashita, Soichi (2004) *No wa eien da* (Agriculture is eternal) (Tokyo: Ienohikari Kyokai) (in Japanese).

Yonekawa, Kazuo (2002) *Enpawamento* (Empowerment) (Tokyo: Tokyo Tosyo Shuppankai) (in Japanese).

Zenkoku nogyo kumiai rengokai (National Federation of Agricultural Cooperative Associations) (2004) *Junia fakuto bukku* (Junior Fact Book) (Tokyo: National Federation of Agricultural Cooperative Associations) (in Japanese).

Part II

Comparing Japan and Developing Countries

5

Women's Participation in Politics and the Women's Movement: The History and Background of Recent Successes of Women Candidates in Local Elections

Kuniko Funabashi

Introduction

Japanese women's participation in the decision-making process, especially in the field of politics, is quite low. The percentage of women in the House of Representatives (the Lower House) after the election of 2003 was 7.1 per cent, putting Japan in 134th place in the Inter-Parliamentary Union (IPU) ranking for the world. The percentage in local assemblies after the nation-wide local elections of 2003 was 7.6 per cent. Why is the political status of women in Japan so low?

> If it were a case of discrimination in a population consisting of two racial groups (rather than two sexes), one would expect riots or an independence movement to break out. The surprising thing is that this situation has gone on so peacefully and quietly. Why? What is the reason why this situation exists and continues unchanged? (Watanabe, 2003, p. 7)

The introduction to the 2003 annual report of the Japanese Political Science Association posed the above question, and said it was the responsibility of political scientists to present some answers to this question.

It is not, however, from an academic interest in politics that I am concerned with this issue, but from a conviction of the importance of political participation for the empowerment of women. It is the abnormally imbalanced relationship between the sexes in political decision-making processes that has reproduced here the old structure of discrimination – the 'predominance of man over woman (*danson-johi*)', as it is expressed in Confucian terms – and this relationship continues to be an obstacle to women's participation in decision-making.

Can a political system in which there are so few female representatives be said to be democratic? Many believe that male representatives cannot fully understand the reality of discrimination against women, and therefore cannot tackle seriously policy issues related to women, issues such as equality between women and men. Women who share that view have started to direct their attention to local assemblies as forums of political participation through which to exercise their right to vote and their right to run for election.

In the 1990s, women started to develop a nationwide strategy that targeted local assemblies as important arenas for political expression. A movement aimed at electing women to local assemblies and supporting women's political aspirations spread throughout the country. As a result, the nationwide local elections of 1999 and 2003 saw an increase in women candidates, and a record-breaking number of those women candidates were elected.

This has taken place against a background of the worldwide expansion of the movement for the elimination of discrimination against women, a movement led by United Nations' initiatives such as the 1975 International Year for Women and the adoption of the 1979 Convention on the Elimination of All Forms of Discrimination against Women. Comparisons with women's situations elsewhere in the world made Japanese women aware of the enormity of the gender bias and the backwardness of policy-making in Japan. Behind women's recognition that being in the power structure was important was also the enactment of gender equality laws in the 1990s and the prioritization of gender equality as a political theme. In the nationwide local elections of 2003, this trend spread not only in urban areas but also in largely rural prefectures such as Nagano, and women began to make visible inroads into local assemblies.

The aim of this chapter is to examine how the women's movement enabled women to establish their political independence, by which I mean to serve in public office, and to analyse its historical and social background. In the second section, I shall describe the current situation, the history of women's election to assemblies and the background to the changes in the 1990s. In the third section, I shall explore the case of Nagano Prefecture.

In Nagano Prefecture, the number of women elected in the local assembly elections of 1947 and 1951 was the highest in the country. After that, the number of female assembly members decreased, but in 2003 a large number of women were elected again. The increase is particularly noticeable in town and village assemblies, where the number of women elected is three times what it was in the mid-1990s. This is in spite of the conservatism of such communities, where family connections and money play an important part in elections, and in spite of the fact that the number of seats was reduced in the 1990s. Although some earlier literature analysed the election of women to municipal assemblies, there is hardly anything published on the background of the election of women to local assemblies in rural prefectures such as Nagano.[1]

In the fourth section, I shall examine, using interviews, what impact the entry of women into the 'public sphere' has had on gender relations at home, in communities, in the assemblies, and on the traditional thinking that views politics as 'the sphere of men' (I shall refer to this as 'gender-based consciousness' in this chapter). The question will also be addressed as to whether the traditional political climate and the structure of gender-based domination are changing. In the fifth section, I shall discuss the case of Korea as indicative of the direction in which the movement to increase female assembly members is moving, and consider what women's election to assemblies means in relation to the elimination of discrimination against women.

My analysis is based on interviews with female assembly members and individuals involved in the movement; the literature on women's policies; various documents, such as the report on a nationwide summit of women representatives; election-related reports; the 'Rural Women's Network Shinano (*Noson-josei-nettowaku Shinano*) report'; newsletters of the Women's Association (*Fujin-kai*); reports on gender equality published by local governments; and literature produced by the Fusae Ichikawa Memorial Association. Interviews were conducted in Nagano Prefecture in August and October 2003 and February 2004, and in Korea in August and October 2003.

History of women's political participation in Japan

Election of women to the Diet

Tables 5.1 and 5.2 show the changes in the percentage of women in the House of Representatives (the Lower House) and the House of Councillors (the Upper House), respectively, in the years since the end of the Second World War II. There has been no big change in the percentage of female Diet members since 1946, when women got the vote. In the 2003 House of Representatives election, thirty-four women (twelve in single-seat constituencies and twenty-two in proportional-representation constituencies) were elected. The number of candidates had decreased from four years previously, and the number of female candidates elected also decreased for the first time in seventeen years. The number of women in the House of Councillors is thirty-eight (seventeen in single-seat constituencies and twenty-one in proportional-representation constituencies), a figure that ranks 29th in the world. In 2001, half the members in the House of Councillors were up for re-election, but the number of women re-elected decreased, from twenty-one in 1995 to eighteen. This shows how hard it is for women to get into national politics.

What are the obstacles? The reasons usually given for the small number of women representatives in politics are as follows: (i) ingrained concepts about the sexual division of labour (discriminatory voter perception of female candidates); (ii) women's own lack of will or capability to run in an

Table 5.1 Female candidates and winners in House of Representatives elections, 1946–2003

Year	Female candidates (total candidates)	Percentage of female candidates out of total candidates	Female winners (total number of winners)	Percentage of female winners out of total winners	Percentage of successful female candidates
1946	79 (2,770)	2.9	39 (464)	8.4	49.4
1947	85 (1,590)	5.3	15 (466)	3.2	17.6
1949	44 (1,364)	3.2	12 (466)	2.6	27.3
1952	24 (1,242)	1.9	9 (466)	1.9	37.5
1953	22 (1,017)	2.1	9 (466)	1.9	40.9
1955	23 (1,017)	2.3	8 (467)	1.7	34.8
1958	19 (951)	2.0	11 (467)	2.4	57.9
1960	21 (940)	2.2	7 (467)	1.5	33.3
1963	18 (917)	2.0	7 (467)	1.5	38.9
1967	15 (917)	1.6	7 (486)	1.4	46.7
1969	21 (945)	2.2	8 (486)	1.6	38.1
1972	20 (895)	2.2	7 (491)	1.4	35.0
1976	25 (899)	2.8	6 (511)	1.2	24.0
1979	23 (891)	2.6	11 (511)	2.2	47.8
1980	28 (835)	3.4	9 (511)	1.8	32.1
1983	66 (953)	3.3	8 (511)	1.6	28.6
1986	35 (838)	4.2	7 (512)	1.4	20.0
1990	66 (953)	6.9	12 (512)	2.3	18.2

Table 5.1   Female candidates and winners in House of Representatives elections
1946–2003   *continued*

Year	Female candidates (total candidates)	Percentage of female candidates out of total candidates	Female winners (total number of winners)	Percentage of female winners out of total winners	Percentage of successful female candidates
1993	70 (955)	7.3	14 (511)	2.7	20.0
1996	127 (1,261)	10.1		2.3	5.5
	74 (808)	9.2		8.0	21.6
2000					
Proportional	102 (504)		22	4.33 (7.29)	
Single seat	166 (1,199)		13	12.22	
2003					
Proportional	76 (745)		20	4.67 (7.08)	
Single seat	132 (1,026)		14	11.11	

Source: Compiled from Ichikawa Fusae Kinenkai (1997, 2003a).

election; and (iii) social and political structures, including the electoral system itself, that place women at a disadvantage (Mikanagi, 1999; p. 89). The first reason cannot be verified because gender statistics on voting behaviour are not available in Japan. The second reason does not apply, as Table 5.1 on the percentage of women elected shows. Therefore the structural factor, given as the third reason, must be considered to be the important one in Japan. I shall now to look briefly at the changes in women's participation in the Diet after the Second World War.

In the 22nd House of Representatives election held in 1946, the first election after the war, and just after Japanese women had gained the vote, eighty-three women ran and thirty-nine were elected (45 per cent of the women candidates). This number has not been equalled since. Earlier research has pointed out several reasons why so many women were elected in the first election after the war. The first is the large-constituency, limited plural-ballot system (*dai-senkyoku-sei seigen-renki*). The second is the shortage of male candidates because of the 'public service purge' carried out in 1946, when members elected to the (all-male) Diet before and during the war were purged. The third reason is the high expectations the public had of women in the pacifist climate of the time. The fourth is General MacArthur's support of women. And the fifth is the fact that the elections were clean because election funds were not available in the war-devastated country (Ogai, 1996, pp. 83–7). In the election held the next year, however, twenty-five women, or 64 per cent of the women candidates, failed to get elected. The change to a medium-district system (*chu-senkyoku-sei*) and the

Table 5.2 Female candidates and winners in House of Councillors elections, 1947–2001

	Female candidates (total candidates)			Percentage of female candidate out of total candidates			Female winners (total number of winners)			Percentage of female winners out of total winners			Percentage of successful by female candidate		
	Proportional	Electoral	Total	Proportional	Electoral	Total	Proportional	Electoral	Total	Proportional	Electoral	Total	Proportional	Electoral	Total
1947	13 (246)	6 (331)	19 (577)	5.3	1.8	3.3	8 (100)	2 (150)	10 (250)	8.0	1.3	4.0	61.5	33.3	52.6
1950	15 (311)	9 (252)	24 (563)	4.8	3.6	4.3	3 (56)	2 (76)	5 (132)	5.4	2.6	3.8	20.0	22.2	20.8
1953	17 (234)	11 (213)	28 (447)	7.3	5.2	6.3	6 (53)	4 (75)	10 (128)	11.3	5.3	7.8	35.3	36.4	35.7
1956	10 (150)	7 (191)	17 (341)	6.7	3.7	5.0	3 (52)	2 (75)	5 (127)	5.8	2.7	3.9	30.0	28.6	29.4
1959	10 (122)	8 (208)	18 (330)	8.2	3.8	5.5	5 (52)	3 (75)	8 (127)	9.6	4.0	6.3	50.0	37.5	44.4
1962	9 (107)	6 (221)	15 (328)	8.4	2.7	4.6	6 (51)	2 (76)	8 (127)	11.8	2.6	6.3	66.7	33.3	53.3
1965	8 (99)	5 (233)	13 (332)	8.1	2.1	3.9	7 (52)	2 (75)	9 (127)	13.5	2.7	7.1	87.5	40.0	69.2
1968	8 (93)	3 (212)	11 (305)	8.6	1.4	3.6	4 (51)	1 (75)	5 (126)	7.8	1.3	4.0	50.0	33.3	45.5
1971	9 (106)	6 (199)	15 (305)	8.5	3.0	4.9	5 (50)	3 (75)	8 (125)	10.0	4.0	6.4	55.6	50.6	53.3
1974	9 (112)	9 (237)	18 (349)	8.0	3.8	5.2	5 (54)	3 (76)	8 (130)	9.3	3.9	6.2	55.6	33.3	44.4

Table 5.2 Female candidates and winners in House of Councillors elections, 1947–2001 *continued*

Year	Female candidates (total candidates)			Percentage of female candidate out of total candidates			Female winners (total number of winners)			Percentage of female winners out of total winners			Percentage of successful by female candidate		
	Proportional	Electoral	Total	Proportional	Electoral	Total	Proportional	Electoral	Total	Proportional	Electoral	Total	Proportional	Electoral	Total
1977	18 (102)	18 (218)	36 (320)	17.6	8.3	11.3	6 (50)	2 (76)	8 (126)	12.0	2.6	6.3	33.3	11.1	22.2
1980	8 (93)	10 (192)	18 (285)	8.6	5.2	6.3	6 (50)	3 (76)	9 (126)	12.0	3.9	7.1	75.0	30.0	50.0
1983	30 (191)	25 (239)	55 (430)	15.7	10.5	12.8	8 (50)	2 (76)	10 (126)	16.0	2.6	7.9	26.7	8.0	58.2
1986	53 (243)	29 (263)	82 (506)	21.8	11.0	16.2	5 (50)	5 (76)	10 (126)	10.0	6.6	7.9	9.4	17.2	12.2
1989	97 (385)	49 (285)	146 (670)	25.2	17.2	21.8	12 (50)	10 (76)	22 (126)	24.0	13.2	17.5	12.4	20.4	15.1
1992	65 (329)	58 (311)	123 (640)	19.8	18.6	19.2	6 (50)	7 (77)	13 (127)	12.0	9.1	10.2	9.2	12.1	10.6
1995	46 (181)	78 (386)	124 (567)	25.4	20.2	21.9	13 (50)	8 (76)	21 (126)	26.0	10.5	16.7	28.3	10.3	16.9
1998	38 (158)	72 (316)	110 (474)	24.1	22.8	23.2	10 (50)	10 (76)	20 (126)	20.0	13.2	15.9	26.3	13.9	18.2
2001	58 (204)	79 (292)	137 (496)	28.4	27.1	27.6	11 (46)	7 (76)	18 (122)	23.9	9.2	14.8	12.4	20.4	15.1

Source: Same as Table 5.1.

fact that not all of the thirty-nine previously elected women were necessarily 'the proper people' (Ogai, 1996, p. 100), many voters in the first election having been influenced by the popularity of women that prevailed immediately after the war, have been cited as reasons for the poor showing.

The number of women elected was as low as around ten, when the small-district system and proportional-representation system[2] were introduced. The number then increased gradually in the proportional-representation constituencies, to twenty-three in 1996, and thirty-three in 2000. This showed that the proportional-representation constituency system favours female candidates, but that the small-district system, where many votes for female candidates were wasted, puts women at a disadvantage. The Democratic Party of Japan, aiming for a change of regime, announced a manifesto. In accordance with this manifesto, the number of candidates recognized by the party in the proportional representation district decreased by eighty and female candidates fell to thirty-four, because the party failed to introduce a policy of putting women higher on its list of candidates.

In the House of Councillors, problems regarding the open-list system in the proportional representation segment, introduced in 2001, include the fact that parties tend to select 'candidates who can win' or candidates with high name recognition and vote-drawing power. It has also been pointed out that the deposit money for running for the House is large.[3] Therefore, structural factors are considered to be the biggest obstacles to women's participation. However, there is still no women's movement for women's participation in national politics, including lobbying of political parties and demanding a reform of the system.[4]

Election of women to local assemblies

Women made gains in local assembly elections in the 1990s, but it is still hard for them to break into national politics. As stated above, women prioritized local assemblies in their strategy to strengthen their political voice, and the movement to send women to local assemblies and to support women's political aspirations spread throughout Japan.

As of June 2003, after the nationwide elections, the total number of women in local assemblies was 4,804, a record high. Although the percentage of women out of the total of 60,200 elected officials totals only 7.6 per cent, it represents a great increase over the 1.4 per cent of ten years earlier. The percentages of women office holders in the respective assemblies are: 6.8 per cent in metropolitan and prefectural assemblies; 12.2 per cent in municipal assemblies; and 5.4 per cent in town and village assemblies. The rate of increase over the number of female representatives four years earlier is high: 26.8 per cent, 19.4 per cent and 22.3 per cent, respectively.

In town and village assemblies, where women had largely been excluded, the percentage of women rose from 0.7 per cent in 1983 to 1.3 per cent in 1987. After that the percentage continued to rise every four years: to 2.1

per cent, 2.9 per cent, 4.6 per cent and 5.9 per cent, and the total number of women elected increased by 200 at each election. As a result, the percentage of assemblies in which there were any women nearly doubled, from 34.2 per cent in 1991 to 62.5 per cent in 2003. Another feature of the 2003 nationwide local elections is that many women ran for the post of local government leader.[5]

This shows that more women are exercising their right to run for public office, not only in metropolitan areas but also in other areas throughout the country. As for the successful candidates' party affiliation, 70 per cent of women elected to town and village assemblies are 'independents' or members of the Communist Party. In the latter half of the 1980s, the Communist Party announced a policy of fielding woman candidates in order to extend the party's influence and gain more votes. In 2003, even more independent women were elected than before.

These election gains are the result of ongoing activism by women in local communities aimed at getting women from the community elected. But the number of women running for office on their own initiative has also increased. Both types of candidates are being elected.

In fact, the increase of female representatives in the 1990s was caused by the increase of female candidates, but there was no big change in the percentage of women elected (see Tables 5.3, 5.4 and 5.5). The fact that more women are running for public office shows that the gender-based political bias that has been the biggest obstacle to women's political participation is weakening.

History and social background of women's election to local assemblies

The changes in women's political participation from the immediate postwar period to the early twenty-first-century are marked by several peaks. The first was the first and second nationwide local elections held after the war. As can be seen from Table 5.6, women in local assemblies numbered 793 just after the 1947 nationwide local elections, and decreased after that. In 1975, the number of women representatives dropped to 218. Women were elected into local assemblies in the first nationwide local elections of 1947 largely because of the activities of an organization in local communities called the Women's Association.[6] Women's political activism in communities started as election campaigning. These activities were influenced by the democratic reforms of the GHQ (Allied Forces General Headquarters) whose objectives included democratization in both the community and in the home, but were based mainly on the consciousness of the women themselves, who had been brought together by these associations immediately after the war. In Nagano Prefecture, six women stood as candidates in the first nationwide local elections[7] for the prefectural assembly, and more than 100 women for municipal, town and village assemblies. Fifty-two women won without political party support. Their strong belief

Table 5.3   Female candidates and winners in Tokyo Metropolitan Government, Hokkaido, and 45 Prefectural Assembly elections, 1947–2003

Year	Female candidates (total candidates)	Percentage of female candidates out of total candidates	Female winners (total number of winners)	Percentage of female winners out of total winners	Percentage of successful female candidates
1947	111 (7,115)	1.6	22 (2,490)	0.9	19.8
1951	99 (6,010)	1.6	34 (2,616)	1.3	34.3
1955	80 (5,556)	1.4	29 (2,613)	1.1	36.3
1959	85 (4,860)	1.7	36 (2,656)	1.4	42.4
1963	79 (4,567)	1.7	39 (2,688)	1.5	49.4
1967	52 (4,340)	1.2	30 (2,558)	1.2	57.7
1971	67 (4,285)	1.6	21 (2,557)	0.8	31.3
1975	126 (4,699)	2.7	29 (2,614)	1.1	23.0
1979	65 (3,922)	1.7	28 (2,646)	1.1	43.1
1983	212 (4,558)	4.7	30 (2,661)	1.1	14.2
1987	180 (4,118)	4.4	52 (2,670)	1.9	28.9
1991	171 (3,810)	4.5	64 (2,693)	2.4	37.4
1995	177 (3,701)	4.8	73 (2,607)	2.8	41.2
1999	323 (4,013)	8.0	136 (2,669)	5.1	42.1
2003	383 (3,854)	9.9	164 (2,634)	6.2	42.8

Source: Compiled from Ichikawa Fusae Kinenkai (2003b).

that 'women's issues should be addressed by female assembly members as their representatives and be solved in assemblies' (Tsujimura) 1968, p. 114) supported the women's movement. Women advanced into politics to solve problems specific to women.

Table 5.4 Female candidates and winners in nationwide City Assembly and Ward Assembly elections, 1947–2003

Year	Female candidates (total candidates)	Percentage of female candidates out of total candidates	Female winners (total number of winners)	Percentage of female winners out of total winners	Percentage of successful female candidates
1947	383 (20,135)	1.9	94 (8,167)	1.2	24.5
1951	466 (20,961)	2.2	152 (8,884)	1.7	32.6
1955	412 (19,395)	2.1	166 (9,972)	1.7	40.3
1959	358 (17,910)	2.0	210 (11,827)	1.8	58.7
1963	363 (18,171)	2.0	207 (13,111)	1.6	57.0
1967	368 (17,917)	2.1	240 (13,086)	1.8	65.2
1971	393 (17,420)	2.3	296 (13,510)	2.2	75.3
1975	505 (17,806)	2.8	381 (13,957)	2.7	75.4
1979	463 (16,551)	2.8	386 (14,038)	2.7	83.4
1983	604 (15,930)	3.8	488 (13,813)	3.5	80.8
1987	777 (15,384)	5.1	637 (13,329)	4.8	82.0
1991	1,064 (14,886)	7.1	839 (13,161)	6.4	78.9
1995	1,239 (14,522)	8.5	1,043 (12,731)	8.2	84.2
1999	1,702 (14,896)	11.4	1,378 (12,332)	11.2	81.0
2003	1,927 (14,289)	13.5	1,552 (11,886)	13.1	80.5

Source: Same as Table 5.3.

In the second local assembly elections, in 1951, two women were newly elected in prefectural assemblies and 78 women in municipal, town and village assemblies. However, in the next election the two women prefectural assembly members were defeated and the number of women in

Table 5.5   Female candidates and winners in nationwide Town Assembly and Village Council elections, 1947–2003

Year	Female candidates (total candidates)	Percentage of female candidates out of total candidates	Female winners (total number of winners)	Percentage of female winners out of total winners	Percentage of successful female candidates
1947	1,784 (231,121)	0.8 %	677 (183,224)	0.4 %	37.9 %
1951	1424 (204,004)	0.7	775 (161,395)	0.5	54.4
1955	326 (55,152)	0.6	206 (43,939)	0.5	63.2
1959	277 (39,085)	0.7	173 (31,252)	0.6	62.5
1963	285 (37,685)	0.8	192 (30,068)	0.6	67.4
1967	250 (34,535)	0.7	163 (27,188)	0.6	65.2
1971	194 (30,701)	0.6	133 (25,063)	0.5	68.6
1975	207 (28,742)	0.7	109 (23,810)	0.5	52.7
1979	163 (26,518)	0.6	120 (23,267)	0.5	73.6
1983	243 (24,923)	1.0	164 (22,303)	0.7	67.5
1987	339 (23,383)	1.4	269 (21,095)	1.3	79.4
1991	515 (22,478)	2.3	432 (20,573)	2.1	83.9
1995	728 (22,287)	3.3	592 20,149)	2.9	81.3
1999	1,040 (21,350)	4.9	867 (18,999)	4.6	83.4
2003	1,192 (19,298)	6.2	1,034 (17,544)	5.9	86.7

Source: Same as Table 5.3.

municipal, town, and village assemblies decreased to fifty-three. It was not until the 1980s that the number of women elected to local assemblies began to increase. I shall now discuss the social background of this decrease in the number of female representatives.

Table 5.6 Female members in local assemblies

Type of assembly	1947	1956	1967	1971	1975	1979	1983	1987	1991	1995	1999	2003
Metropolitan Tokyo, Hokkaido and 45 Prefecture Assemblies	22	31	39	28	34	34	36	63	82	90	153	194
City assemblies	94	206	301	341	464	504	648	848	1,157	1,492	1,976	2,360
Town and village Assemblies	677	411	304	232	218	255	321	509	791	1,114	1,635	2,050
Total	793	648	644	601	716	793	1,005	1,420	2,030	2,696	3,764	4,604

Notes: Town assemblies include government designated cities and special wards. In 1999, the number of female members first reached over 10% of the total members in city assemblies (including government-designated cities).

Source: Same as Table 5.3.

The decrease in the number of women elected in the third election, in 1955, was connected to a change in the social structure, as well as to a reduction in the total number of assembly members that resulted from mergers of towns and villages throughout the country. The process of industrialization in Japan ten years after the war ushered out 'the post-war period' in terms of the structure of production, as an economic White Paper of the time declared. The beginning of a sustained period of high economic growth led to the proliferation of materialism in rural as well as urban areas. The 'urbanization' of the Japanese lifestyle produced a population of consumers and an increase in the number of farm families engaged in non-agricultural employment. With rural women also beginning to work in factories, the division of labour by sex was strengthened, and the postwar, female-centred, 'livelihood improvement' movement and the activities of local women's associations stagnated. The development of a male-centred social system by creating divisions between men and women in all spheres of life paralleled the decrease in the number of female assembly members.

In the latter half of the 1960s, however, problems that accompanied economic growth surfaced, such as environmental pollution, the harmful effects of medicines, price increases, the pollution of agricultural products, and uneven regional development. These gave rise to neighbourhood and citizens' protest movements that lobbied the government.

The second peak was caused by the women's liberation movement, which began in 1970. The women's liberation movement recognized the political dimension of everyday discrimination against women and called for the women's political movement to pursue a 'revolution in daily life'. However, developments like the 1975 International Year for Women and the United Nations Decade for Women that followed made women question their political independence.

Women came to realize that '"women's votes" supported "men's power" and did not change the situation of women' (Mizoguchi, 1995). This led to a movement among feminists to have one of their activists, Yoshitake Teruko, elected in the national constituency in the 1978 House of Councillors election so that she could work for the implementation of their policies in the Diet. Although she lost the election, the network of women at the grassroots with no party affiliation who worked on her campaign played a pioneering role in the movement that followed, a movement whose slogan was 'from the women's liberation movement to legislative assemblies'.

The third peak was seen at the time of the establishment of a local political party (*Seikatsusha* Network) whose base was the *Seikatsu* Club Consumers' Co-operative Union (*Seikatsu Kurabu Seikyo*).[8] Women from the group won seats in cities such as Tokyo and Kanagawa, through a new participatory politics under which they were representatives speaking for 'housewives' as ordinary citizens. In this sense, it was political participation from the standpoint of housewives – individuals responsible for homemaking and bound by the sexual division of labour. It was also a time that saw, in the election of 1987, women who had participated in NGO forums at the second World Women's Conference of 1980 and the third conference of 1985 stand on platforms that called for the elimination of discrimination against women and the realization of equality between women and men. This represented a new move and was based on networks of people who shared a feminist philosophy.

The fourth peak was in the 1990s, when a lot of women were elected to legislative assemblies because many women stood as candidates and many networks for supporting them were established.

There were a number of changes in the women's movement and the background that helped to produced so many female assembly members in this period. First, there were the achievements of the women's liberation movement and the expansion of the worldwide networks of grassroots women that began in the 1980s. Japanese women realized anew how far behind they were in terms of representation in legislative assemblies in Japan and, with slogans like 'Send women to legislative assemblies!' and 'No assemblies without women!', started diverse campaigns for the nationwide local elections of 1999.[9] Throughout the country women at the grassroots level started organizing classes on politics to support women who wanted to run for public office. Traditional perceptions of politics and politicians began to be replaced with new ones, thanks to the growing power of these women's networks.[10]

Second, in response to this nationwide movement to increase the number of female assembly members, organizations were established to provide information and funds, and to support networking.[11]

Third, women's centres established by local governments were an important indirect factor. At these centre, many women learnt about the reality of discrimination against women and the structure that reproduces discrimination, and went on from there to run for public office.[12]

In addition, adult education programmes funded by local governments enabled women not only to participate in workshops but also to take responsibility in organizing conferences. Women have been empowered in the discussions and decision-making process. An example is the 'Women's Conference Japan', a conference sponsored every year since 1984 by a local government. Women organize the committees that plan and run these 3,000-participant conferences, sometimes clashing with the administrative officials with whom they work. Women's participation in politics is always one of the many workshop themes at these conferences, where women have the opportunity to encourage each other, exchange information, and share experiences. A programme sponsored by a local government in which women 'representatives' ran a mock assembly also functioned effectively for the empowerment of women (Ogai, 2003, pp. 123–38).

Women's participation in politics and the women's movement in Nagano Prefecture

Table 5.7 shows changes from 1987 to 2003 in the number of female assembly members in Nagano Prefecture. In the general election held in 2003, 190 women were among 1,992 newly elected assembly members in the prefecture. This is 9.5 per cent, a considerable increase over the 6 per cent of four years earlier, when 140 female candidates were elected. Back in 1983, the twenty-one successful women candidates accounted for only 0.9 per cent of the total, so the figure for 2003 is more than ten times that of twenty years before. The number of assemblies in Nagano with female members has been increasing. In 1987, there were only twenty-seven assemblies out of a total of 122 that had any female members, but this low rate, 22 per cent, climbed to 45.5 per cent in 1995, on to 65.3 per cent in 1999, and to 75.2 per cent in 2003. The equivalent nationwide averages in 1995 and 2003, at 43.1 percent and 62.5 per cent, respectively, are lower. The Nagano Prefecture Assembly ranks third in the nation in terms of female participation, with women accounting for 13.8 per cent of mem-

Table 5.7 Female assembly members in Nagano by type of assembly

		1987	*1991*	*1995*	*1999*	*2003*
Prefecture assembly	Number of seats	62	62	62	62	58
	Female members	0	1	2	4	8
	Ratio of female members (%)	0	1.6	3.2	6.5	13.8
	Nationwide ratio of female members (%)	1.9	2.8	3.1	5.3	6.8
City assembly	Number of seats	501	483	477	453	437
	Female Members	12	23	30	46	59
	Ratio of female members (%)	2.4	4.8	6.3	10.2	13.5
	Nationwide ratio of female members (%)	4.8	5.7	7.4	10.0	12.2
Town and village assembly	Number of seats	1,677	1,632	1,605	1,570	1,497
	Female members	23	33	51	90	123
	Ratio of female members (%)	1.0	1.9	3.2	5.7	8.2
	Nationwide ratio of female members (%)	1.3	1.8	2.6	4.0	5.4
	Total seats	2,240	2,179	2,144	2,085	1,992
	Total Female members	35	57	83	140	190
	Ratio of female members (%)	1.6	2.6	3.9	6.7	9.5

Source: Same as Table 5.3.

bers. Throughout the nation there are 150 town and village assemblies located in thirty-seven prefecture-level areas (including Tokyo, Osaka Prefecture and Hokkaido). Taking the top ninety-eight in terms of the number of female members, Nagano's share is the largest, with sixteen local assemblies having female members. At the previous election there were only six assemblies with any female members.

As mentioned earlier, Nagano Prefecture experienced ups and downs in the number of women elected to local assemblies. While it was the top-ranking prefecture in the 1947 and 1951 general elections, there was a decline that continued until 1999 and 2003, when Nagano experienced a remarkable rise, producing more female elected officials than other prefectures. What was behind this favourable change? The Network for Increasing Female Assembly Members – 'Shinano' (hereinafter called Network Shinano), established in 1996, contributed directly. How did Network Shinano, formed through the merging of the main streams of the women's movement, further women's participation in the political arena? In examining the background of the women with party affiliation who were elected to local assemblies in Nagano, one finds that they ran under the auspices of two main streams of the women's movement, the Women's Association and the Rural Women's Network. The latter is an organization originally set up for the purpose of livelihood improvement. How, then, did these two streams of the women's movement create an environment favourable to accelerating women's participation in politics, and how did they come together in Network Shinano?

Women's Association movement and women's participation in politics

Nagano Prefecture is located in the central part of Honshu, surrounded by mountains that rise some 3,000 metres sea level, forming the Japan Alps/South Alps mountain ranges, often referred to as the 'roof of Japan'.

Eighty per cent of the prefecture is covered with forest, and farmland – including rice fields – accounts for only 10 per cent of the land area. Mountain ranges dominate the landscape, leaving only limited space for cultivation in the basins or along the valleys on terraced fields with poor productivity. The people of the prefecture are said to have a penchant for higher education because of the limited expectations for returns from labour on the land. Members of the Women's Association movement in Nagano Prefecture are also said to be strongly motivated to learn.

This characteristic of the Women's Association goes back to prewar days. The Women's Association was established in the 1880s by women in towns such as Ueda and Matsumoto, the Articles of Association encouraging members to reform old customs and to co-operate to raise the status and consciousness of women. In 1891, women in Iida City established the Shimoina Women's Association and sponsored a lecture by Ms Chiseko Ushioda, the leader of the campaign to abolish licensed prostitution. The

Nagano Women's Association was established in 1918 and its members, led by educated middle-class women, published a journal, *Shinshu Fujin* (Shinshu Women). In 1922, they sponsored a summer college jointly with Shinshu University, at which issues like women's liberation, birth control, and household innovation were discussed (Shinano no josei-shi kan ko-kai 1994, p. 52). After the outbreak of war with China, all women's organizations were of course co-opted by the wartime regime.

There were signs of the re-emergence of the Women's Association soon after the end of the Second World War, and towards the end of 1945, sixty-six groups formed a new, postwar Women's Association. Occupation policies to transform Japan into a democratic country and the expectation that women would play an important role in this influenced and supported these moves. Women in various regions started working together in the reconstruction of their lives and to help rebuild their regions. Then in May 1946 the Federated Women's Association of Nagano Prefecture was inaugurated and immediately began studying politics, moved to action by a stunning event the previous month.

Hatsu Ando was an ordinary housewife who ran a dressmaking business. She had never been involved in women's liberation or other social movements, but she was elected to the House of Representatives in the election which took place in April 1946. She was the only female among seventy-six candidates and she eventually gained the largest number of votes. She was neither representative of the Women's Association nor representative of the community; she seemed to have sprung out of nowhere. The Women's Association records from that period describe the shame the directors of the Association felt on seeing the success of Ms Ando (Tsujimura, 1968, p. 102). Their chagrin was reflected in a resolution passed by the Federated Women's Association of Nagano Prefecture in November 1946 calling on chairs of the Women's Association in counties and cities to run for election to the prefecture assembly, and chairs in towns and villages to run in local assembly elections (Tsujimura, 1968, p. 104). As a result, six women ran for election in the prefecture assembly election and more than 100 women in town and village assembly elections. In all, fifty-two women won the honour of becoming members of the regional and local assemblies. While many had run by Association fiat, in some villages the local Women's Association carried out their own voting to select the candidates themselves rather than simply obeying the resolution of the Federated Women's Association. Members reportedly continued to study politics to enhance their knowledge with a view to getting more women elected to assemblies.

In the meantime, the Women's Association sponsored lectures, symposia and discussion meetings on topics such as the Constitution, the Civil Code, and fair elections. These programmes aimed at stimulating the political consciousness of women bore fruit in the next regional and local elections in 1951; more female candidates were elected in Nagano Prefecture than anywhere else. The Coalition of Women's Associations in Shimoina set up a political section in order to enhance women's awareness of politics and to carry out activities in the political field (Tsujimura, 1968, pp. 108–12).

The Federated Women's Association of Nagano Prefecture took part in a movement in 1953 against a US military training base on Mt Asama that succeeded in getting the use of the base cancelled. This incident showed the high-spirited political thinking of the women in the organization.[13]

As mentioned above, the activities of the Women's Association of Nagano Prefecture were concentrated on election campaigning at an early stage but eventually expanded to encompass the study of other aspects of politics as its members became more politically conscious. The local Women's Association during this period was an independent entity and had become indispensable to women in the local communities. Nevertheless, as has been mentioned already, since 1955 the momentum that had resulted in an increase in the number of female assembly members declined continuously until, by 1993, the number had fallen to a low of 0.9 per cent of all assembly members. Women were being kept out of the regional and local assemblies, while the number of Women's Association members, which at one time reached 200,000 also gradually decreased over the same period, mainly because young women were not interested in joining. However, even in this adverse situation, the Women's Association, composed of politically aware women and inspired by the International Women's Year in 1975, challenged the old gender structure prevailing in the regional and local assemblies. Ms Michiko Tarukawa, a co-ordinator of 'Network Shinano' who will be referred to again in the fourth section, urged women to bring a political consciousness to the activities of the Women's Association.

The rural women's network and political participation

According to Nagano Prefecture statistics for 2003, the employment rate in the prefecture was the highest in the nation. The female employment rate was 52.6 per cent (national average 46.2 per cent) and that of the elderly 32.1 per cent (national average 22.2 per cent), while the total unemployment rate was 3.9 per cent, lower than the national average of 5.4 per cent. The high female employment rate is closely related to the good day-care environment in Nagano Prefecture. Statistics for five-year-old children show that 72 per cent are enrolled in day care centres, far in excess of the percentage enrolled in kindergartens. More than 90 per cent of the demand is met in terms of nursery school. This agricultural prefecture has a history of struggle to set up day care centres to liberate women in the farming villages.

Agriculture and primary industry comprise 11.3 per cent of Nagano Prefecture's industry, very high compared with the national average of 5 per cent. Nagano also ranks as the agricultural region with the largest number of farming households in Japan.[14]

As was seen in chapter 4, women play an important role in agriculture throughout the country, and Nagano is no exception. Women represented 57 per cent of the total farming population of 155,620 in the year 2000. Because many male farmers are engaged in jobs outside the farm, women necessarily bear the responsibility for both farming and everyday affairs, and thus gain practice in becoming independent.

The Rural Women's Network originated from the Livelihood Improvement Movement.[15] In 1950, when this movement was beginning, members of a committee to popularize the ideas of livelihood improvement were sent to the villages to encourage women to change the lifestyle in farming homes. In less than five years, 206 livelihood improvement groups existed, consisting of 4,484 members living in various parts of the region.

Eventually women began activities on their own or in groups to obtain loans for remodelling their kitchens, activities that led to networking among women. In 1972, the Liaison Conference in Nagano Prefecture for Livelihood Improvement Groups was established. By participating in the Conference's 'rural women's classes', women became aware of the problems in their agricultural communities and gained know-how in the 'theory and practice' of transforming the community. They were inspired and motivated to do away with old customs in the village and to take part in social affairs. Their group activities expanded into the processing of agricultural products and arrangement of direct sales outlets. In 1998 the name of the network became 'Rural Women's Network in Nagano' and at the time of writing there are 360 groups with about 3,000 members.[16]

These women's activities have been strengthened by the gender equality policies for rural areas promoted by Livelihood Improvement extension workers, as discussed in Chapter 3.

Nagano Prefecture got started on issues of gender equality earlier than other regions. In 1991, the 'Action Plan for Rural Women' was drawn up. In 2003 there were 249 women in Nagano on the Agricultural Committees that make administrative decisions on important issues such as the conversion of farmland to other uses, including residential use. Although this involves only 11.5 per cent of the 2,167 members, it is still the highest rate in the nation, and about three times the national average of 3.7 per cent.[17] The number of Nagano farm household that concluded 'family management agreements', a scheme promoted by the government to empower rural women, exceeded 1,600, a very high figure compared to the rest of the country.[18]

These advances by rural women in Nagano Prefecture were the result of seminars held in connection with the Action Plan for Rural Women,[19] seminars that stimulated women to take an active part in agricultural management and changed women's consciousness about traditional village customs and gender equality. The prefecture's 'meister system' for rural communities,[20] and the large number of women appointed to the agricultural committees, stimulated the emergence of female community leaders. As of the last election in 2003, seventeen of the female assembly members elected had either served on an agricultural committee or been certified as a rural 'meister'. Below are some examples of women from farm villages who became regional and local assembly members:

- Ms A, who was engaged in farming as well as in another business, was elected to the village assembly in 2001. She had been appointed to the Agricultural Committee in 1999 while active in setting up a group for young wives, involving herself in activities of the Women's Association, and promoting gender-equality policies as a Gender Equality Communicator.[21]
- Ms B, who joined the Women's Association and the women's section of the Japan Agricultural Co-operatives (JA) after her marriage, was elected to the village assembly in 1999 after becoming chair of the Women's Association in 1998. She had been made a rural life meister in 1994 because of her contribution to the Livelihood Improvement Program, and in 1997 she organized a Livelihood Improvement group.
- Ms C had been selected to various posts, such as branch manager of the women's section of JA, chairwoman of the Women's Association, and member of the Agricultural Committee, after thirty-eight years in the Women's Association and the women's section of JA, and twenty-six years with the Consumers' Association and the Association for Dietary Improvement.
- Ms D, who came from Tokyo, married a full-time farmer. She was elected to a city council in 1998, after a busy career that included chairing the National Council for Female Farmers while holding the positions of rural life meister and Agricultural Committee member. At the time of writing, she is serving her second term.

These examples show clearly that the accumulated achievements of the women and their dedicated service on the Agricultural Committee, Women's Association and so on were important advantages when running for election.

Network Shinano and the women's movement

In Nagano Prefecture, a substantial number of women have made their way into the regional and local assemblies, beginning a new phase in women's involvement in politics, and Network Shinano played a very important role. Network Shinano was started in 1996 to create a supportive environment to increase the number of female assembly members in Nagano Prefecture. Currently the network comprises 700 members, mainly engaged in non-partisan activities. In 2003, Nagano Prefecture had 190 female assembly members and (eighty-six) nearly half belonged to Network Shinano, testifying to the Network's successful pursuit of its goals.

Thirty women, many of whom were current or former assembly members, defeated candidates, and supporters of these were involved in the establishment of Network Shinano, but its central figure was Ms Michiko Tarukawa, its head. She served four terms, from 1983 to 1999, as an assembly member in Shimosuwa Town, during which time she worked to bring Network Shinano into existence. She is the only woman to have served as vice-chair of the Nagano Prefecture Assembly. Ms Tarukawa proposed the setting up of the Network, and this gifted woman undoubtedly played a crucial role at the start as well as in the women's movement that followed.

However, it was not possible for her to do this on her own, without the support of other women. Network Shinano succeeded in consolidating women's political power: how did the women acquire this power?

Network Shinano has its origin in the Women's Issues Research Group in Nagano Prefecture that started in 1978 under the initiative of women's movement leaders who sought to eliminate discrimination against women in line with the National Plan of Action drawn up by the Japanese government during International Women's Year in 1975. The group's journal, *Ayumi* (Advancing step by step), published from 1978 to 1996, vividly describes the group's activities. A theme taken up in all sixteen issues was women's participation in policy-making (*Ayumi*, no. 16). Ms Michiko Tarukawa, the head of Network Shinano, launched the Network in 1996, a year after the twentieth anniversary of the Women's Issues Research Group, which she also headed.

Ms Tarukawa had organized the Network to 'put theory into practice' and to increase the number of female assembly members, a goal already seen in her activities during the two years she served as the chairperson of the Coalition of Women's Associations. During this time she organized two mock assemblies as part of a political learning process for women. This experience made women aware of politics and resulted in the setting up of a political study group in 1982. The objective of this study group, called *Shinpukai* (New Wind Group) was to elect female assembly members and support them in office. The group's name indicates the women's intention to send a new breeze into stale, male-dominated politics. Some 800 women joined *Shinpukai* within a week of its founding, under the encouragement of the Women's Association. Women in Shimosuwa were driven to take action out of a sense of disgust with the election campaign for town mayor. This election split the 25,000 voters into two factions, one on the side of the mayor and the other on the side of the chair of the town assembly, and women wanted a change in the political climate that governed elections in their town. *Shinpukai* sponsored a seminar on politics which was reported on the front page of a local newspaper and discussed in its editorial.[22]

The significance of the emergence of female assembly members

Fighting against male-dominated election campaigns

In this section I shall examine how women's entry into the public sphere has had an impact on the traditional political climate, the home and community, gender relations in assemblies, and gender-biased norms, and what is the significance of women's participation in policy-making.

Women first of all challenged the bad practices seen in traditional elections in the community. Males, touted as 'representatives of our community', are usually the candidates put up by male-dominated communities and in general dominate politics in local communities to an even greater extent in rural areas than in cities. Since the 1980s, women have tried to change this, establishing lateral networking and advocating 'ideal' campaigns without the expenditure of large sums of money. As in the case of Michiko Tarukawa, the head of Network Shinano, who, with the endorsement of the coalition of Women's Associations, ran in the 1983 local assembly election and was elected.

It is not easy for non-hierarchical women's organizations such as the Women's Association to field female candidates against male candidates who have the endorsement of the neighborhood self-governing body or of an administrative organization in a village community. And members of the Women's Association themselves often feel under an obligation to support male candidates. Almost everywhere, men fill the posts of president in neighbourhood self-governing bodies, and in Nagano Prefecture too it is almost impossible for a woman to receive community endorsement as a candidate. Female candidates can usually only look to political parties for endorsement. Since the 1980s, however, women throughout the country have been challenging bad election practices based on local power, kinship and money through campaigns led chiefly by Women's Association members run along more 'ideal' lines.[23] Women's campaigns challenged such traditional practices as bribery by developing new ways of garnering support, and in this, their experiences as housewives proved to be positive assets.

The impact on gender relations at home and gender-based consciousness

Next I shall look at the impact that the election of women to assemblies has had on gender relations at home, and gender-based consciousness, based on interviews or questionnaires with assembly members in Nagano Prefecture, most of whom have no party affiliation. I will also draw on research on seven female assembly members and five of their husbands conducted by the Nagano Prefecture Department of Agricultural Administration. My research has revealed the trends discussed below, but a quantitative analysis could not be made because the sample was too small.

The questions in this research include the following:

(i) How was the female representative's husband involved in the election campaign after she decided to run?

(ii) Did gender relations, gender-based consciousness, and sex-role stereotypes change after the election? and

(iii) What is the significance of the existence of female assembly members?

To the first question, about the reaction of husbands of female representatives when they decided to run, answers fell into two groups. Some husbands objected initially to the decision but became more co-operative later, while other husbands co-operated from the start. One of the reasons why husbands and family members were against the woman's decision was based on anxiety that their family lives might be changed if the woman was elected. However, even family members who had been against the decision eventually co-operated in some way.

One way in which husbands co-operated was by distributing the candidate's newsletter. Ten female representatives responded that they would not have been able to run if their husband had not co-operated in caring for elderly family members and doing the housework. Five husbands answered that they started to learn how to do housework, including cooking, thanks to their wife's campaign. In other words, these husbands could not have carried on their daily life if they had been bound by gender-based consciousness or sex-role stereotypes. Real needs rectified the sexual division of labour at home. From this research I found that the women I met were not bound by sex-role stereotypes or the sexual division of labour.

In other ways, too, women's election to assemblies has been significant. For one thing, male assembly members been made conscious of the existence of women in the assemblies. Women voters have also become more involved, and the decision-making process for local ordinances has become more transparent. Every female assembly member I interviewed publishes a newsletter reporting on the assembly. Issues in which female representatives are particularly interested include the promotion of policies for gender equality, education, environment, fair spending of taxes, and freedom of information. Their previous experiences in voluntary activities in the community are useful to female representatives in their activities in the assemblies. One questionnaire response said that the female representative's questions in the assembly about gender equality policies led to the promotion of such a gender equality policy. Another response was that male representatives have begun to recognize the importance of women's participation in committees, including the assembly steering committee. The increase of female representatives on assembly steering committees owes a lot to the influence of networking among female representatives. The

Alliance of Feminist Representatives,[24] consisting mainly of non-party-affiliated representatives currently in office and the National Summit of Female Representatives,[25] organized by the network for increasing grass-roots women's representatives, have been arenas for the exchange of experiences and discussion. Themes of their reports include such things as how male-centred assemblies have changed through women's participation, and how the main issues of local politics are changing from traditional 'development' and profit-orientated policies to politics in which people's daily lives are regarded as important. And as news of these effects of female representatives' activities reach women in the community through the media, momentum for more change will grow.

Prospects and future challenges: what we can learn from Korean women's experiences

The significance of the emergence of female assembly members has been discussed above, but the fact remains that it is difficult for female representatives to pursue women's interests in assemblies, because they comprise less than 10 per cent of members.[26] Furthermore, female representatives are not always feminists. Therefore it is essential to increase the number of representatives with a feminist standpoint. How can this be done?

I shall look now at the situation in another East Asian country, the Republic of Korea. As in Japan, discrimination against women in South Korea has long flourished under the ideology of Confucianism. However, the institutionalization of women's policies and the representation of women in the National Assembly there have been promoted strongly since the 1990s. In the 2004 national election, the number of female National Assembly members increased hugely, more than doubling from sixteen (5.86 per cent) in the year 2000 to thirty-nine (13 per cent) of the 299 representatives. This marks a record increase in the history of the National Assembly in South Korea. In the proportional-representation constituencies, the number of women increased from eleven to twenty-nine, and in the regional constituencies, from five to ten. Similar advances by women candidates were also seen in the local elections of 2000. In the 2002 nationwide local elections, the number of female assembly members reached sixty-three out of 682 representatives (9.2 per cent). Among them, forty-nine out of seventy-three representatives (67.1 per cent) were elected in proportional-representation constituencies, and fourteen out of 608 representatives (2.3 per cent) in regional constituencies. For city, county and district councils, seventy-seven women (2.2 per cent of 3,459 representatives) were elected. The high percentage of women in the proportional-representation constituencies was because of the 2002 revision of the electoral system which introduced the system of 'two votes for one voter' in municipal and provincial councils (one vote for a candidate in a regional constituency and one vote for a political party in a proportional-representation constituency) and the quota system for female candidates (50 per cent) in the proportional-representation constituencies candidates who did not follow the revised system could not register for the election. This system was not applied in the elections for city, county and district councils. However, if more than 30 per cent of the candidates put up by a party were women, the party was given an additional government subsidy and the campaign deposit money was reduced. This was one of the demands of women's organizations and it benefited female candidates as well as small and weak parties who lacked campaign funds. Many of the representatives elected in the proportional-representation constituencies, and in the national election, were people who had long been involved in workers, peasants or women's movements. For example, Open Uri Party representatives who were elected include a co-leader of the Korean Alliance of the Handicapped, a human rights activist, and a leader of a women's organization; and Democratic Labour Party representatives include a 'worker' secretary of a labour union and the chair of the South Korean General Federation of Women Peasants' Unions. Their election owed much to the revision of the electoral system.

The revision of the electoral system was the achievement of the 'movement for introducing a quota system everywhere' started by a coalition of women's organizations in 1994.[27] Although there are opinions both for and against a quota system in Korea, most women leaders in the country agreed with the necessity of a quota system as a temporary measure to rectify discrimination against women. In fact, a quota system has been introduced in other countries where women's political participation has been promoted, including Norway and Sweden.

The importance of women's participation in the policy-making process has been recognized increasingly by the Korean women's movement since democratization in 1987, and the scope for promoting women's political participation has been expanded. Until then, the Korean League of Women Voters had been the centre of organizations specializing in political issues. Since that time, increasing numbers of organizations focused on 'women and politics' have been established, and they have become the driving force behind the movement. Such organizations include the Korean Institute for Women and Politics (1990), the Korea Women's Political Caucus (1991), the Korean Women's Development Institute (1994), and the Korean Women's Political Solidarity (1999). Women's civil organizations like these, as well as the Korean Women's Development Institute, a governmental organization established in 1987, conduct research, including analysis of women's voting behaviour, and provide education and training for candidates, support women candidates, and submit recommendations or proposals to political parties.

This movement is an extension of the most important feature of the women's movement in the 1980s. As one activist put it, 'the women's movement started to play a leading role in presenting policy issues for women to tackle and make demands to the government' and 'the change in relations between the state and the women's movement has led to a great change in the decision-making process of women's policies as a whole' (Hwang, 2003). In the 1990s, several institutional measures were taken in order to improve women's status. It included the establishment of the Ministry of Gender Equality in 2001, by a presidential order. Han Myong-Sook, a leader of the movement for democratization and a leader of the present women's movement, ran for the National Assembly as a representative of the women's movement and took office as Minister. Gender mainstreaming was further promoted by the advancement of women from women's organizations or academia into the bureaucracy: 'The appearance of the first generation of "femocrats" in Korea shows not only empowerment of women through their advancement into the male-centered bureaucracy, but also the potential for introducing a female-centered viewpoint in the administration of the state' (Hwang, 2003, p. 114).

Women's participation in the policy-making process in Korea has been the result of the women's movement giving top priority to institutional reforms. However, because of the prioritization of the institutional approach, Korean women have faced a disparity between the institutions, including the law, and people's consciousness when they are implemented. There is criticism that the women's movement itself has been institutionalized and is becoming conservative, as a result of the participation of the movement's leaders in the establishment, a criticism reflected in the newly coined expression, 'state feminism'.[28]

In Japan, which, unlike Korea, has no quota system or other institutional support, women have developed the movement to get women elected to local assemblies through day-to-day activities at the grassroots level all over Japan. However, at the national level, Japanese women face tough obstacles to getting more women elected to the Diet. To overcome these, the Japanese women's movement should strengthen and enlarge its network to promote the reforming of institutions, including the electoral system, as did the Korean women's movement. Moreover, routes should be established through which to put forward suitable candidates. In Korea, women's organizations submitted lists of potential female candidates to political parties and elected leaders of the women's movement to the National Assembly. Japan also needs a movement like this. If candidates can be elected who can help to bring about change, the present low voter turnout can be improved and more voters will have a voice in changing politics.[29] As it is, the Japanese movement's emphasis on gender consciousness-raising has meant that the kind of specific actions for institutionalizing election reform pursued by the Korean women's movement have been neglected.

Conclusion

This chapter has analysed the background of the victory of women candidates in the 1999 and 2003 nationwide elections, elections which saw the largest number of female representatives elected in the history of Japan. Through an examination of the situation in Nagano Prefecture, a rural area, the following results were observed.

The women's political movement in Nagano started as election campaigning when women gained the vote after the Second World War, with the Women's Association playing the leading role. Women's solidarity contributed to spreading learning about politics and promoting ideal election campaigns. Nagano Prefecture was at the top in terms of the number of women candidates elected in two nationwide local elections after the war. Behind the achievement of this figure, there was a history of activities of the Women's Association organized as a voluntary study group in the early 1900s, which played a role in the formation of a political group by women in communities after the war. However, how the case of Nagano Prefecture has a place in the activities of the Women's Association in Japan before and after the war is an issue that should be analysed further in the future.

The number of women in local assemblies decreased with Japan's high economic growth, which encouraged the sexual division of labour and an increasingly male-centred society. During this period, farmers in Nagano Prefecture took other jobs. While women also began to take outside jobs, they found themselves responsible for the farm work their husbands had formerly undertaken.

The rapid increase in the number of women elected to assemblies in the 1990s symbolizes a weakening of the conventional gender-related consciousness. It is the result of two types of political movement after the 1980s. One is exemplified by the case of Nagano, and consists of the empowerment of women in rural communities through activities (not necessarily based on feminist consciousness) related to farm management, including the movement to introduce the Family Management Agreement. The other was the consciously feminist movement aimed at making women more active in politics and getting them elected to public office. Many women from the former type of movement who were elected to public office have since become more aware of gender issues. Whatever their background, however, the women recently elected represent an important, but still embryonic, trend.

At the national level, much can be learned from the experiences of the women's movement in Korea, where women who are closely linked to the women's movement have been elected in record numbers. In Japan, most female Diet members are not linked to women's organizations. At the national level, Japan too might benefit from the introduction of a quota system and from a system in which parties accept as candidates women recommended by women's organizations.

It is most important that the feminist movement gets more female representatives elected to legislatives bodies – women who will stand up for women's rights and protect women's interests. It is equally important not to divide or stratify women as a result of the promotion of women's participation in the policy-making process, which is seen as being important for women's liberation.

Notes

1 Yoko Kunihiro and Tokuko Ogai analyse the Ordinary Citizens' Network movement as a case of women's political participation in cities. Ikumi Haruki examines three female prefecture assembly members who were elected from urban constituencies in the 1999 nationwide local elections.
2 The total number of representatives is 480. Their term of office is for four years unless the Diet is dissolved in mid-term. The country is divided into 300 small districts, each of which has a single seat. In the proportional-representation system, the country is divided into eleven blocks. Seats are allocated to parties in proportion to the number of votes obtained, and the candidates whose names appear highest on the party's list of candidates are given those seats. Candidates who are also standing in the small districts are often given identical rankings in the party list. The winner in this case is decided by looking at the ratio of the margin of defeat – that is, the margin compared to the candidate who obtains the largest number of votes among candidates who stand, both in the small constituency and the proportional-representation constituency.
3 The total number of representatives is 242. Their term of office is six years, and half the representatives are up for re-election every three years. There is both a regional constituency and a national constituency. In the regional constituency, the number of seats for each prefecture is decided in proportion to the population. In national constituencies with large electoral districts, a non-binding list system is adopted, where each political party submits names of candidates and the order is decided according to the number of votes obtained by a candidate. The deposit money, 6 million yen (about US$ 56,000), is required by a candidate, and 60 million yen (about US$ 560,000) for ten candidates on the list of a party.
4 In 1974, sixteen organizations, including the League of Women Voters of Japan, submitted an opinion to the prime minister opposing small-district constituencies. And in 1990, the International Women's Year Liaison Group, a group of forty-eight organizations established in 1975 (and reorganized in 1980), submitted demands to political parties asking them to put up more women candidates in elections for the Upper House and Lower House, and in 1992 submitted to the government a demand for the promotion of women's advancement into national politics and a reform of the electoral system.
5 Eight women ran for governor in the eleven prefectures where gubernatorial elections were held, and one of them was elected, raising the number of female governors to four. Seventeen women ran in mayoral elections and three were elected, to bring the number of female mayors to six. Eleven women ran in elections for ward chief in Tokyo, but none was elected. Seventeen women ran for the heads of towns and two were elected.
6 The Women's Association is a village-level organization, the village-level associations being united at the level of the prefecture into coalitions called the United Women's Association. Although membership is not compulsory, most

women joined in the past to keep in step with the rest of the community. Activities included political education. Unlike many other organizations established after the war, the Women's Association was not dependent on assistance from the local administration. It is the biggest women's organization in Nagano Prefecture, with 2 million members at its height, but at the time of writing has only 20,000. The decrease in membership is mainly because of the diversification of women's activities and needs, and its failure to attract young women.

7   In the 1947 nationwide local elections, the number of women elected was largest in Nagano Prefecture, followed by Saitama and Gunma. These prefectures are silkworm-producing districts, where women's labour was highly valued.

8   This is a political party that originated in the co-operative movement and consists mainly of women working on such issues as safe foods, the environment and community development. The party puts up housewives as its candidates in local assembly elections, who campaign on an 'ordinary citizens' platform. It has proved its political muscle in cities such as Tokyo, Kanagawa, Chiba and Fukuoka. See also Note 1.

9   This campaign, the first grassroots campaign in the country on 'Women and Politics', was started by fifteen women who had participated in the Conference on the Global Network for Women and Politicians held in Manila in 1998. See '(2003 Josei to Seiji Kyanpen' Yobikakenin jimukyoku, 2003). *Report on 2003 Campaign for Women and Politics: Fifty per cent of Representatives for Women*, published in 2003 by the Secretariat of the Campaign for Women and Politics

10   The first such training programme, the 'School for Women and Politics', was established by Yoriko Madoka, then a member of the former Japan New Party (*Nihon-shin-to*), who at the time of writing belongs to the Democratic Party of Japan, and the number of women who have participated in the School exceeds 500. This move is represented by the 'Centre to Promote Women's Involvement in Politics', established in 1994 by a foundation called the Fusae Ichikawa Memorial Association for the 1995 nationwide local elections. It changed its name to the 'Centre for Political Participation' in 1996. The centre was started with the participation of sixty-one women from nineteen prefectures in ten programmes in the first term, and thirty-two women in five programmes in the second term. The participants were activists in women's and civil movements, and assembly members currently in office, who were candidates and their supporters. In the nationwide elections one year later, thirty-three women among ninety-three participants stood for the elections, and twenty-four women (66%) were elected. Grassroots 'back-up schools' were established around the time of the Beijing Conference.

11   In 1997, two funds were established – the Women's Solidarity Fund, whose Empowerment Prize supports women's organizations working to elect women to local assemblies, and WINWIN (Women In New World, International Network), which funds women who want to go into politics, mainly national politics.

12   For example, the basic course on gender equality organized by the Centre for Gender Equality in Nagano Prefecture produced graduates who went on to become representatives in seventeen city, town and village assemblies.

13   In June 1953, the chair and other officials of the coalition of Women's Associations in the prefecture asked the Diet to revoke the use of the manoeuvre site on Mt Asama, and the Diet did so in July.

14   There are many Nagano products whose outputs are the highest in Japan, including vegetables such as lettuce, celery and Chinese leaf, and fruits such as *Kyoho* grapes, blueberries, apricots, Chinese quinces and walnuts.

15 The Livelihood Improvement Movement promoted improvements in rural houses such as introducing safer cooking stoves in the kitchen, and better nutrition and work clothing. The movement also proposed simpler, less expensive weddings and other ceremonies. In accordance with the 1998 revision of the Law for Promoting the Improvement of Agriculture, members take part in training programmes to improve farming methods and become farmers.

16 See the thirtieth anniversary report of the Rural Women's Network Nagano (*Noson Josei Nettowak Nagano*) (2002).

17 This is an administrative committee in cities, towns and villages for the approval of transactions and loans to farmland for its efficient use. The committee also works to promote the development of rural management and the training of the agricultural workforce. The number of committee members depends on the area of farmland and the number of farms. Although the number of women only reached ten (2.2%), in 1993, because of the implementation of the Plan for Rural Women (see Note 18 below), its percentage has become the highest in Japan.

18 The Plan for Rural Women in Nagano Prefecture: Towards More Affluent Farms and Rural Life and the Establishment of a Gender-Equal Rural Society, published by the Nagano Prefecture Department of Agricultural Administration was passed in 1993 and subsequently revised three times.

19 The family management agreement is an agreement among members of farm families on items such as the allocation of remuneration for farm work, transfer of management, and holidays. The Ministry of Agriculture, Forestry and Fisheries promotes this agreement as a means of furthering the advancement of women in the management of farms, and the modernization of farm management.

20 This is a system started in 1992 in which Nagano Prefecture recognizes 'meisters', or community leaders, who tackle, from a woman's perspective, issues such as the promotion of agriculture in their communities, improving farmers' lives, and village development.

21 Nagano Prefecture recognizes them as leaders on gender equality in communities.

22 *Josei nyusu* (Women's news) (of 20 July and 30 July 2000, and my interview with Michiko Tarukawa, conducted on 16 February 2004).

23 Documented in *Shimosuwa-machi no Onnashu Senkyo sono shogen* (Women and the election in Shimosuwa Town: their testimonies) by Michiko Tarukawa, and *Tobucho fujin-giin tanjo no ashiato: Riso senkyo o susumete* (The track of the birth of a female representative in *Tobucho*: developing the ideal election campaign) edited by the Group for an Ideal Election Campaign, the election committee of the candidate Hisako Ono.

24 The National Alliance of Feminist Representatives was established in 1992 and consists of 200 members. It published *Ochakumi no seijigaku* (Politics of the service of tea).

25 In 2000, the Second Summit of Female Representatives in Shinano was held in Nagano Prefecture, with 1,000 participants from all over the country, including members of the Diet and of local assemblies.

26 In the Chiba Prefecture Assembly, for example, only nine out of the ninety-six members were women when a bill on gender-equality was introduced (following the 2003 election, there were only eight women). Because of the opposition of the Liberal Democratic Party, all the members of which are male, the bill was scrapped.

27 There are five women's organizations at the centre of the national movement: the Korean Women's Political League; the Korean League of Women Voters; the Korean Institute for Women and Politics; the Korean National Council of Women; and the Korea Women's Associations United. About eighty organiza-

tions, including the YWCA and the Korean Women's Link, each of which has some 100,000 members, join with their activities.

28 'The reality and challenges of the Korean Women's Movement', an oral report by Chang Mi-gyong, a member both of the Korean Women's Institute and Korean Women's Political Solidarity. It was given at the Exchange Seminar on Human Rights between Korea and Japan on 27 August 2003.

29 In the 2003 election of the Lower House, the voter turnouts were 60.03% for women and 59.68 for men in the small constituencies, and 59.99% for women and 59.63% for men in the proportional-representation constituencies, which is the lowest since 1996.

References

Hara, Taro (1958). 'Fujin to sono seiji katsudo: Nagano-ken Chikumachimura Fujinkai' (Women and their political activities: Women's Association in Chikumachimura, Nagano Prefecture), *Gekkan: shakai kyoiku* (Monthly social education). May. Also in *Nihon josei no shutai keisei* (Establishment of contemporary women's independence in Japan) (1996) vol. 3, pp. 444–52 (Tokyo: Domesu shuppan (in Japanese).

Haruki, Ikumi (2000) 'Josei to seiji: Yamaguchiken ni okeru josei kenkai-giin tanjo no haikei' (Women and politics: the background of the birth of female assembly members in Yamaguchi Prefecture), *Hyoron: Shakai kagaku* (Review: Social science), vol. 61, pp. 23–53 (Kyoto: Doshisha University Society of Humanities – Doshisha daigaku jinbun gakkai) (in Japanese).

Haruki, Ikumi (2003) 'Kankoku ni okeru kokkai-giin no tanjo katei: Porityikaru riku-rutomento to shuhyo-kozo' (The process of the birth of Diet members in Korea: political recruitment and the structure of gathering votes), Ph.D. dissertation (Kyoto: the Department of Literature, Doshisha University) (in Japanese).

Hwang, Chang-mee (2003). 'Kankoku josei seisaku no tenkai katei' (Women's policy paradigm in Korea: between development and democratization), *Toa keizai kenkyu* (Asian economic studies), vol. 61, p. 475 (Yamaguchi: Toa Keizai Gakkai, Yamaguchi University) (in Japanese).

Ichikawa Fusae Kinenkai (Fusae Ichikawa Memorial Association) (1987, 1991, 1995, 1999 and 2003) *Fujin sansei shiryo-shu: Zen chiho-gikai fujin-giin no genjo* (Local assemblies: Handbook of data on Japanese women in political life) (Tokyo: Ichikawa Fusae Kinenkai (in Japanese).

Ichikawa Fusae Kinenkai (1997) *Josei sansei goju-shunen kinen josei sansei shiryoshu* (The fiftieth anniversary of women's suffrage: handbook of data on Japanese women in political life) (Tokyo: Ichikawa Fusae Kinenkai) (in Japanese).

Ichikawa Fusae Kinenkai (2002) *Dokyumento chiho-seiji: Ichikawa Fusae Seiji Senta de manabu 47-nin no chosen* (Document local politics: challenge of 47 women learning at the Ichikawa Fusae Kinenkan for political participation) (Tokyo: Ichikawa Fusae Kinenkai (in Japanese).

Ichikawa Fusae kinenkai (2003a) *Josei sansei shiryoshu 2003* (handbook of data on Japanese women in political life, 2003), Tokyo: Ichikawa Fusae kinenkai.

Ichikawa Fusae Kinenkai (2003b) *Josei sansei shiryoshu: zen chiho gikai fujin giin no genjo* (Handbook of data on Japanese women in political life: the status of female members in all local assemblies) (Tokyo: Ichikawa Fusae Kinenkai) (in Japanese).

Iwamoto, Misako (1999) '1999 nen no toitsu-senkyo ni okeru josei no shinshutsu: mutoha-giin wo chushin ni shite' (The advancement of women in the 1999 nation-wide local elections: focusing on the non-partisans), *Seisaku kagaku* (Policy science), vol. 8, no. 3, (December, pp. 21–38 (Kyoto: Ritsumeikan University) (in Japanese).

Iwamoto, Misako (2003) 'Josei to seiji: Nihon ni okeru gensetsu bunseki' (Women and politics: a discourse analysis in Japan), in *Nihon seiji gakkai nenpo: 'Sei' to seiji*

2003 (Annual of the Japanese Political Science Association: Gender, sexuality and politics), (Tokyo: Iwanami Shoten), pp. 15–44 (in Japanese).

'2003 Josei to seiji kyanpen' yobikakenin jimukyoku (eds) (2003) *2003 Josei to seiji kyanpen* (2003 campaign for women and politics) (Tokyo: '2003 Josei to seiji kyanpen' yobikakenin jimukyoku) (in Japanese).

Kunihiro, Yoko (1993) 'Josei no seiji sanka no nyu uebu' (A new wave of women's political participation) in Sumiko Yazawa (ed.), *Toshi to josei no shakaigaku* (Sociology of cities and women) (Tokyo: Saiensu-sha) (in Japanese).

Mikanagi, Yumiko (1999) *Josei to seiji* (Women and politics) (Tokyo: Shinhyoron) (in Japanese).

Mizoguchi, Akiyo, Yoko Saeki and Soko Miki (eds) (1995) *Shiryo: Nihon uman ribu shi* (Resources: history of the women's liberation movement in Japan), vol. 3 (1975–81) (Kyoto: Women's Store Shoka-do) (in Japanese).

Nagano-ken Fujin Mondai Kenkyukai (Nagano Research Group on Women's Issues). (1987–96) *Ayumi* (Reports: Advancing step by step), vols 1–16 (Nagano: Hokushin Insatsu) (in Japanese).

Nagano Prefecture, Agricultural Technology Section, Department of Agricultural Administration (2002) *Noson josei no shakai sankaku ni kansuru chosa hokokusho* (Report of the research on the social participation of rural women) (Nagano: Ryuo-shobo) (in Japanese).

Nakamura, Ryuko (2002) *Shinshu josei-shi* (Women's history in Shinshu) (Nagano: Ryuo-shobo) (in Japanese).

Noson Josei Nettowaku Nagano (Rural Women's Network Nagano) (2002) *Sanju-shunen kinenshi: Mirai wo kizuku* (Thirtieth anniversary report: Creating the future) (Nagano: Noson Josei Nettowaku Nagano) (in Japanese).

Ogai, Tokuko (1993) 'Chiho-gikai ni okeru josei giin no "keishi" to ishiki no henyo: Tokyo-seikatsusha nettowaku no jirei yori' (The 'birth' of female representatives in local assemblies and the change in perceptions: the case of ordinary citizens' network in Tokyo), Ph.D. dissertation, Ochanomizu University (in Japanese).

Ogai, Tokuko (1996) 'The Stars of Democracy: The First Thirty-nine Female Members of the Japanese Diet', *U.S.–Japan Women's Journal*, English Supplement no. 11, pp. 81–117.

Ogai, Tokuko (2003) 'Josei mogigikai to iu josei seisaku: Onnatachi no keiken no seijika katei' ('Evolution of women's simulation assembly: a case study of women's political participation), in *Nihon seiji gakkai nenpo: 'Sei' to seiji)* (Annual of the Japanese Political Science Association: Gender, sexuality and politics) (Tokyo: Iwanami Shoten), pp. 113–34 (in Japanese).

Shimoina Rengo Fujinkai (Coalition of Women's Associations in Shimoina) (1957) *Junen no ayumi* (History of ten years) (Nagano: Shianano Kyoiku-kai Shappanbu) (in Japanese).

Shinano no josei-shi kankokai (Group for Publishing Women's History in Shinano) (ed.) (1994) *Shinano no josei-shi* (Women's history in Shinano) (Nagano: Kyodo-Shuppansha) (in Japanese).

Shinano no josei-shi kanko-kai (eds.) (1994) *Shinano no josei-shi* (Women's history in Shinano) (Nagano: Kyodo Shuppansha) (in Japanese).

Tilly, Louise A. and Patricia Gurin (eds) (1992) *Women, Politics and Change* (New York: Russell Sage Foundation).

Tsujimura, Teruo (1968) *Sengo Shinshu josei-shi* (Women's history of Shinshu after the Second World War) (Nagano: Federated Women's Association of Nagano Prefecture) (in Japanese).

Watanabe, Hiroshi (2003) 'Joron (Preface)', in *Nihon seiji gakkai nenpo: 'Sei' to seiji* (Annual of the Japanese Political Science Association: Gender, sexuality and politics) (Tokyo: Iwanami Shoten) (in Japanese).

6
Has Socialism Contributed to Gender Role Changes? A Comparison of Gender Roles in Cuba and Japan

Kanako Yamaoka

Introduction

Gender issues in socialist countries have been discussed by many scholars. Most of them acknowledge that socialism succeeded in sending women to work outside their homes, while the domestic burden was not lifted from their shoulders, even when they had jobs. Therefore, women have dual responsibilities, both at work and at home. This is also true in the Cuban case. In spite of the progressive Family Code of 1975, which provides for husbands and wives sharing domestic work and child care, there have been few couples who honour this provision. Cuban *machismo* is still fully alive under the socialist regime.

This chapter aims to analyse to what extent socialist policy has succeeded in changing this tendency under the revolutionary government that has ruled Cuba for more than four decades. In particular, I shall focus on the changes starting in the first half of the 1990s, under the severe economic crisis created by the disintegration of the Soviet Union. There are many gender studies on Cuba, from both inside and outside the country. Mayda Álvarez has studied masculinity in terms of cultural and psychological frameworks.[1] The Federation of Cuban Women (Federación de Mujeres Cubanas – FMC), a mass organization for women, has led both movement and research, and has organized various study projects on gender issues in Cuba, especially in terms of empowerment (Álvarez *et al.*, 1994; Álvarez, 1998, 1999). These studies focused mainly on Cuban women's empowerment processes through labour and political participation. Sheryl Lutjens analysed the impact of the rectification process in the second half of the 1980s, focusing on Cuban women's political participation (Lutjens, 1995). Yet there are few studies that focus on gender roles and their transformation. Bunck discussed that in Cuba, gender issues were introduced, led and funded by the revolutionary government, not by spontaneous civil movements or individuals, and implied therefore that most Cuban women, from upper to lower classes, were not ready to participate in paid work, as many of them wanted to be housewives if the conditions permitted (Bunck, 1994, p. 101). According to Bunck, there are two reasons that women generally wished to stay at home as housewives. (1) Even before the disintegration of the Soviet Union, upper and middle class women had felt that domestic work became more time-consuming because of a shortage of consumer goods and because husbands were obliged to leave home for long periods participate in various revolutionary missions, and anyway women needed to spend more time in domestic work. (2) The meaning of earning money was not so important, because goods were always scarce, and money supply was relatively abundant, and even if a women worked and brought extra income, there was few more things to be able to purchase (Bunck, 1994, p. 101). However, the author's interest mainly focused on the historical point of view, especially the adaptation period during the 1960s. It dealt with the situation until the beginning of the 1990s. I would like to contribute to the gender role situation of the most recent period. In Cuba the Cuban journal *Bohemia* published an article on gender roles, with the results of a small survey on this issue (Rodríguez *et al.*, 2001). According to the survey, values in traditional gender roles have not changed as much as had been expected. Helen Safa's study provided much inspiration and information for this chapter (Safa, 1995). After conducting an interesting field survey on woman workers in a textile factory on the outskirts of Havana, she concluded that the revolution had contributed greatly in changes in gender relations. She observe differences in gender roles among generations of female workers: younger-generation couples were more likely to share domestic work and child care, while older women were more tolerant of their husbands' or partners' traditional attitudes. But her survey was conducted in 1987, before the economic crisis, and the impact of the crisis on gender relations was not fully predicted by her.

In order to evaluate how and to what extent the Cuban Revolution and its socialist policies have affected Cuban gender roles, in this chapter I first analyse what policies of the government improved the situation of women in both their homes and workplaces before the disintegration of the Soviet Union. Then I examine how the economic crisis has affected women's condition and gender roles. Finally, in order to prove the effect of socialism on changes in gender relations in households, I will compare the Cuban case with that of Japan. The transformation of gender roles in both countries seems to run parallel to one other, in terms of women's labour force participation rates in since the 1960s, but the factors that influenced those changes are different.

The transformation of Cuban women's labour participation in the post-revolutionary period

Gender role changes and their economic impact

In this section, I first describe the main accomplishments of the Cuban Revolution in gender relations: women's employment policy and supporting social services. Second, I will examine how the economic crisis has affected working patterns in the 1990s.

It is widely believed that socialist countries should enjoy gender equality, at least more than capitalist countries, since socialism encourages women to work outside the home, according to Marxist principles, and also because socialist countries do not suffer resistance from the private sector. As long as women's labour force participation is concerned, Cuba has recorded quite a significant improvement. In 1955, the women's full-time labour force participation rate was 13 per cent, and the majority gave up their jobs on marriage. In 2000, that rate was 39 per cent. Obviously, women's participation has increased since the revolution of 1959, and it is likely that the revolutionary government has encouraged this trend by providing enough employment to welcome women into the labour force, as well as nursery schools and other public facilities to support families with working parents.

Yet it is also well known that women's participation in the labour force has imposed dual responsibilities on them: to work full-time at their workplace and at the same time to bear full responsibility for domestic work; the government has approved women's rights to work outside their homes, but it has not been able to make their husbands or partners share in domestic work and child-raising. This is the problem of gender roles, or the legacy of traditional Latin *machismo*. Nevertheless, women how enjoy a new-found authority and economic independence through their labour force participation, and even if this has imposed dual responsibilities on them, it is significant that women's economic participation is one of the most important factors in the changes brought about in gender relations.

Women's labour force participation before and after the collapse of the Soviet Union

The decline of living standards and its impact on women's labour force participation

Before the revolution, women's participation in the labour force was low – only 13 per cent in 1955. The participation rates increased gradually through the 1970s and 1980s, and in 1990, it reached 34.8 per cent (Safa, 1995, p. 26. Table 1.7). The data in Table 6.1 cannot be compared directly to that of Safa's data Table 6.1 because they are based on different sources, but nevertheless the proportion of working women in the total working-age population (both sexes and female only) has decreased gradually since the disintegration of the Soviet Union.

Table 6.1 Women's labour force participation rates, 1990–96 (percentages)

Year	Women's participation rates	
	In total labour force population	In female working age population
1990	38.9	46.7
1993	37.0	44.1
1996	37.2	42.1

Note: In Cuba, women's economically active ages are 15 to 55.
Source: Oficina Nacional de Estadísticas (1999), p. 138.

Table 6.2 Labour force participation rates by age and sex, 1990 and 1996 (percentages)

Age groups	Women		Men	
	1990	1996	1990	1996
15–16	1.7	1.0	3.0	8.1
17–19	20.7	20.1	58.7	53.5
20–29	55.1	50.1	84.1	79.9
30–59	55.9	49.1	92.5	84.8
60 and older	3.5	2.3	22.7	18.1
All ages (over 15)	42.2	37.7	72.4	68.0

Source: Oficina Nacional de Estadísticas (1999), p. 139.

It is generally agreed that before the revolution, the majority of working women were young and unmarried, and they were expected to give up their jobs once they got married. Safa explains this as a result of traditional gender segregation (*casa/calle* distinction) (Safa, 1995, p.127). Their husbands did not allow them to continue working, because they believed that men belonged to the street (*calle*: the world outside the home) and women in the house (*casa*). In the 1990s, that tendency was no longer observed. The highest rates of women's labour force participation are in the age cohorts 20–29 and 30–59 (see Table 6.2). This means that most female workers continue to work even after getting married and having children. Also, Cuban women's labour force participation rate has been the highest in Latin America. If the revolution has made this possible, it is indeed one of its most remarkable accomplishments.

Women tend to choose jobs that are related to caring for other people, such as in public health, education and social assistance. In Table 6.3, it can be seen that women workers are concentrated in education, public health and social assistance, while there are fewer women workers than men in the industrial sector and construction. In each sector, 61.5 per cent

Table 6.3 Distribution of working population by economic sector, 1996 (percentages)

Economic sector	Women	Men
Industrial sector	18.3	30.6
Construction	3.7	11.2
Agriculture	5.0	10.7
Transportation	2.9	6.5
Communication	0.7	0.4
Commerce	13.3	10.4
Education	22.3	8.3
Public Health, Social Assistance, Sports and Tourism	18.3	6.6
Finance and Security	1.1	0.4
Administration	4.8	3.7
Other	9.6	11.2
Total	100.0	100.0

Source: Oficina Nacional de Estadísticas (1999), p. 141.

of workers in education are female, 62.1 per cent in public health, sports and tourism, and 60.7 per cent in the financial sector. Male workers are concentrated more in construction (83.8 per cent), transportation (79.2 per cent) and agriculture (78.1 per cent). In reality, it is seldom that one sees male workers in nursery schools and primary schools in Cuba. At senior citizen's homes (*hogares de ancianos*), the majority of workers are women, from directors to care workers.[2] In the public health sector, many family doctors (*médicos de familia*) are women, while in big hospitals most physicians are men.[3]

In Cuba, for men, work is a social obligation, and the labour law of 1971 provides for this, but women are permitted not to work. Therefore, while around 70 per cent of the male population worked in the 1990s, the female labour force participation rate was about 40 per cent. Yet female workers tend to have a higher level of education than male workers, and to obtain more professional jobs. Table 6.4 shows that the 18.9 per cent of female workers completed higher education, in 2001 compared to 11 per cent of male workers. This tendency reflects the proportion of female workers in the blue-collar and administrative categories in Table 6.5. On the one hand, for the total number of female workers, which is less than half of the number of male workers, women occupy many administrative jobs. On the other hand, far fewer women work in blue-collar jobs.

Table 6.5 shows the fluctuation of numbers of workers in each category. For both sexes, the number of the total workers recorded a significant drop in 1995; but apart from that year the numbers have increased. In 1995, the decrease reflects drops in technicians and administrative categories. That year, the Cuban government implemented an economic rationalization

Table 6.4 Education level of workers, by sex 2001 (percentages)

	Proportion (%)	
	Male	*Female*
Primary or less	18.3	9.8
Middle	33.7	22.9
Higher middle	36.9	48.4
Higher	11.1	18.9
Total	100.0	100.0

Source: Oficina Nacional de Estadísticas (2003), p. 128.

policy: a kind of austerity policy to rationalize lazy or inefficient state enterprises, seek an equilibrium in the state budget, and control the monetary flux. The government closed down inefficient state enterprises and restructured section of the government, and in doing so it cut jobs. It is likely that the government's drastic action caused the drop in the size of the labour force.

A similar tendency is observed in the female labour force participation in Table 6.5. While the drop was recorded for both male and female workers in 1995 only, in 1996 it barely increased. The technical and administrative categories recorded drops then, but for women workers, employment in all categories except the managerial category decreased. The male labour force participation rates fluctuate in a slightly different manner. In 1995, the workers' category maintained the same level, but technician, administrative and managerial categories recorded drops. The difference between female and male participation is that, while the number of female workers was lower in the blue-collar category, male workers decreased at the managerial level.

More importantly, Table 6.1 shows that the female labour force participation rates decreased in the 1990s, in both total labour force population and the female working-age population. This means that during the worst period of the economic crisis, women are more likely to have give up their jobs. And from the gender difference in the labour force participation pattern (see Table 6.5) described in the previous paragraph, I presents a hypothesis that women who have professional or higher positions in their careers remained in the labour force through the economic crisis, but blue-collar working-class women were more likely to have given up their jobs.

There is another possible explanation for the women's retreat from 'official' labour force participation: they may have left the formal sector and started working in the informal market. This also explains the fact that male workers have left the managerial category. Male managers, free from domestic responsibilities, probably did not hesitate to enter the newly developed economic sectors.

158

Table 6.5 Distribution of labour force, by occupational category and sex, 1992–2002 (000s workers)

Year	1992	1993	1994	1995	1996	1997	1998	1999	2000	2001	2002
Both sexes											
Workers	1951.5	1858.0	1854.9	1838.6	1463.1	1882.2	1897.2	1921.8	1929.2	2000.3	1986.2
Technical	872.4	904.2	917.7	739.7	824.8	792.9	779.2	788.6	810.9	849.3	880.5
Administrative	218.1	225.1	226.5	168.8	212.9	170.5	159.3	158.8	153.7	146.9	148.3
Service	524.2	545.6	556.5	567.4	853.2	570.8	624.9	657.5	645.6	670.8	708.8
Managerial	260.2	282.2	284.2	276.5	272.7	288.8	293.0	294.6	303.6	301.6	300.3
Total	3826.4	3815.1	3839.8	3591.0	3626.7	3705.2	3753.6	3821.3	3843.0	3968.9	4024.1
Female											
Workers	364.9	354.3	360.9	344.3	297.7	340.6	345.5	359.7	358.5	324.4	362.9
Technical	488.9	511.0	511.4	478.0	527.9	507.6	503.6	513.3	527.7	579.6	577.2
Administrative	176.9	175.0	173.0	144.4	142.8	139.8	135.7	134.0	130.1	133.2	125.2
Service	295.3	299.3	312.3	303.8	303.0	300.1	325.9	329.9	333.9	353.6	349.2
Managerial	66.8	72.0	74.6	79.7	79.6	87.6	88.1	91.5	95.4	94.1	101.3
Total	1392.8	1411.6	1432.2	1350.2	1351.0	1375.7	1398.8	1428.4	1445.6	1484.9	1515.8
Male											
Workers	1586.6	1503.7	1494.0	1494.3	1165.4	1541.6	1551.7	1562.1	1570.7	1675.9	1623.3
Technical	383.5	393.2	406.3	261.7	296.9	285.3	275.6	275.3	283.2	269.7	303.3
Administrative	41.2	50.1	53.5	24.4	70.1	30.7	23.6	24.8	23.6	13.7	23.1
Service	228.9	246.3	244.2	263.6	550.2	270.7	299.0	327.6	311.7	317.2	359.6
Managerial	193.4	210.2	209.6	196.8	193.1	201.2	204.9	203.1	208.2	207.5	199.0
Total	2433.6	2403.5	2407.6	2240.8	2275.7	2329.5	2354.8	2392.9	2397.4	2484.0	2508.3

Source: Oficina Nacional de Estadísticas, Anuario estadístico de Cuba, Edition 2000, p. 123, and Edition 2002, p.129.

Table 6.6   Economic growth rate, 1989–2003 (percentages)

Year	Growth rate (%)
1989	0.7
1990	−2.9
1991	−10.7
1992	−11.6
1993	−14.9
1994	0.7
1995	2.5
1996	7.8
1997	2.5
1998	1.2
1999	6.2
2000	5.6
2001	2.4
2002	1.1
2003	2.6

Sources: Oficina Nacional de Estadísticas (2001), and information from the Cuban Embassy in Japan.

Women's labor force participation pattern during the economic crisis

The collapse of the full employment policy and decline in general living standards[4]

Since the disintegration of the Soviet Union, the Cuban economy has been rather sluggish. The economic crisis was especially severe in the first half of the 1990s (see Table 6.6). Cuba was suddenly excluded from the CMEA (Council for Mutual Economic Assistance, or COMECON) bloc and lost most of its main trading partners. The country suffered severe material shortages, including fuel, spare parts, and other inputs, as well as foodstuffs and other basic necessities.

Cuba traditionally depends heavily on trade and imports most of its staples (rice and wheat) and other foodstuffs, as well as most industrial goods. Without the Eastern bloc, Cuba lost its main suppliers of these products, and the people's daily lives were affected directly by that suspension. During the Soviet era, Cuba had had a very favourable barter agreement with the USSR – Cuban sugar for Soviet petroleum. Most of the time, Cuba benefited more from that agreement because the USSR sold its oil to Cuba at prices lower than that on the international market, and bought Cuban sugar at higher prices. There were some exceptions when the oil price became lower than on the international market, such as during the Oil Crises in 1973 and 1979, and when the world sugar prices were extremely high at the beginning of the 1980s, but in most cases, the barter agreement

160

Table 6.7 Monthly food rations in Havana City, February 2004 (per person)

Item	Quantity	Price per unit (pesos)	Total price (pesos)	Price in US dollars[7]
Rice	6 lb	0.25	1.50	5.8
White kidney beans	10 oz	0.02	0.20	0.8
Peas	10 oz	0.01	0.10	0.4
Refined sugar	3 lb	0.15	0.45	1.7
Brown sugar	2 lb	0.10	0.20	0.8
Vegetable cooking oil	0.5 fluid 03	0.40	0.20	0.8
Bath soap	1 bar	0.25	0.25	1.0
Laundry soap	1 bar	0.20	0.20	0.8
Toothpaste	1 tube[5]	0.65	0.65	2.5
Ground coffee	8 oz	0.05	0.40	1.5
Cigarettes (strong type)[1]	3 packs	2.00	6.00	23.1
Cigarettes (mild type)[1]	1 pack	2.50	2.50	1.0
Salt	1 pack	0.35	0.35	1.3
Spaghetti	0.5 lb	0.50	0.25	1.0
Potatoes	4 lb	0.40	1.60	6.2
Chicken legs	1 lb	0.70	0.70	2.7
Minced meat from beef and soya beans	0.5 lb	0.70	0.35	1.3
Fish	2 lb	0.70	1.40	5.4
Egg	16 eggs	0.15	2.40	9.2
Fruit purée[2]	5 packs	0.06	3.00	11.5
Lactic powder[3] or milk chocolate	2.2 lb	1.50	1.50	5.8
Cow's milk[4]	33.8 fluid 03.[6]	0.25	7.5[8]	28.8[8]
Yoghurt	67.6 fluid 03.	0.50	1.00	3.8
Bread	2.603 lbs per day[6]	0.05	1.50[8]	5.8
Total amount (1 month = 30 days)			34.20	

Notes:
1 For adults only.
2 For babies less than one year of age.
3 Only for adults over 65 years old. It contains soya beans, cow's milk, chocolate and multivitamins.
4 Only for children less than 7 years old.
5 1 tube per household.
6 Per day.
7 Total quantity calculated at the current unofficial rate of 1 US dollar = 26 pesos. The unit is
8 For 30 days.
9 In Cuba weights and measurements are those of the USA 1 fluid 03 = 29.6 ml; 1 oz = 28.3 g 1 lb = 0.454 kg.

was more favourable for Cuba than for the Soviet Union. Furthermore, Cuba could sell redundant oil in the international market, which was one of the most important sources of hard currency income for the country.

The fall of the Soviet Union took away from Cuba all these favourable conditions, and the living standard of the people dropped sharply, with little food in ration stores and few cars on the streets. In the 1980s, a food rationing system guaranteed a basic food supply with which the people could sustain a certain standard of living. For example, limits were not placed on rations for eggs and fish (sardines and other inexpensive fish) and a family could purchase as much as it wanted. Cans of powdered milk and condensed milk were often distributed not only within the rationed schedule but also as additional supplies. But in the first half of the 1990s, this entire situation changed, and even the rationing schedule was compromised. People were obliged to seek these products on the black market, where prices were extremely high for those earning at the level of public-sector workers.

As a result of the economic crisis, the entire economy was dollarized, and the black market exchange rate with the US dollar became more and more unfavourable for the Cuban peso. Figure 6.1 shows how the exchange rate became extremely unfavourable for the Cuban peso, especially before October 1994, when the farmers' markets reopened. At that time, the average salary was 185 pesos (in 1994); in US dollars its value was only two to three dollars. One bottle of vegetable oil (one litre) at that time cost almost three dollars at hard currency shops, which meant that one month's salary of an average worker was equivalent to just one bottle of cooking oil.

Furthermore, the economic crisis had a serious effect on the public infrastructure, lowering living standards and increasing the burden of domestic work on women. Thermal electric plants did not work because of lack of petroleum, a large amount of which used to come from the Soviet Union. Consequently, severe and frequent power-failures occurred.[5] And not only electricity, but also gas and water supplies became scarce.[6] The rationing system no longer guaranteed the minimum level of food for survival (see Table 6.7). Table 6.8 is based on information for 2003, when the situation of the rationing programmes had improved considerably over that in 1994 and 1995, but the amount of monthly rations still only supplies enough for 10–14 days of the month.[7]

The impact of the economic crisis on patterns of women's labour force participation

In order to understand women's labour force participation in the 1990s, it is necessary first to see the structural transformation of industries and economic sectors. Most of both heavy and light industry disappeared as the Soviet supply of primary resources and spare parts, as well as machinery, was suspended. Today, only a part of the mining industry, largely of nickel, survives, with the co-operation of foreign investors. The sugar industry, Cuba's traditional locomotive industry, became sluggish because of its

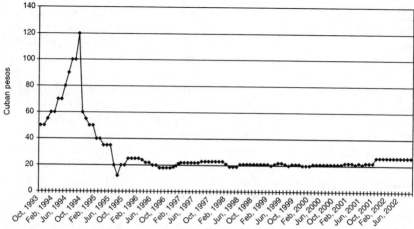

Sources: Data to 1998 calculated by the author; data from 1999 from US—
Cuba Trade and Economic Council, *Eye on Cuba*

Figure 6.1   Fluctuation of black market, or unofficial exchange rate (Cuban
pesos ts one US dollar)

inefficient structure. In 2002, government officials finally admitted to the
problem and closed down half of the sugar mills. The tourism industry has
been the main hard currency earner of Cuban economy.

Table 6.8   Average monthly salary of Cuban workers in the
state sector and joint ventures, 1989–2002 (Cuban pesos)

Year	Average monthly salary
1989	188
1990	187
1991	185
1992	182
1993	182
1994	185
1995	194
1996	202
1997	206
1998	207
1999	222
2000	234
2001	245
2002	261

Sources: Oficina Nacional de Estadísticas (ONE), *Anuario estadístico de
Cuba* 1996, 1999, 2000, and 2002.

In 1993, the government permitted self-employment within limits. Yet the job categories were limited to those that did not require the formation of a company or group. Concretely, these business comprise plumbing, house and vehicle repairs, private taxis, small restaurants (*paladares*), and house and room rentals for tourists.

Furthermore, the black market and other informal sectors became active in the 1990s, in spite of the government's occasional and strong control. The growth of these sectors partly reflected the necessity of many workers in the public sector also to work in the informal sector to compensate for the low level of their salaries. Table 6.8 shows the average salary of Cuban workers, and Figure 6.1 shows the black market, or unofficial, exchange rate of Cuban pesos to US dollars. The average salaries, which were paid in unconvertible Cuban pesos, fell in value to less than five or ten US dollars. In fact, it became almost impossible for workers to maintain their lives and their families on just several dollars a month, even with food rations and free healthcare and education. This is why many workers have gone to work secretly in the informal sector, where they can earn much more. Also, many public-sector workers take advantage of their access to the state's resources to resell them on the black market. For example, truck and bus drivers take petrol from their vehicles and sell it on the black market at a price a little lower than state-owned, hard-currency gas. Workers in cafeterias and restaurants steal food and sell it. People working for state-run shops of all types (*bodegas*, shops for rationed goods; and *shoppings*, hard currency shops) bring merchandise home to sell to their neighbours. The government, of course, is aware of these activities, but also knows that workers cannot live only on their salaries, so has no choice but to overlook them, although the police sometimes carry out missions to control them. Table 6.9 shows the sharp differences in monthly income between the public sector and private and informal sectors.

Under this transformation, it has become more difficult for women to maintain labour participation. First, the burden of domestic work has become much heavier and more time-consuming, and it has become much harder to do both paid work and domestic work. Rodríguez Reyes claims that it is not true that Cuban women have returned to being housewives, because from 1995, women's labour participation began to increase (Rodríguez Reyes, 1999, p. 9). According to government statistics, her claim is correct, and perhaps it is also right that many Cuban women remained in the labour force because they wanted to maintain their favourable conditions as salaried workers and their social participation via employment (Rodríguez Reyes, 1999, p. 10). It was easier for them to keep their jobs because of loose work ethics and various factors such as a lack of public transportation that allowed workers to be absent from work.[8] Also, at the time of writing, the conditions of workers in the public sector have improved, and there are more incentives to remain in their jobs.

Table 6.9 Monthly income in Havana City, March–April 2002

	In Cuban pesos	In US dollars[1]
State sector		
Minimum pension	100	4
Minimum wage	100	4
Teachers, primary and secondary schools	200–400	8–15
University professors	300–560	12–22
Engineers, physicians	300–650[2]	12–25
Garbage collectors	300–500	12–19
Police (ordinary order)	200–500	8–19
Police (security for tourists)	700–800	27–31
Military officers	350–700	13–23
Cabinet ministers	450–600	17–23
Private sector		
Domestic workers	520–1,040[3]	20–40
Private farmers	2,000–20,000[5]	77–1,923
Private bus service (in vehicles with capacity for 20–60 passengers)	10,000–20,000	385–770
Prostitutes (*qineteras*)	[4]	240–1,400[6]
Rental business of rooms and houses	[4]	250–4,000
Artists and musician (celebrities)	[4]	600–6,000[7]
Self-employed restaurant (*paladares*) owners	[4]	12,500–50,000

Notes:
1 Unofficial exchange rate at this time was US$1 = 26 pesos.
2 Older physicians can reach an agreement with the government to undertake private practice, which permits them to earn 10 to 20 times more than in the public sector.
3 Higher income for work in prestigious neighbourhoods such as Miramar.
4 Workers in these professions usually charge in US dollars.
5 Farmers who own less land earn less. Those who own many acres of land or who produce park or items or that are more in demand earn more.
6 Calculation based on the assumption that prostitutes earn US$10 to $50 per night = US$70 to $350 per week.
7 Artists and musicians who are not famous earn US$10 to US$13 a month. The late Compay Segundo, a famous musician at the Buena Vista Social Club, earned US$6,000 net income for a one-night show. Silvio Rodríguez (musician), Jorge Perugorría (film actor) and los Van-Van (music group) earn as much as US$200,000, but a percentage of their income is paid to the government.

Sources: Mesa-Lago, Carmelo (2003) *Economía y bienestar social en Cuba a comienzos del siglo XXI* (Madrid: Colibrí), p. 80.

Yet a more serious obstacle is that jobs that promise higher incomes now require much more worker dedication in output, as the worst economic crisis in the history of the Cuban Revolution (see Table 6.6) has had a serious effect on the government's full employment policy. Many Cuban women could obtain jobs, and consequently more authority, in their households, but that was possible only when the full employment policy was in effect. With the economic crisis, the government was no longer able to maintain that policy, because it was obliged to exercise the most drastic structural reforms and rationalization in its revolutionary history. Many state enterprises that had depended heavily on the generous input of Soviet production and technical assistance were paralysed, and were obliged later to close down. They no longer remained indulgent of inefficient management and lack of cost performance. They needed to cut back on the number of employees the government had kept on to provide full employment. The unemployment rate rose, even according to government statistics. The rate was 5.5 per cent in 1989, started to rise in 1993, and reached as high as above 9 per cent in 1995. The level of unemployment recovered gradually after 1995, and in 2000 returned to the same level as it had been in 1989, but the Cuban economic structure and its employment patterns had changed.

Workers in high-earning sectors need to work at night if the employer requires this, and must work for longer hours than the legal requirement, because of the nationwide structural reforms (*racionamiento*) and because of the participation of foreign investors. Safa pointed out that socialist countries are in the better position 'to combat gender discrimination, because they do not have to face resistance from the private sector' (Safa, 1995, p. 165), but since the 1990s this favourable condition has been disappearing, except in state sectors where salaries are low in US dollars. Women who bear dual responsibilities find it more difficult to work in such sectors. According to Popowski Casañ (1999), there were more women than men, in both 1970 and 1980, working in the state-owned sectors and political and mass organizations, and fewer women than men worked in non-state-owned sectors. In 1970, 98.3 per cent of women worked in the state-owned sectors, while 86.9 per cent of total workers worked in that sector. This means that fewer men worked at state-owned jobs than women. Similarly, in 1998, while 86 per cent of women worked in the state sector, 75.5 per cent of all workers did; and 1.4 per cent of women worked in political and mass organizations, while only 1.1 per cent of total workers work in that sector, and there were more women than men working there. This means that women tend to earn less than men, and their economic independence through employment has diminished. Workers in the state sector also have reasons to continue working – for example, because the workplace supplies lunch in the workers' cafeteria,[9] which is a saving for the worker, and there are regular payments to be made in Cuban pesos, such as for public utilities, so it is not totally meaningless to receive a salary in pesos.

Gender bias in labour participation patterns

As depicted above, many men with a higher education level gave up their jobs and started to work in the self-employed sector and farmers' markets or the black market, for example, where they could earn much more (see Table 6.9). Thus a similar transformation could have occurred in the case of female workers. It is, however, not easy for women to enter these newly developed economic sectors. The job categories in the self-employed sector are rigidly determined by the government – from plumbing to small-scale restaurants – and the majority of the workers in this sector are male. According to Pepowski Casañ (1999) in 1998 fewer women than men worked in joint ventures and the private sector, in which there are more opportunities to earn hard currency. More women tend to work in the government sector, and political and mass organizations. The only profession in which Cuban women dominate and also allows them to earn a large income is prostitution for foreign tourists (see Table 6.9). Furthermore, women's labour-force participation rate decreased in the 1990s (see Table 6.1), according to official government data, which does not include the informal sector.

One of the reasons that fewer women are seen in the high-income sectors is their dual responsibilities. When there was much less food available for households, and there were power-failures and cuts in water and gas supplies, domestic work became even heavier. Cuban women were obliged to bear the responsibility of finding food, clothing for children and so on. When electricity and water supplies were irregular, it was impossible to make plans for domestic work; the women had no way of knowing when and for how long they would be able to do, or complete, each household chore. They did not know when electricity would be available, for example. The water supply might dry up in the middle of doing the laundry, and the gas supply could be cut off for days so that people could not cook. There was (and is) severe material shortage, and when some products were made available, a long queue formed at the shops. When the farmers' markets were reopened in October 1994, the food shortage was modified a little, but prices were high for the average worker. There were still long queues to buy food at the farmers' market and even dollar shops, and women needed to get up before dawn to buy better products. The number of farmers' markets and hard currency shops, both built by the government, was limited, and many people needed to walk for several kilometres to go shopping.

The situation at the time of uniting is much better. There are more free markets and dollar shops, and therefore shorter queues and they are closer to home. There are fewer power cuts, as domestic oil production has increased to satisfy 50 per cent of national consumption after the year 2000, and as Cuba has become almost self-sufficient in electricity production through thermal power plants (95 per cent in 2003). Nevertheless, during the 1990s, women's burden of domestic work prevented them from continuing working outside the home. It is, however, still true that the domestic workload in Cuba is generally much heavier than in developed countries. There is little part-prepared or ready-made food on sale, and electric appliances are expensive, sold only in hard currency. Most women do the laundry by hand, and it is heavy daily labour because people change their clothes often in the hot and humid climate.

The requirements of the new jobs with high incomes are also a negative factor for women's labour force participation. While the public sector has allowed loose working discipline,[10] the new economic sector demands a rather capitalistic work ethics from its workers. It is not easy to obtain leave to nurse sick family members, for example, and if a worker arrives late at the workplace, even for a socially understandable reason, such work incentives as additional bonus may be deducted.

The above two reasons (heavier domestic work and more rigid work discipline) caused the decline of Cuban women's labour force participation in the mid-1990s (see Table 6.1). Nevertheless, the Cuban women's labour force participation rate is still the highest in Latin America, and it is possible that as the economy stabilizes, more women will try to get jobs. The educational level of women in Cuba is high, and this is another remarkable accomplishment of the Cuban Revolution. Especially in the higher middle and higher education levels, the number of the female students is higher than that of male students. The high level of education among Cuban women leads to more and better job opportunities.

Economic independence, even if it is supported by the government's generous social policy (especially social assistance), may have been a factor influencing the rise in divorce rates. Table 6.10 shows the fluctuation in the divorce rate after the revolution. Divorce rates continued to increase from 1960 until 1993, then fell a little, and became stable. Accordingly, the number of female heads of households increased. Comparing the year 1995 with 1981, the number of female heads of household was higher in all age

Table 6.10   Divorce rate in Cuba, 1960–96

Year	Divorce rate (%)
1960	0.5
1970	2.9
1980	2.5
1990	3.5
1991	4.1
1992	5.9
1993	6.0
1994	5.2
1995	3.7
1996	3.7

Source: Oficina Nacional de Estadísticas (1999), p. 44.

groups among the female population.[11] The increase in the older age groups can be explained by the ageing of the population, which started in the middle of the 1980s, but the same tendency occurred in younger age groups, such as 15–19 years and 20–24 years, and may be a result of the increasing number of divorces. On the other hand, the women's labour force participation rate decreased in the 1990s, and possibly their economic independence and authority have also decreased. The stabilized divorce rate can be explained by more women choosing not to divorce because they were concerned about economic difficulties after getting divorced.

Gender roles: how to share domestic work

As mentioned in the Introduction, the most significant accomplishment of the government regarding gender roles is the Family Code of 1975, which for the first time legitimized the equal obligation of both sexes to share domestic work. Article 27 provides that 'if one of the couple contributes only to work in the household and care for the children, the other party must contribute to the tasks for subsistance, *without prejudice to co-operate in the other tasks.*[12] In an interview with a staff member of the FMC, the interviewee pointed out that this article in the Family Code contributed at least to a change in the attitude of men, who used to look down on husbands who were willing to do domestic work.[13] In fact, several Cubans told me that the Family Code of 1975 officially approved of men who were ready to do domestic work and take care of their children, and has succeeded in silencing the traditionalists who used to speak ill of men who shared in domestic work.

The 'demonstration effect' of the Family Code is probably one of the contributing factors to changes in gender relations and gender roles among the younger generations. In particular, those who were educated after 1975 are more likely to have been taught in schools that it is a valuable for men to share domestic work and child care. Even if their parents have not accepted this new lifestyle, they are likely to learn this through formal education and the activities of mass organizations such as the Organización de Pioneros José Martí,[14] Federación de Estudiantes de la Enseñanza Media (FEEM),[15] and Unión de Jóvenes Comunistas (UJC),[16] as well as the FMC. However, even after three decades, the reality has not caught up with what the law provides. In this section, I shall analyse some findings of the national research survey of time use in Cuba.

There is not much research data available in Cuba. In 2000–1, one of the most prestigious Cuban journals, *Bohemia*, which was started before the Second World War, published an article on masculinity (Rodríguez *et al.*, 2001). A poll was conducted for that article among 272 people (136 women and 136 men) in five provinces. Las Tunas, Sancti Spíritus, Havana Province, Havana City (the capital city) and Pinar del Río. University degrees were held by 56.9 per cent of the sample, and 31.9 per cent were senior high school graduates. This sampling represents a highly educated portion of the Cuban population, but their attitude towards masculinity and gender roles were traditional. The majority of those questioned believed that men's role was to maintain the household economically, and women were responsible for cooking and child care. Maternity was considered the first attribute of women, by 96 per cent of respondents, while those of men were capacity, integrity, honesty and strength, with only a few selecting paternity. The poll shows that women are still bound strongly to the traditional maternal image, in the minds of both the women themselves and men, while men are largely free from any paternalistic identity. It is interesting that more than half of the samples had a university degree and were assumed to be highly educated, but they still maintained a traditional gender image.

The Cuban government's statistical agency, la Oficina Nacional de Estadísticas (ONE), has carried out four time-use surveys, (and I could obtain a part of the 1997 survey and a full report of the 2001 survey). The 1997 survey was nationwide, and the 2001 focused on only five places – two (Pinar del Río City and San Juan y Martínez) in Pinar del Río Province, two (Bayamo and Guisa) in Granma Province, and the other in Habana Vieja, the oldest district of Havana City. The 2001 survey was not conducted nationwide because of financial constraints. Both surveys were conducted with the co-operation of the FMC, in order to analyse and improve the situation of Cuban women.

There was another survey on domestic work by the FMC, which showed a less traditional tendency. The FMC's research institute, Centro de Estudios de la Mujer (CEM), conducted a survey of 1,125 families in the 1990s (Reca *et al.*, 1996). The category of the traditional model, where mainly wives or female partners did the domestic work, was 59.4 per cent, and the category of the 'perspective model', where husbands and wives share domestic work, was only 3.8 per cent. The category of the transitional model, where the couple do not yet share domestic work, but where the male partner or husband is gradually learning to do so, is 17.6 per cent (Reca *et al.*, 1996, p. 60). Class, educational levels and women's labour participation influence these tendencies. There are fewer cases of the traditional model among intellectual workers than among blue-collar workers, and also fewer if the wives have jobs (Reca *et al.*, 1996, pp. 61–2). Families in which wives or female partners work at the managerial level have the fewest traditional models, and the most perspective models (Reca *et al.*, 1996, p. 62).

The rest of this section aims to study the difference in gender roles before and after the revolution, and before and after the collapse of the Soviet Union. Helen Safa's survey in 1986–7 shows a change in gender roles before and after the revolution. In order to compare the transformation under the economic crisis since the 1990s, I shall analyse the two time-use ONE surveys mentioned earlier. These two surveys show how women and men share domestic work, and how the distribution of labour for domestic work changed after the collapse of the Soviet Union. Safa's research shows the situation of women workers in the second half of the 1980s, and the contribution of the revolution to gender roles.

Safa's interview survey: gender roles in the Soviet era

In 1986–7, Helen Safa carried out a research survey with the co-operation of the FMC (Safa, 1995, pp. 130–2). She did her research on the outskirts of Havana, where she interviewed 168 female workers as random samplings at a textile factory which employed 1,289 female workers. In order to cover all the age groups to see the generational transformation, she chose an over-sampling in the age group of over 50, more than their proportion in the total cohort. Of the sampled women, 154 were production workers and the remaining fourteen were technicians. The interview for each sample took around two hours, and interviewees were questioned about work experience, family life, political attitudes and participation in mass organizations. FMC researchers conducted most of the interviews at workers' homes from May 1986, and then in 1987 Safa carried out more interviews herself.

I utilize the results of Safa's research, because she also describes the transformation of gender roles through the generations. Most of the female workers who had worked in the factory since the pre-revolutionary period had not completed the first nine years of schooling, which is now compulsory in Cuba. In contrast, their children have achieved much higher education levels, and they (the mothers) considered higher education to be a great accomplishment of the revolution.[17]

Safa points out that there are some examples that show the transformation of gender roles by generation. She highlights Rosalía (mother) and Alicia (daughter) as one of the examples (Safa, 1995, pp. 126–7). Rosalía was 55 years old at the time of the interview and belonged to the pre-revolutionary generation, as the Cuban Revolution took place in 1959, and the research took place in 1986–7. She had seven children. Her ex-husband had fought in the July 26 Movement led by Fidel Castro before the triumph of the revolution. He was still very active in Communist Party activities, which meant that he was often absent from home, where Rosalía took charge of all domestic work and child care. After their divorce, he still exercised a high degree of authority over Rosalía and their children, even after he remarried. Safa implies that it is because he paid child support when the children were young. In another case, a young woman worker named Odalys, 23 years of age, said in her interview that she did not receive and did not wish to receive support for her children from her ex-husband, because she did not want him to exercise any authority over her children (Safa, 1995, pp. 133–4).

There are obvious differences of opinion between Rosalía and her daughter Alicia about how to deal with a husband. Alicia, who was probably in her twenties, got divorced from her first husband, who was thirteen years her senior, because he did not allow her to work or to participate in activities of mass organizations. At the time of the interned she had a newborn baby with her current husband, who was more open. She did not allow him to go out alone often, leaving her at home with their baby (Safa, 1995, p. 127). Interestingly, Alicia's mother Rosalía insisted that Alicia allow him to go out alone, because he is a man, and that men are from the street (*calle*). But Alicia responded that not only men but also women were from the street, and taking care of the baby was the responsibility of both husband and wife. Safa observes that the traditional house/street (*casa/ calle*) distinction was no longer accepted by the women of younger generations. The *casa/calle* distinction confined women to the home, and Alicia's mother Rosalía still believed in that value, but Alicia refused to accept it (Safa, 1995, p. 127).

Safa points out that most of the sample women of the 45 years and older age group continued to do most of the domestic work, and that 'the only household tasks in which men actively participate are paying the bills, doing the shopping, and taking out the garbage' (Safa, 1995, p. 137). She quoted the example of Raquel's case. Raquel had been married for thirty three years, and she and her husband worked in the same factory. But she did most of the domestic work and said that it was 'too late to get her husband to change' (Safa, 1995, p. 137). Raquel said that her daughter and son-in-law worked in the same factory and shared cooking and other household tasks.

Safa writes that there were very few husbands of sampled women workers who asked their wives to stop working. Of all married women, 65.6 per cent contribute to the household economy, and Safa considers that this helps women to increase their authority in the household (Safa, 1995, p. 137). Another sample, Ana María, said that life was expensive and raising children costs a lot, implying that husbands must allow their wives to earn and contribute to the household economy (Safa, 1995, p. 138).

Safa considers the revolutionary government's policy of redistribution a significant contribution to the transformation of gender roles. Ana María, who belongs to the older generation, compared the time when she was raising children alone after her divorce and the time when the research took place. She said that it was very difficult for her to find a job and take care of her children, and that now women can raise their children alone, because there are a lot of jobs and also more facilities for working women (Safa, 1995, p. 139). It is true that the government provided many facilities so that women could work after getting married and having children. Although there are not enough places for all the children who wished to enrol in nursery schools, as Rosalía and Alicia complained in the interview

(Safa, 1995, p. 126), the government built many child care centres after the revolution. The fee that parents pay is low, considering the total cost, which is determined by the parents' income; the maximum is 60 pesos, and the state bears most of the cost.

Findings from the time-use surveys

The 1997 time-use survey

The 1997 survey on time-use shows a great difference between men and women in terms of their use of time for domestic work. The survey was conducted only with men and women who both had jobs. According to this survey, men spent twelve hours a week on domestic work, and women spent thirty-four hours. The hours the respondents spent on paid work were not so different (men forty-three hours; women thirty-nine hours). The data shows that women did much more domestic work than men, in this data almost three times as much, even when both women and men had jobs.

I could not obtain data of previous time-use surveys, but Lutjens (1995) had some results of a 1988 time-use survey. According to her, women spent 'more than 22 hours each week,' while men dedicated 'nearly 4 hours' (Lutjens, 1995, p.109). If this data is correct, the time use for domestic work for both men and women increased significantly, 22 to 34 hours for women, 4 to 12 hours for men. Compared in ratios, proportion between women and men for time use for domestic work in 1997 was 2.8 (34 hours / 12 hours), and that in 1988 was 5.5 (22 hours / 4 hours). While the absolute quantity of time use increased for both sexes, the ratio between sexes dropped significantly. This indicates that men in 1997 did much more domestic work than those in 1988, although women's burden became heavier in 1997, too.

Tables 6.11 shows the relationship between sex and educational level to the contribution to paid and domestic work. On the one hand, as the educational level rises, men's contribution to domestic work declines. On the other hand, as the educational level rises, more women tend to do paid work, but their burden of domestic work does not change in value no matter what level of education the woman has. As the educational level rises, men also have a tendency to do more paid work, but that tendency is not as clear as that for women.

Also, according to the research results, the time share of domestic work per day is 20–30 per cent among all female age groups above 25 years of age.[18] The age group 61–64 has the highest percentage. Women in this group spend more than 25 per cent of their time doing domestic work. The second highest age group is 26–30, which records 25 per cent. It is probably because many of the women of this group have younger children, who require the most time and care. The significant difference between the 61–64 and 26–30 groups is the tendencies of the men of those groups. Men

Table 6.11 Time use for domestic and paid work, by educational level and sex, 1997 (hours and minutes)

Educational level	Below primary school level	Primary school level	Second-ary school level	Skilled labour level	High school level	Univer-sity level
Men						
Domestic work	2:28	2:21	1:41	2:07	1:41	1:42
Paid work	1:36	3:04	3:49	5:48	4:48	5:48
Total (domestic and paid)	4:04	5:25	5:30	7:55	6:29	7:30
Women						
Domestic work	5:04	6:01	5:10	4:38	4:48	4:48
Paid work	0:26	0:42	2:12	4:35	3:36	4:51
Total (domestic and paid)	5:30	6:43	7:22	9:13	8:24	9:39

Source: Compiled by the author from Oficina Nacional de Estadísticas (1999), p.149.

of the age group of 61–64 have the highest percentage of domestic time use among men in all age groups. The domestic work share of men in this age group is around 10–15 per cent, much higher than for any other age group. Therefore, both men and women of this age group (61–64) spend the highest percentage of their time in domestic work: women spend more than six hours, while men spend about three hours. This is probably because people of this age group include widows and widowers, or more people care for their sick spouses. In contrast, men of the age group 26–30 do less domestic work than most other age groups – less than 5 per cent. It means that while men of this age group spend a little over one hour a day on domestic work, women in this group spend six hours on domestic work.

Men in the age group 31–50 spend a little more than those of the 26–30 group, around 5–10 per cent –, that is, one to two hours. Women in this group spend a little less time than women in the 26–30 age group – about 21–22 per cent.

Among all the women, those who are married spend the most time on domestic work – almost 350 hours a month.[19] Interestingly, married women spend more time than divorced women, who spend around 250 hours a month. In Cuba, most divorced women are single mothers, who are considered to be socially the most vulnerable, but the time use for domestic work by single mothers is less than that of married women. Married women spend more time because they take care of their husbands, whereas single mothers usually live with their parents and receive their support, although many married women also live with their parents or in-laws.

The 2001 time-use survey

The time-use survey of 2001 was conducted in March in three provinces (Pinar del Río, Habana Vieja, and Granma). In Pinar del Río Province, the city of Pinar del Río (the provincial capital) and San Juan y Martínez were surveyed. Habana Vieja is the oldest district of the City of Havana, a part of the capital city of Havana. In Granma Province, Bayamo (the provincial capital) and another small town, Guisa, were surveyed. In all these places, both urban and rural areas were surveyed, apart from in the old district of Havana, which is totally urban. Interviewers were sent with questionnaires to the households, and within each household, all members above 14 years of age were surveyed.

Women in the rural area of Pinar del Río spent the longest time on domestic work – 12 hours and 14 minutes (734 minutes) (see Table 6.12). In the other town in Pinar del Río Province, San Juan y Martínez, women in both urban and rural areas spent almost 11 hours. According to this survey, women in Pinar del Río Province, in Pinar del Río City and San Juan y Martínez, spent the longest time. Contrary to Granma Province's reputation as one of the most conservative *Oriente* (Eastern) provinces, women in the capital city of Bayamo, and in Guisa, spent less time than women in Pinar del Río, but longer than those in Habana Vieja. There was not much difference between the urban and rural areas of Bayamo and Guisa, though women in the rural area of Guisa spent almost the same amount of time as women in San Juan y Martínez.

Regarding men's participation in domestic work, men in the urban area of the city of Pinar del Río spent the longest time – almost 8 hours (454 minutes). The second-longest time recorded is the case of men in the rural area of Bayamo. Men who spent the least time are those in Habana Vieja – 5 hours and 29 minutes (329 minutes).

Finally, we examine the proportion of the use of time for domestic work by women compared to that by men. This value shows the difference in responsibility for this between women and men. The rural area of Guisa shows the biggest difference, and women spent more than twice as much time as did men. The rural area of the city of Pinar del Río and the urban area of San Juan y Martínez record the second-largest differences. The third largest is Habana Vieja.

Women in the rural area of Guisa certainly do much more domestic work than their male counterparts, and possibly there are tendencies that in rural or remote areas in *Oriente* men to do much less domestic work than women. Yet in the rural area of Bayamo a large difference in domestic work load between women and men does not exist. According to this research, Pinar del Río Province, the province to the west of Havana Province, records a heavy responsibility for domestic work for women, and relatively large differences in responsibilities between women and men.

Table 6.12 Domestic work and care work for minors and adults, by area and by sex, 2001 Average for the persons engaged in the activity (hours and minutes)

Name of the place researched	Habana Vieja		Pinar del Río		San Juan y Martínez		Bayamo		Guisa	
Participants in the activity	*Women*	*Men*	*Women*	*Men*	*Women*	*Men*	*Women*	*Men*	*Women*	*Men*
Urban area	8:29	5:29	8:12	7:34	10:32	6:21	9:12	6:42	9:11	7:00
Proportion of women/men	1.55		1.08		1.66		1.37		1.31	
Rural area		12:14	7:21	10:31	10:20	9:27	7:26	10:28	4:34	
Proportion of women/men			1.66		1.02		1.27		2.29	

Source: Compiled by author from data of Oficina Nacional de Estadísticas (2003), p. 63.

Nevertheless, in general, you can see the difference in time-use for domestic work between Western (*Occidente*) and Eastern (*Oriente*) parts of the country. Compared between two places in Pinar del Río Province and other two places in Granma Province, you can see that apparently the women's time spent for domestic work in Bayamo and Guisa, Granma Province 4 hours and 39 minutes and 5 hours and 15 minutes, consecutively, in average for all persons, are greater than that in Pinar del Río City and San Juan y Martínez, Pinar del Río Province, 3 hours and 53 minutes and 4 hours and 34 minutes. Also, the men's time spent in Granma, 1 hour and 28 and 1 hour 48 minutes, consecutively, are less than those in Pinar del Río, 1 hour and 45 and 1 hour and 50 minutes. The same tendency is observed in the average for the persons engaged in the activity. The difference between men and women can be seen in proportion of women/men. The ratio in Pinar del Río Province, 2.22 and 2.49, are lower than that in Granma Province, 3.17 and 2.92. It means that there is less difference between men and women in time use for domestic work in Pinar del Río than in Granma. You can see the same tendency in the proportions in average for the persons engaged in the activity. Habana Vieja, old part of Havana City is exceptional, because it is in the middle of data of Pinar del Río and Granma Provinces. Habana Vieja is famous for many immigrants from poor eastern part of the country. I assume that many residents in Habana Vieja still maintain their traditional gender role model from *Oriente*, while surely they have received influence from other part of the city, which is more progressive.

There is some improvement in gender roles between the two time-use surveys. According to the 1997 survey, while women spend thirty-four hours a week on domestic work, men spend twelve hours (ONE, 1999, p. 149). This means that women spend 2.3 times as much time as men on domestic work. The 2001 survey shows that the ratio of men's domestic work time to women's is between 1.02 and 2.29 in the participant average (see Table 6.12).

Table 6.13 shows the difference between the all persons who were surveyed in this poll, and those who actually engaged in domestic work. The table shows only people in urban areas, but you can see the tendency. Generally the proportion between men and women are much smaller in the case of those who actually did domestic work. There is no apparent difference among regions in Table 6.12, but some in Table 6.13. The difference between Tables 6.12 and 6.13 is if it contains carework. It implies that men do more carework than domestic work.. The difference between the average for all persons and the average for persons engaged in domestic work is greater in men's case than women's. The difference in women's is less than 30 minutes, but that in men's is over 30 minutes, sometimes over one hour. It may indicate that there are more men than women who do none or very little of domestic work at home.

Table 6.13 Domestic work, by sex, by participation, 2001 (Urban area) (hours and minutes)

Name of the place researched	Habana Vieja		Pinar del Río		San Juan y Martínez		Bayamo		Guisa	
Participants in the activity	Women	Men	Women	Men	Women	Men	Women	Men	Women	Men
Average for all persons	3:55	1:17	3:53	1:45	4:34	1:50	4:39	1:28	5:15	1:48
Proportion of women/men	3.05		2.22		2.49		3.17		2.92	
Average for the persons engaged in the activity	4:21	2:20	4:18	2:44	4:53	2:39	5:06	2:06	5:38	2:32
Proportion of women/men	1.86		1.57		1.84		2.43		2.22	

Source: Compiled by author from data of Oficina Nacional de Estadísticas (2003), p. 65.

To compare the data of 1997 and 2001 is not easy, as each poll was realized in different conditions. The 1997 survey was conducted only with workers, without students and pensioners who had no jobs. The 2001 survey dealt with all types of the population, but it only covered several areas of the country. Also the results of the 1997 survey are not as extensive as in 2001. The 1997 survey includes so-called domestic work and child care. In the 2001 survey, domestic work includes only house-keeping; unpaid work includes domestic work and care for minors and adults. That is probably the reason that there are significant differences between values of urban area in Table 6.12 and ones of Table 6.13. In Table 6.12 the ratio between men and women is not as great as Table 6.13, and it means that men are more ready to take responsibilities to take care of children and especially of senior citizens, but I cannot say the men in the 2001 survey, domestic work more in unpaid work than those in 1997, because the 1997 survey did not include data on unpaid work.

Yet it is a new finding that more Cuban men participate in care work, not only shopping, house repair and gardening, which have been considered traditionally rather masculine works. That may reflect not only the severe economic crisis but also Cuba's very rapid population aging. Cuba's pattern of population aging is similar to that of Japan, and many young couples have only one child. Unlike Japan, generally daughter-in-law in Cuba do not take a major part in care for elders, and if the elder has only one son, he, not his wife, must be obliged to take care of his elder parent. Nevertheless, as the author could not obtain data of the other surveys before these two, I would see some changes in spite of those limits described above. It is rather difficult to determine if there is some change in the ratios between time spent for domestic work by women and men. As written above, the general ratio in 1997 was 2.83. The simple and rough average of ratios in 2001 shown in Table 6.12 is 1.47 (not shown in the table), but it is of only persons engaged in domestic work and care for minors and adults. A rough average of values in all persons of Table 6.13 is 2.77 (not shown in the table), a little less than average of the 1997 survey, but it is not sufficient to say that the ratio between men and women is getting smaller. The ratio between men and women is the lowest in 'under primary school level,' and the second lowest is 'skilled labour level'.

Men in high school level and university level do domestic work for the shortest time. On the contrary, Table 6.14 shows the similar comparison in the 2001 survey, and in that survey, men who completed only primary education do domestic work for the longest time among all male categories, and men who received higher education do the least, which I can say common with the 1997 survey (Table 6.10). Yet there is little difference among the rest of the categories. There are no clear reasons to explain the difference by education, why men at the lowest educational level do more domestic work. In the case of women, the higher she receives her educa-

Table 6.14   Domestic work and free time per day, by educational level, Habana
Vieja, 2001 (hours and minutes)

Educational level	Domestic work		Free time	
	Women	Men	Women	Men
Below primary education	5:12	2:06	4:16	5:45
Primary education	5:07	2:51	4:57	5:59
Secondary education	4:17	2:16	3:58	5:20
Higher secondary	4:15	2:19	3:54	5:03
Higher education	3:07	1:35	4:30	4:45

Source: Oficina Nacional de Estadísticas (2003), p. 66.

tion, she tends to do paid work, but her burden for domestic work does not
reduce so much in both surveys, and there is no clear transformation of
women's pattern in both.

Table 6.15 shows the relations between paid work and unpaid domestic
and care work. The difference between women and men becomes sharper.
In Bayamo and Guisa, women need to spend almost or more than twice the
time for domestic work as for paid work, while men spend 21 to 32 per

Table 6.15   Distribution of paid and domestic work, by area and sex, 2001 (urban
area population older than 15 years of age/hours per day)

	Time for paid work (hours)	Time for domestic work (hours)	Ratio of women's domestic work/ men's domestic work	Ratio of domestic work/paid work
Habana Vieja				
Women	3:26	3:33	3.03	1.03
Men	5:35	1:10		0.21
Pinar del Río				
Women	3:08	3:32	2.43	1.13
Men	5:14	1:27		0.28
San Juan y Martínez				
Women	3:22	4:20	2.89	1.29
Men	6:09	1:30		0.24
Bayamo				
Women	2:25	4:23	3.43	1.82
Men	6:05	1:17		0.21
Guisa				
Women	2:06	5:09	3.48	2.45
Men	4:34	1:29		0.32

Source: Expanded by the author from the data of Oficina Nacional de Estadísticas (2003), p. 60.

cent of the time on paid work. Possibly less women in these two cities have paid work. This difference is also seen in all the other places. It means that in Cuba, the life pattern is still quite traditional, where men dedicate more time to paid work outside of the home, while women bear the brunt of more unpaid domestic work.

Also in comparison with the data of Table 6.12 which shows data of persons who actually engaged in domestic work, men who are willing to do domestic work sometimes do as much as women do, in the case of San Juan y Martínez where the ratio of women's and men's is 1.02. The ratio of Table 6.14, which data is for all persons, shows that there is much more of a burden on women (2.43 to 3.48 times) than in Table 6.16. It means that there are more men than women who do not participate in domestic work at all.

Table 6.14 shows part of the survey conducted in Habana Vieja. It details the relationship between time for domestic work and for free use, and its relationship to educational level. According to this table, as women's educational level rises, they tend to spend less time on domestic work. Yet it does not necessarily mean that women's free time increases as their educational level rises, although there is a slight tendency to increase. In the case of women with higher education levels, women spend much less time on domestic work and have more free time, almost the same amount as the men with the same educational level.

Men tend to spend almost the same amount of time on domestic work, regardless of their educational level. Only men with higher education levels spend a great deal less time on domestic work, although their free time is the lowest among all male groups. Men, apart from those with higher education levels, have almost the same amount of free time, although there is a slight tendency that as the educational level rises, men have less free time. The reason for this is probably, that men with higher education levels spend the least time on domestic work and have the least free time became they do paid work for longer hours than those with other educational levels.[20]

A critical evaluation of Safa's study

Safa's research was conducted in 1986–7, when Cuban ties with the Soviet Union were still very stable, Soviet assistance was generous, and the Cuban economy was already sluggish but not at that time in a serious crisis. The government guaranteed full employment and relatively abundant rationing programmes, which disappeared after 1991, when the Soviet Union disintegrated. Safa's study was published in 1995, but her chapters on Cuba do not reflect well enough the drastic changes that occurred in the economy and society in the 1990s.

Consequently, now Cuban women are under less favourable conditions to become economically independent. It has become more difficult for a woman to raise children alone, even with her family's assistance, and her dependency on her husband or male partner has become stronger. Women's authority decreased because of a drop in good job opportunities to achieve high earnings, the subsequent weakening of economic independence, and the revival of the traditional pattern of division of gender roles. Table 6.10 shows a decrease in the divorce rate after the fall of the Soviet Union. The fall in the divorce rate could explain, at least partly, the possible drop in women's economic independence.

Another factor determining gender roles, to which Safa did not attach importance, is the role of the state in the transformation of gender roles. She did make some references in the conclusion to her chapter on Cuba: 'women look to the state to provide these services rather than expecting their husbands to take more responsibility, as mandated by the Family Code' (Safa, 1995, p. 163). She also pointed out that women 'depend on the state to solve their problems rather than requiring more from their husbands' (Safa, 1995, p. 163). In other words, the socialist state policy for gender issues has allowed men to avoid their responsibility for domestic work, as provided in Article 27 of the Family Code. Women have succeded in dedicating in paid work thanks to the state, not to their husbands.

The ironical fact is, however, that the state has not only successfully promoted women's labour force participation but also implemented a generous social policy that has made children's education and medical care free of charge, lowered the burden of obtaining housing, and subsidized a part of food expenses through the rationing program, all of which have lightened the economic burden on households.[21] Because the government required only the men to participate in compulsory work in 1971, while women did not have this obligation, the male breadwinner model could be applied in general to Cuban society, but its real economic impact on increasing purchasing power was not as great as Safa thought before the disintegration of the Soviet Union.[22] Safa also points out that couples tend to live with one set of parents, a situation that means men 'never learn responsibility' (Safa, 1995, p. 136). This is probably true of all countries where young couples tend to live with their parents or in-laws, but the Cuban government has reinforced the tendency by providing generous social services to its people through social policy and by not providing sufficient housing in urban areas. In capitalist countries, the traditional gender role model requires men to bear economic responsibility almost exclusively throughout marriage, with much less support from the government. Men are considered the 'breadwinners', and Safa considers this concept to be the main source of male authority, not a source of obligation and economic burden for which men are obliged to work. I believe that the role of breadwinner is the main source of both authority and obligation. The Cuban state social policy decreased men's obligations as breadwinner, much as it lessened the restrictions placed on women's by the *casa/calle* segregation, which Safa describes. As a result, if a man wishes to take advantage of the state system, he can easily abandon his economic responsibilities, because the state supports the most important part of the household economy in any case.

Safa points out that one of the principal reasons that women worked was economic need and the increasing cost of living (Safa, 1995, pp. 29, 140), but this economic need is probably mainly demands for consumer products, such as food and clothing, not for savings, housing or education of the children. The meaning of money in socialist countries is much less important than in capitalist countries. Furthermore, Safa wrote that 'nearly 90 per cent of these husbands contribute more than half of their salary to the household' (Safa, 1995, p. 140). Yet one of Safa's tables shows that more than 82 per cent of married women in her survey contributed 50–100 per cent of their salaries to their households (Safa, 1995, p. 134, table 5.2), and the economic contribution of husbands and wives are almost equal, in spite of the disproportion of their contribution to domestic work. Under the economic crisis at the time of writing, the meaning of money (especially US dollars) has become very important, and professions in which workers earn hard currency is not favourable for people who have domestic responsibilities. The question over the sharing of domestic work and economic responsibility is becoming similar to that in capitalist countries.

Under these circumstances, three patterns of authority between men and women can be identified: (i) when the role of breadwinner is less important in Cuba, male contribution to the household is more likely to be through participation in domestic work, and therefore men tend to do more domestic work; (ii) If a man thinks he is free from both economic responsibility and domestic work, he does nothing for his household, but it does not necessarily mean that he loses his authority; and (iii) if a husband earns a high income, working in the tourism industry, for example, his authority over his wife, coming from economic power, increases, and a more traditional division of labour may be revived.

Summary of all the survey findings

Safa's study shows that Cuban women gained economic independence and authority through the revolutionary government's encouragement of their labour participation, as well as a social policy that made it possible for women to find paid work. Safa's interviews describe the steady advance of women's labour participation, with support from their husbands. Although men's participation in domestic work has not become common, women of the younger generation have become much less tolerant of the traditional gender role model. The revolutionary government's contribution to this change is great and obvious.

According to the two ONE time-use surveys, men's participation in domestic work is not sufficient, since the major part of domestic work is still done by women. Yet after the disintegration of the Soviet Union, the absolute amount of domestic work increased, and, at first, women's labour participation rate dropped. But in the second half of the 1990s, it went up again, to recover to the level it was at before the collapse of the Soviet Union. At the same time, men's burden of domestic work and care for minors and elders increased. This might be the result of a transformation of gender roles and, also of Cuba's population aging.

The survey conducted by the Centro de Estudios de la Mujer (CEM) in the 1990s shows that the families (i) whose profession is intellectual (white-collar) work;[23] (ii) whose female member(s) have jobs; and (iii) whose female member's job category is managerial, have less of a traditional gender role pattern in the division of labour in the household, although more than half of the families still practise the traditional division of labour. Although the first time-use survey at the beginning of the 1990s shows that men who have higher education degrees tend to do the least amount of domestic work among all males sampled, this CEM survey shows that white-collar workers tend to have less traditional gender role patterns.

The *Bohemia* survey was the second most recent among the surveys, next to the 2001 time-use survey. It focused mainly on gender image, and while the respondents have higher educational levels than the national average, their gender image is traditional: the dominant image of women is maternity, and men's image is diverse and does not emphasize paternity.

In sum, according to the time-use surveys of 1988, 1997 and 2001, the economic crisis following the disintegration of the Soviet Union and advancing population aging in Cuba might have influenced men to share more domestic work and care for minors and adults, while the absolute amount of domestic work of both women and men increased. Although women still bear the greater burden of domestic work, the proportion of their share in the total amount of domestic work is tending to decrease. It is probably because women bear domestic work to their limits, and their husbands feel obliged to help them so that women do not get sick. And also it is because younger generations are transforming their values in gender roles. While Bohemia 2001 survey shows that the image that Cubans have in gender roles is quite traditional, the FMC 1996 survey shows that the family tends to have less of a traditional gender role pattern in the case of family members with higher educational levels, or when women work as managers, while the majority of those sampled still maintain the traditional pattern.

In general, I assume that the gender role pattern in Cuba after the disintegration of the Soviet Union is going closer to that in most capitalist countries. Women's labour participation rate decreased in 1995–96, and it shows that many women quit their jobs and became housewives. There is no data of that rate after 1996, and I cannot judge if, as Rodríguez Reyes asserts, women return to work again after that, although the total number of female labour force is increasing after 1996.

There are more men than women who work in newly developed economic sectors such as self-employment, joint ventures and other dollar-earning sectors, probably because the working conditions of these sectors are less favorable for women who need to take care of their families, and that means that women tend to work in peripheral sectors of low wages, which is the public sector in the Cuban case. Therefore, more men earn much, work for a long time, leaving their women to bear domestic and care work. This situation seems very similar to that in Japan, as I depict later, where men tend to work for longer time than the other developed countries and therefore, men do not have time to share domestic work with their female partners.

If women also earn much, they hire maids in the informal or black market. Table 6.9 shows that domestic workers earn 20 to 40 dollars a month. That indicates that elite women who hire domestic workers should not be ordinary public sector workers whose average salaries are around 20 dollars or less. In capitalist Latin American countries, elite women in upper or upper-middle classes continue their career by hiring women in lower poor classes as domestic workers. This becomes possible when there are large differences in the distribution of wealth, and domestic workers can be hired at relatively low wages. For now, Cuba is one of the most egalitarian countries in Latin America, thanks to its socialist revolution. Yet the difference in the distribution is widening now, because of economic crisis and new wealth in dollar-earning sectors. If the difference becomes greater, Cuban female workers could be categorized in two patterns: (1) elite women who can hire domestic workers and continue their career; (2) women who work in the public sector where their earnings are relatively low. In the second category, women have to choose if they keep working by asking their male partners to share domestic and care works, or ask their female family members to share that work, or she bears all the paid and unpaid work anyway until she becomes sick. It is exactly the situation that now Japanese women are confronting.

Comparison with Japan

Overview of Japanese trends in the gender role model

Unlike in the case of socialist Cuba, Japan has been a capitalist economy. For many decades, in addition to the private sector's strong support for the male breadwinner model, the government has also promoted that model strongly by providing favourable tax and social insurance systems for families where the husband bears only the economic responsibility and the wife works only as housewife. A tax exemption applies to families where the wife earns up to around US$10,000 a year. Also, the old age pension system and the universal medical insurance favour a traditional gender role model by exempting from contribution wives who earn less than around

US$10,000 a year, placing its costs on non-traditional families, such as cases in which both husband and wife work full-time, or single persons. This policy favouring the traditional gender-role model still continues, but the government's attitude towards gender roles has been changing since it presented the concept of 'Society of Co-Participation of Men and Women' in the mid-1990s. In this concept, the government officially admitted that it should establish programmes and policies so that both men and women shared unpaid domestic work.

The Ministry of Education has introduced home economics class for both female and male students in secondary schools: in junior high school in 1993 and senior high school in 1994. Until then, home economics class in the public education system had been only for female students, and boys had the opportunity to take home economics only in primary school. Yet this change has been criticized as ineffective in changing gender role models, because the new home economics class is divided into three courses, only one of which teaches of housekeeping. And boys do not have to choose housekeeping from among the three courses.

On 16 February 1998, Prime Minister Ryutaro Hashimoto delivered his annual address on administrative policies at the 142nd session of the Diet, to point out that it was important to change the traditional gender role model in which men do paid work and women do domestic work and child care, and to produce a society where both men and women participate, sharing both joys and responsibilities. Then he said that the government would submit a bill to promote this new policy the following year. On 23 June 1999, the Gender Equality Law (if translated literally from the original Japanese title, the Law of Society for Co-participation of Men and Women)[24] was promulgated and enforced. Its preamble defines the society for the co-participation of men and women as one where both men and women respect each other's human rights, as well as share their responsibilities and give full rein to their abilities and individuality. This law is still insufficient for the promotion of 'gender equality' as its English translation provides, because it touches only vaguely on the problem of the traditional division of labour in the household. It says that both men and women should participate in various activities, free from traditional gender role models, and also that both men and women should share tasks to maintain the household, but it does not mention the problem of division of labour in the household. Therefore, the law does not refer to the gender role change, or the necessity for both men and women to share domestic work.

The Cabinet Office established a new bureau to implement this new policy, the Bureau for Co-participation of Men and Women (officially, Gender Equality Bureau, in English). However, the work that this new bureau has done is (i) the promotion of female participation in national and local governments' decision-making and its employment in the public sector; (ii) the protection of women from domestic violence; and (iii) the publication of statistics and White Papers on gender equality. The only work related to gender equality is in item (iii).

At the time of the promulgation of the law, more than half of the female working-age population had to work, full- or part-time, in another type of employment. Japanese women's labour participation rate in 2001 between the ages of 20–59 was 66.4 per cent, and even for the age group of 30–34 (the lowest percentage, because of marriage and child care) was 56.5 per cent, still more than half. More women continue to work after marriage and childbirth. As for the working-age population (age group of 15 to 64), 62.1 per cent of women worked in 2001, a 1.2 per cent increase over 1981. This is a recent drastic change in women's labour force participation, but the majority of women still also do the greater part of domestic work at home.

Among the developed countries, Japan is the least developed in gender equality. The Gender Equality Bureau of the Cabinet Office publishes every five years a comparative survey on gender equality in Japan, South Korea, the Philippines, the USA, Sweden, Germany and the United Kingdom (Gender Equality Bureau, 2003). The result of the 2002 survey shows that in 90.1 per cent of households in Japan, wives or female partners mainly take charge of house cleaning, and 92.6 per cent do the cooking. This is the highest proportion among all seven countries, higher even than South Korea and the Philippines, economically less developed countries.[25] In comparison with the 1982 survey, the proportion of the households in 2002 where wives or female partners carry house cleaning and cooking responsibilities has fallen greatly in the three EU countries (Sweden, Germany and the UK), while in Japan there has been a drop, but it is much smaller.

According to Ito's (1993) analysis, the main reason that Japanese men have not been able to participate in domestic work and child care is their long working hours. He points out that male workers who share domestic work and child care are those who have chosen to get out of the career competition in their companies or who have jobs in which they can manage their own working hours, such as self-employed workers (Ito, 1993, pp. 78–9). The average working hours of Japanese workers in the manufacturing industries each year is about 2000 hours – 500 hours more than their German counterparts. They leave home early in the morning and return late at night, and have virtually no time to do domestic work (Ito, 1993, p. 51).

The Gender Equality Bureau's comparative survey also does research on each respondent's support for traditional division of labour in the household, whether men should do paid work and women should be responsible for domestic work. Japan and the Philippines recorded the highest support for the traditional division of labour: Japan 36.8 per cent and the Philippines 44.8 per cent. In the other developed countries, the proportion is much lower: the USA, 18.1 per cent; Sweden, 4.0 per cent; Germany, 14.5 per cent; and the UK, 9.7 per cent. South Korea recorded 13.2 per cent, a similar level to that of the other developed countries, apart from Japan and the Philippines. Yet in comparison with the comparative survey of 1982, the proportion in Japan also dropped greatly, from 71.1 per cent (1982) to 36.8 per cent (2002). This means that Japanese people's thinking on gender roles has changed over twenty years, but still more Japanese support the traditional gender role model than the other developed countries and South Korea.

Japanese women's labour participation rate drops between the ages of 25 and 39, when they get married and, in most cases, when they have children. The Ministry of Public Health and Labour published statistics in March 2004 indicating that the 61 per cent of women who had jobs stopped working at the birth of their first child and had not returned to work eighteen months later. Other developed countries in the 2002 comparative survey also used to have a similar tendency, but nowadays they do not. Only Japan maintains this tendency, though it is gradually disappearing. Ito and others point out that an image still persists in the private sector that women are not responsible workers (Ito *et al.*, 2002, pp. 138–9). If women remained housewives, men would have more reason to follow the traditional gender role model, because women would have more time and a reason to take charge of domestic work and child care.

Results and evaluation of time-use surveys

The results of the time-use surveys conducted by the Japanese government statistics bureau every five years since 1981 are shown in Tables 6.16, 6.17, 6.18, 6.19, and 6.20. Table 6.16 shows women's time use, especially in terms of sleep, paid work, and domestic work and child care. The time for sleep has been gradually decreasing between 1981 and 2001. Because the time for primary activities is gradually increasing, even if time for sleep is decreasing, the other parts of primary activities (meals, bathing and so on) are increasing. Because the time spent on paid work is also decreasing in the case of the average for all persons, the reduction in the time for sleep is not a result of the increase in paid work.

In all respondents, female time-use for paid work has been decreasing since 1981, and women who spend more time doing paid work (rather than domestic work) work for a shorter time, from 6 hours 42 minutes in 1981 to 5 hours and 55 minutes in 2001 Table 6.16. According to Table 6.17, men's time use for paid work has also been decreasing between 1986 and 2001, and this is a general tendency. The reasons for this phenomenon is the diffusion of the five-day working week and the start of an economic recession in the 1990s.

Table 6.19 shows Japanese men's time use for sleep, paid work, and domestic work and child care. It is quite impressive that, while their time

Table 6.16 Japanese women's use of time: their work and contribution to domestic work, 1981 and 2001 (hours and minutes)

	Sleep	Work (paid)	Domestic work and child care[1]	Primary activities[2]	Secondary activities[3]	Tertiary activities[4]
1981						
Women (15 years old or older)						
All Total						
Weekly average	7:48	3:11	3:59	10:44	8:01	5:15
Weekday	7:44	3:29	3:58	10:38	8:24	4:58
Saturday	7:47	3:07	4:04	10:44	7:58	5:17
Sunday	8:15	1:48	4:01	11:18	6:08	6:34
With a job						
Weekly average	7:36	5:54	3:05	10:28	9:33	3:59
Weekday	7:31	6:28	2:57	10:21	10:04	3:36
Saturday	7:34	5:44	3:10	10:28	9:26	4:06
Sunday	8:04	3:14	3:41	11:06	7:07	5:47
With a job, who mainly work rather than do domestic work or are without a job						
Weekly average	7:38	6:42	2:16	10:29	9:42	3:49
Weekday	7:31	7:27	2:02	10:20	10:19	3:21
Saturday	7:36	6:18	2:22	10:29	9:24	4:07
Sunday	8:10	3:22	3:15	11:12	6:53	5:55
Without a job						
Weekly average	8:01	0:17	4:56	11:01	6:23	6:36
Weekday	7:57	0:17	5:02	10:55	6:38	6:27
Saturday	8:00	0:18	5:02	11:01	6:24	6:35
Sunday	8:25	0:17	4:23	11:30	5:06	7:24
2001						
Women (15 years old or older)						
Total						
Weekly average	7:38	2:27	3:34	10:42	7:01	6:17
Weekday	7:29	2:52	3:32	10:31	7:37	5:53
Saturday	7:49	1:46	3:43	10:55	6:08	6:57
Sunday	8:16	1:03	3:35	11:26	4:55	7:39
With a job						
Weekly average	7:20	4:51	3:00	10:20	8:31	5:09
Weekday	7:09	5:41	2:49	10:06	9:19	4:34
Saturday	7:35	3:29	3:22	10:36	7:16	6:09
Sunday	8:02	2:04	3:28	11:10	5:45	7:05

Table 6.16 Japanese women's use of time: their work and contribution to domestic work, 1981 and 2001 (hours and minutes) *continued*

	Sleep	Work (paid)	Domestic work and child care[1]	Primary activities[2]	Secondary activities[3]	Tertiary activities[4]
With a job, who mainly work rather than do domestic work or are without a job						
Weekly average	7:21	5:55	2:16	10:20	8:50	4:50
Weekday	7:09	7:00	2:00	10:04	9:48	4:08
Saturday	7:40	4:02	2:47	10:40	7:13	6:06
Sunday	8:08	2:19	3:03	11:16	5:35	7:09
Without a job						
Weekly average	7:52	0:05	4:35	11:03	5:28	7:29
Weekday	7:45	0:05	4:43	10:54	5:46	7:20
Saturday	8:01	0:05	4:30	11:14	5:05	7:41
Sunday	8:22	0:05	4:04	11:38	4:23	7:59
Without a job, who do domestic work only						
Weekly average	7:39	0:04	5:53	10:51	5:58	7:11
Weekday						
Saturday	7:46	0:05	5:41	11:00	5:46	7:13
Sunday	8:05	0:04	5:06	11:21	5:10	7:29

Notes:
1 This category includes housekeeping, child care and shopping. From the survey of 1991, it also includes care-giving (mainly senior members of a household).
2 Primary activities mean biologically necessary activities such as sleeping and eating.
3 Secondary activities mean obligatory activities to lead a social and economic life, such as paid work and domestic work.
4 Tertiary activities mean leisure and other activities.
Sources:
Data for 1981: Statistics Bureau, Prime Minister's Office, Japan (1982).
Data for 2001: Statistics Bureau, Ministry of Public Management, Home Affairs, Posts and Telecommunications (2002a).

use for paid work has been decreasing gradually, the time use for domestic work and child care has increased very little, just a few minutes in fifteen years. In contrast, the increase in their time use for tertiary activities was greater (5:16 to 5:38 (22 minutes) for those who have a job; 5:13 to 5:32, (19 minutes) for those who do paid work rather than domestic work) than that spent on time use for domestic work and child care (0:16 to 0:27

Table 6.17 Japanese men's use of time: their work and contribution to domestic work, 1986 and 2001 (hours and minutes)

	Sleep	Work (paid)	Domestic work and child care[1]	Primary activities[2]	Secondary activities[3]	Tertiary activities[4]
1986						
Men 15 years old or older; average for all persons						
Total						
Weekly average	7:56	5:58	0:18	10:20	7:41	5:59
Weekday	7:48	6:45	0:13	10:11	8:36	5:13
Saturday	7:51	5:36	0:22	10:16	7:13	6:31
Sunday	8:37	2:29	0:40	11:12	3:36	9:12
With a job						
Weekly average	7:49	7:24	0:16	10:12	8:32	5:16
Weekday	7:42	8:23	0:09	10:02	9:33	4:25
Saturday	7:44	6:54	0:19	10:08	8:02	5:51
Sunday	8:31	3:02	0:43	11:06	3:59	8:55
With a job, who mainly work rather than do domestic work or are without a job						
Weekly average	7:49	7:31	0:15	10:11	8:36	5:13
Weekday	7:41	8:31	0:08	10:01	9:37	4:22
Saturday	7:44	7:00	0:18	10:08	8:04	5:49
Sunday	8:31	3:02	0:43	11:06	3:59	8:55
2001						
Men 15 years old or older, average for all persons						
Total						
Weekly average	7:52	4:56	0:31	10:30	6:51	6:39
Weekday	7:41	5:49	0:23	10:17	7:55	5:48
Saturday	8:04	3:34	0:46	10:44	5:14	8:02
Sunday	8:35	1:50	0:54	11:21	3:05	9:34
With a job						
Weekly average	7:39	6:48	0:27	10:13	8:09	5:38
Weekday	7:27	8:02	0:18	9:58	9:25	4:37
Saturday	7:52	4:55	0:45	10:30	6:13	7:17
Sunday	8:26	2:30	0:57	11:10	3:43	9:07

Table 6.17 Japanese men's use of time: their work and contribution to domestic work, 1986 and 2001 (hours and minutes) *continued*

	Sleep	*Work (paid)*	*Domestic work and child care*	*Primary activities*[1]	*Secondary activities*[2]	*Tertiary activities*[3]
With a job, who mainly work rather than do domestic work or are without a job						
Weekly average	7:38	7:01	0:26	10:12	8:16	5:32
Weekday	7:26	8:19	0:17	9:57	9:35	4:29
Saturday	7:51	5:02	0:44	10:30	6:17	7:13
Sunday	8:26	2:30	0:58	11:11	3:41	9:08

Notes:
1 Primary activities mean biologically necessary activities such as sleeping and eating.
2 Secondary activities mean obligatory activities to lead a social and economic life, such as paid work and domestic work.
3 Tertiary activities mean leisure and other activities.

Sources:
Data for 1981: Statistic Bureau, Prime Minister's Office (1982).
Data for 2001: Statistics Bureau, Ministry of Public Management, Home Affairs, Posts and Telecommunications (2002).

(11 minutes) for those who have a job; 0:15 to 0:27 (12 minutes) for those who do paid work rather than domestic work). This tendency, however, does not necessarily prove that men generally worked less and had more free time for leisure. The Japanese unemployment rate has been increasing since the beginning of the 1990s, as a result of the economic recession, and those who have a job need to work even harder. In 2001, married men with jobs worked a weekly average of 8 hours and 39 minutes per day (see Table 6.18). In 1981, the figure was 8 hours and 21 minutes (see Table 6.19). So the working time of married men with jobs has increased.

Nevertheless, married women's dual responsibilities have not decreased. Married working women spend long hours on both paid and domestic work (see Tables 6.18 and 6.19). While married women who have jobs, whose participation rate for paid work was 39.0 per cent in 2001, spent 6 hours and 13 minutes on paid work in 2001, over 4 hours on domestic work, 3 hours on child care and 1 hour on shopping. In 1981, married

Table 6.18 Average time spent on activities by participants, 2001 (hours and minutes)

	Sleep	Work (paid)	Domestic work	Caring or nursing	Child care	Shopping
With a job, who mainly work						
Married women[1]						
Weekly average: average for all persons	7:18	2:27	3:48	0:06	0:36	0:41
Weekly average: average of activities by participants	7:18	6:13	4:04	2:07	3:14	1:07
Participation rate (%)	100:0	39:0	93:5	4:8	18:7	61:0
With a job						
Weekly average: average for all persons	7:09	4:29	3:12	0:05	0:17	0:34
Weekly average: average of activities for participants	7:09	6:20	3:29	1:53	2:13	1:00
Participation rate (%)	100:0	70:0	92:0	4:0	12:7	57:4
Married men[1]						
Weekly average: average for all persons	7:46	5:49	0:15	0:02	0:05	0:14
Weekly average: average of activities by participants	7:46	8:36	1:39	2:01	1:37	1:12
Participation rate (%)	100:0	66:2	14:8	1:3	5:2	18:3
With a job						
Weekly average: average for all persons	7:37	6:57	0:09	0:01	0:06	0:12
Weekly average: average of activities by participants	7:37	8:39	1:22	1:47	1:33	1:09
Participation rate (%)	100:0	78:6	10:9	1:0	5:8	15:8
Married men with working wives[1]						
Weekly average: average for all persons	7:31	7:06	0:13	0:01	0:06	0:12
Weekly average: average of activities by participants	7:31	8:54	1:15	1:56	1:32	1:01
Participation rate (%)	100:0	77:5	16:4	1:1	5:9	16:1

Note: (1) Here 'married' means both legal marriage and informal cohabitation. The women declared that they spend more time on paid work than on domestic work.

Source: Statistics Bureau, Ministry of Public Management, Home Affairs, Posts and Telecommunications (2002).

Table 6.19 Average time spent on activities by participants, 1981 (hours and minutes)

	Sleep	Work (paid)	Domestic work and Childcare	Shopping
Married women				
Total				
Weekly average	7:49	6:43	4:17	1:12
Weekday	7:44	6:52	4:19	1:07
Saturday	7:47	6:29	4:19	1:15
Sunday	8:15	6:13	4:06	1:34
With a job				
Weekly average	7:36	6:57	3:19	1:03
Weekday	7:31	7:05	3:14	0:56
Saturday	7:35	6:41	3:21	1:07
Sunday	8:04	6:30	3:42	1:33
With a job, who mainly work rather than do domestic work or are without a job				
Weekly average	7:38	7:40	2:40	1:01
Weekday	7:31	7:52	2:30	0:52
Saturday	7:37	7:17	2:43	1:09
Sunday	8:10	7:07	3:25	1:38
Without a job				
Weekly average	8:02	4:00	5:18	1:21
Weekday	7:57	3:59	5:27	1:18
Saturday	8:00	3:58	5:21	1:23
Sunday	8:26	4:06	4:32	1:35
Married men				
Total				
Weekly average	8:07	8:16	1:52	1:22
Weekday	8:00	8:31	1:47	1:16
Saturday	8:03	8:00	1:58	1:28
Sunday	8:42	7:16	2:13	1:46
With a job				
Weekly average	8:01	8:21	1:39	1:21
Weekday	7:54	8:36	1:29	1:14
Saturday	7:59	8:04	1:50	1:29
Sunday	8:39	7:23	2:14	1:47

Table 6.19   Average time spent on activities by participants, 1981 (hours and
continued   minutes)

	Sleep	Work (paid)	Domestic work and childcare	Shopping
With a job, who mainly work rather than do domestic work or are without a job				
Weekly average	8:01	8:24	1:36	1:22
Weekday	7:54	8:39	1:26	1:15
Saturday	7:59	8:08	1:49	1:29
Sunday	8:39	7:26	2:13	1:47
Without a job				
Weekly average	8:31	4:04	2:19	1:24
Weekday	8:28	3:57	2:21	1:19
Saturday	8:22	4:19	2:20	1:26
Sunday	8:59	4:28	2:08	1:42

Source: Statistics Bureau, Prime Minister's Office (1982).

women had jobs, worked for 7 hours on weekdays, and spent over 3 hours
on domestic work and child care. Generally, married men worked longer
hours than women, over 8 hours on weekdays in both 1981 and 2001, but
there are few men who share domestic work and child care with their wives
or female partners. As a result, the time use of working women for secondary activities, which include both paid work and domestic work and
child care, is almost always longer than that of men with jobs (see Tables
6.16, 6.17 and 6.18). In 2001, only 10.9 per cent of married men who had
jobs did domestic work, and 5.8 per cent did child care. Men who participate in these activities actually spend almost as much time as do women (see
Table 6.17), but the problem is that those men are an absolute minority.
Moreover, according to Table 6.20, in both 1996 and 2001, husbands with
working wives spent less time on domestic work (25 minutes) than husbands whose wives did not work (32 minutes), although in both cases, little
time was spent on domestic work. All the men surveyed in Table 6.20 have
jobs, and thus, even if a woman has a job, her male partner has a traditional gender role model.

One of the reasons for the low participation rate of men in domestic
work and child care is, in addition to the problem of gender role and long-
standing tradition, men's long hours devoted to paid work. Many married
men return home tired, after a long day at work, with no energy or time
left to do domestic work. When they arrive home, the children are already
asleep. Their wives is waiting for them, to dine together, or perhaps the

Table 6.20   Time use for domestic work by women with and without paid work,
1996–2001 (hours and minutes)

Year	Both husband and wife have paid work				Husband has paid work, wife does not			
	1996		2001		1996		2001	
	Husband	Wife	Husband	Wife	Husband	Wife	Husband	Wife
Paid work	7:18	4:47	7:01	4:29	6:55	0:05	6:51	0:03
Domestic work	0:21	4:10	0:25	4:12	0:26	7:05	0:32	6:59

Source: Statistics Bureau, Ministry of Public Management, Home Affairs, Posts and Telecommunications (2002b), p. 23.

wives are asleep along with the children. It is common for men to return home after midnight, and this working habit prevents Japanese men from sharing more domestic work with their wives. This tendency has become stronger in recent years, and men who have a job and worked more than 11 hours a day on weekdays, increased by 1.8 per cent between 1991 and 2001. Yet part-time male workers, most of whom are young, and unemployed men, suffer from economic instability, but do not necessarily participate more in domestic work, especially when they live with their parents. This phenomenon is perhaps more related to the problem of masculinity.

Women's time use for domestic work and child care has decreased gradually but steadily over the years between 1981 and 2001, and their time spent on paid work has also tended to decrease. One of the main reasons for the drop in time spent on domestic work is the development and diffusion of more advanced and automated electrical appliances in the household, which has made it much easier to complete domestic work. Another reason is the popularity of pre-cooked or part-cooked meals, which saves cooking time. To buy automated electrical appliances and cooked meals was regarded as a sign of laziness among married women in the past, but this sentiment has been gradually disappearing.

The main reason for the small drop in women's work time is the change in employment patterns. Many women, especially those who gave up work upon marriage or childbirth and returned to the labour market later, at around 40 years of age, usually have no options other than part-time jobs. Part-time labour is characterized as low-wage labour, lacks the protection of social security, and work contracts are for short periods of time and less stable than those of full-time workers. This is convenient for the private sector, because companies can hire part-time women workers at low cost, and dismiss them easily when the company has financial difficulties.

In short, Japanese women's labour force participation became easier and more common partly because of the general improvement in living standards, which made it possible to purchase electrical appliances and pre-cooked meals, as well as to enjoy the well-established infrastructure that allowed women to be able to participate in the labour market. Yet general work habits, especially of men who work long hours, have made it difficult for men to participate in domestic work and child care, or the nursing of older family members.

Because of Japan's economic recession that started in the 1990s, employment has been polarized. In the case of men, full-time workers, who represent the majority of male workers, tend to work for longer hours. Women's labour participation rate is increasing, but it is because of the increase in married part-time female workers. The female labour force is divided into three sections: many single full-time workers; many married part-time workers; and a small number of married full-time workers who have the resources to continue working, especially after childbirth. The only change now observed is found among the younger generation, because young men feel uncertain about lifetime employment, and they feel that their female partners should work to lessen the economic risks of the household.

Conclusion

Socialist Cuba has improved the gender situation, most significantly in the field of women's labour participation. The revolutionary government succeeded in the promotion of universal education for both boys and girls, and provided for the employment of women, as well as providing nursery schools and other facilities so that women could continue to participate in paid work. Furthermore, through the universal education system and legislation, especially the Family Code of 1975, and through continuous efforts of semi-governmental mass agencies such as the Federation of Cuban Women, the government has educated the people to respect women's rights to work and to expect husbands or male partners to share in domestic work. All these have helped in transforming gender relations, which have in turn encouraged women's self-esteem and economic independence. These accomplishments have been realized mainly because of the state's social policy. But in spite of all these government efforts, in reality Cuban women still carry dual responsibilities. At the same time, the state socialist policy has decreased men's responsibility as breadwinner, as the state sustains household economies via various universal social programmes other than wages. Cuban men are freer from economic responsibility, and therefore freer from the traditional role model of husbands.

The disintegration of the Soviet Union has complicated the situation of gender relations and gender roles. First, the quality of the government's social policy has deteriorated because of the severe economic crisis, and the public support for female workers has weakened accordingly. Second, partial economic reforms have generated new economic sectors that have more capitalistic labour relations and less favourable working conditions for female workers who have domestic responsibilities. Cuban data show that women tend to remain in the public sector and most have not entered the new sectors that pay higher wages. The economic crisis has caused severe material shortages, and shopping, cooking, and all other domestic work has become much more difficult. Yet women have returned to the labour force after the most severe period of the crisis – the first half of the 1990s – and at the time of writing their labour participation rate has recovered to the level of the Soviet era.

According to the time-use surveys, the absolute quantity of domestic work has increased for both sexes. On the other hand it is now presumed that Cuban women have less economic independence and need to depend more on men's support to economically maintain households, especially when their male partners work in a newly developed economic sector, such as joint ventures and the tourism industry, which bring in high incomes (often in hard currency) to the workers and their families. It can be presumed from the slight drop in the divorce rate in recent years.

On the other hand, it is generally said that the younger generation, especially those born in or after the 1970s, is much less traditional, and men of that generation are more willing to share domestic work. This coincides with the enactment of the Family Code of 1975. This is also clear from Safa's survey. If this tendency continues, over time the transformation of gender roles and the division of labour in the household will advance, in spite of the impact of the economic crisis and disadvantageous conditions for female workers. In sum, the burden of Cuban women inside the household has increased since the disintegration of the Soviet Union, as the absolute amount of domestic work increased. Women's authority in households tends to decrease as women's economic independence has been lessened. The only lighter sphere is, although I have little concrete evidence, seemingly younger generations have been changing their gender values to a more equal and fair direction. The 2001 *Bohemia* survey shows that people's gender values are quite traditional even among most educated citizens, but the ratio of use of time for domestic work between women and men has been less than in the 1980's, and at least men are beginning to participate more in domestic work.

Japanese women's labour participation rate increased in the 1980s and 1990s, but they are in the same situation as Cuban women in the sense that, even if women have jobs, they still have dual responsibilities. Women's burden in domestic work has been decreasing since the 1980s, but it is not because their male partners share in domestic work, but rather that women are able to utilize pre-cooked meals and have more electrical appliances to save time on cooking and other housekeeping work. This is a result of Japan's high economic development after the Second World War. Japan has maintained more traditional gender relations and gender role model than other developed countries. Yet Japanese work habits, which oblige most workers to work longer hours, has impeded workers from returning home early enough to do domestic work, and it is one of the main reasons that fewer married men share in domestic work at home. The situation is difficult because private companies will not comply easily with requests to change the working style, certainly not until they feel that it is advantageous for their survival.

Japan's capitalist economic development has made it possible for women to participate in the labour market since the 1980s. The Japanese government's policy and legislation is much less advanced than the Cuban government's in terms of gender equality, because Japanese legislation for gender equality does not refer to gender role transformation or the sharing of domestic work between spouses. Probably because of the private sector's resistance, the government has not abolished its support for the traditional gender role model through favourable programmes for tax, social security and medical insurance for housewives. Economic development has made it possible for women to save time on domestic work, but this has not been successful in bringing men to share in it.

On the other hand, Japan's economic development has had a positive effect on gender relations. The improvement of living standards in Japan has made it possible for individuals to live independently. This has helped to implant in young men's minds a sense of responsibility for their wives and children. In Cuba, because of the economic difficulties, mutual assistance among extended family members is very common, and the society does not expect that a young man should be economically independent. As a result, young Cuban men do not need to make great efforts to become economically independent in order to be considered a man, nor do they need to have sense of economic responsibility for their wives and children. Furthermore, economic difficulties in Cuba have prevented women from being economically independent even when they have full-time jobs, and it is therefore more difficult for women to get divorced if they do not have help from their parents or other family members.

In spite of the differences in political and economic systems and level of economic development, neither Japan nor Cuba have been able to establish new gender relations, where men and women share domestic work, especially when the wife has a job. Cuban socialism has not been able to realize new gender roles fully. It has only achieved it partially, through the government's social policy and full employment policy, and legislation such as the Family Code of 1975. After the disintegration of the Soviet Union, partial economic reforms have changed the economic structure and labour relations into a form closer to those of capitalist economies where workers need to dedicate their time and energy more intensly in work. Because younger generations tend to have values favouring a non-traditional gender role model, more people may try to change gender relations, but if men need to work for long hours to maintain the household economy, women will probably need to take on more domestic work, as is the case in Japan. Most Cuban women have come to lead more severe lives after the collapse of the Soviet Union, with more domestic work and less economic independence, and the only possibility of their burden being lessened is the change of their male partners' attitude in gender roles. The Japanese government presented much less developed legislation on gender roles, partly because of the resistance of the private sector. It is advantageous for Cuba that it has only a small private sector, but if the working pattern of Cuban workers becomes similar to the capitalistic pattern, and if they need to work longer hours in a more cost-effective way, traditional gender relations may be revived, in spite of the fact that the younger generation has been educated to prefer a non-traditional relations.

Notes

* I am sincerely grateful to Dr Mayda Álvarez Suárez, Director of the Centro de Estudios de la Mujer (CEM) of FMC, for her assistance and comments during my research, and Prof. Gladys C. Hernández Pedraza, of the Centro de Investigaciones de la Economía Mundial (CIEM), for her comments during the 8th Workshop 'Cuba-Japón,' held in Havana on 6–8 October 2004.
1 For example, Álvarez (2002).
2 I visited one nursery school, two state-run and two private elder citizens' homes, two orphanages, and one facility for severely disabled children from October to November 2003. All the institutions, except one of the orphanages, were located in Havana. The only exception (an orphanage) was in Matanzas City (the capital of Matanzas Province). A part from one of the private elder citizens' homes, the orphanage in Matanzas, and the home for physically disabled children, all the directors of the institutions were women. Even in those that had male directors, most of the other workers were women.
3 This is the author's personal impression, based on her stay in Cuba for two years, from 1994 to 1996.
4 I consider that the economic crisis was caused mainly by the inefficient socialist system and by Cuba's extreme dependence on the CMEA bloc. The Cuban government has asserted that US economic sanctions against Cuba since the 1960s are the main reason for its economic crisis, but this is only a minor reason, although I agree that the US embargo has affected Cuban economy to some extent.
5 I lived in Havana from January 1994 to February 1996. Especially in the first year, power failures were serious. In many cases they continued for more than twelve hours. The government carried out planned shutdowns to make the people suffer power cuts equally, but they occurred more often than was reported by the government.
6 In Havana City, for many years, water was available only every other day. But during the power cuts, water pumps do not work, and people who live in collective housing must carry water in buckets from the pump to their apartments.

7 This is true when ordinary Cubans consume as much as they used to, before the crisis. The rationing programme still guarantees that the people do not starve. I personally know some people who lived only on rationed food, and they told me that they had lost around 40 to 50 pounds in weight, apparently were malnourished and easily fell ill but at least they did not die of hunger, as in some other developing countries.

8 Many Cuban workers enjoy the loose work ethics. During the worst period of the economic crisis, around 1992–6, for example, they could easily be absent from work because of a lack of public transportation or floods after heavy rains, and could often get sick leave as physicians easily gave them permission for this. If there was no electricity in the office or any other trouble that was not covered by the workers' responsibility, the workers could go home and do their domestic work. Many workers were able to keep their jobs during the worst period of the economic crisis because of these factors.

9 Previously, the quality of lunches at workers' cafeterias was not good by Cuban standards, and food was not really an incentive for workers, but these days the quality has improved.

10 When I lived in Havana in the midst of the economic crisis (1994–96), many workers could not go to work because of lack of public transportation, for example. When buses come only every three or four hours, even if a worker was absent from the office for another reason, it was impossible to find out what the real reason was. If lunch was not served at the workers' cafeteria for whatever reason, the work shift that afternoon was cancelled, and all the workers left the workplace. When a worker fell ill, the public sector allowed him or her to take leave with few limitations, plus 60 per cent of wage compensation. But the new sector demands more output from each worker, and it is more difficult for a worker to ask for leave, as there is a large supply in the labour market for the new sector.

11 Oficina Nacional de Estadísticas (ONE) (1999), p. 48, Figure 4.3. This figure does not show exact values of the rates of female heads of household in each age group, but the rates for 1995 are higher than those for 1981 in all age groups.

12 Translated by the author from the original Spanish text.

13 Interview with Ms Isabel Moya Richard, editorial director of FMC's journal *Mujer*, 3 November 2003. Yet Dr Mayda Álvarez Suárez, director of Centro de Estudios de la Mujer (CEM) of FMC commented that various and continuous efforts of FMC is the main contributor of the transformation. Of course, I do not deny the fact that the continuing efforts of that mass organization and every Cuban woman to change the situation of gender roles have worked more than one piece of legislation.

14 The mass organization for primary school students. Almost 100 per cent of the students become members.

15 The mass organization for secondary school students.

16 Cuban Communist Party's subordinate organization for young communists. The members are selected as candidates to be future leaders of the party.

17 Safa (1995), p. 152. Safa writes, 'more than half the daughters and over two-fifths of the sons have gone beyond secondary school, including some who have gone to the university'.

18 ONE (1999), p. 147, Figure 9.6. The data is shown in figures, and exact data values are unknown, so here only the tendency can be identified.

19 Ibid., p. 147, Figure 9.7.

20 There is no data on paid work hours classified by men's educational level.

21 Cubans do not need to save a part of their salaries for their children's education, or for unexpected illness in the family. The meaning of money in Cuba or other socialist countries is much less important than in capitalist economies. All these decreased the traditional responsibility of male breadwinners, and men tend to become economically less responsible for their families.

22 Safa writes that because the rationing was reduced from 95 per cent to 30 per cent of consumer items from 1970 to 1980, and because in 1981 the government raised retail prices, people had more incentive to work (Safa, 1995, p. 29). She refers only to consumer products such as food and clothes, not to housing or education.

23 In this survey, the work category was divided into only two: intellectual work and blue-collar (*obrero*), and the number of respondents in these two categories is almost the same. Therefore, 'intellectual work' covers a much broader working category, from technical and professional to so-called intellectual jobs.

24 The Japanese government's official English translation of the law is 'Gender Equality Law'. But the original Japanese title (Law of Society for Co-participation of Men and Women) represents more clearly its less progressive character than the official English title of 'gender equality'. The law was able to pass through the Diet with the support of the private sector because private corporations wanted more female workers.

25 Results from other countries in 2002: in South Korea, in 79.9 per cent of the samples, women do house cleaning and 92.3 per cent cook; the Philippines, 69.2 per cent do house cleaning, 76.2 per cent cook; the USA, 70.9 per cent do house cleaning, 74.8 per cent cook; in Sweden 58.5 per cent do house cleaning, 67.6 per cent cook; in Germany, 65.5 per cent do house cleaning, 73.9 per cent cook; in the UK, 73.0 per cent do house cleaning, 71.5 per cent cook.

References

Cuba

Aguilar, Calorina (ed.) (1999) *Algo más que palabras: el post Beijing en Cuba: acciones y evaluación* (Havana: Editorial de la Mujer).

Álvarez Suárez, Mayda (1998) 'Mujer y poder en Cuba', *Temas*, no. 14, April/June, pp. 13–25.

Álvarez Suárez, Mayda, (1999) *Mujer y poder en Cuba* (Havana: Centro de Estudios de la Mujer (CEM) Federación de Mujeres Cubanas (FMC) and UNICEF).

Álvarez Suárez, Mayda, (2002) 'Construcción socio-cultural de la masculinidad', Paper presented at the Seminario Nacional de Capacitación sobre Género en la Communicación y Sexismo en el Lenguaje, Federación de Mujeres Cubanas (FMC).

Álvarez, Mayda, Carolina Aguilar, Perla Popowski, Reina Muro and Alicia Gómez (1994) 'Mujer y poder: las cubanas en el gobierno popular', Mimeo, Havana, June.

Álvarez, Mayda, Inalvis Rodríguez, Perla Popowski, and Ana Violeta Castañeda (2001) *Situación de la mujer y la familia en Cuba* (Havana: Centro de Estudios de la Mujer (CEM), Federación de Mujeres Cubanas (FMC) and UNICEF.

Bunck, Julie Marie (1994), *Fidel Castro and the Quest for a Revolutionary Culture in Cuba*, (University Park: Pennsylvania State University Press).

Lutjens, Sheryl L. (1995) 'Reading Between the Lines: Women, the State, and Rectification in Cuba', *Latin American Perspectives*, vol. 22, no. 2 pp. 100–24

Oficina Nacional de Estadísticas (ONE) (1999) *Perfil estadístico de la mujer cubana en el umbral del Siglo XXI* (Havana: Oficina Nacional de Estadísticas).

Oficina Nacional de Estadísticas (ONE) *Anuario estadístico de Cuba* (Havana: Oficina Nacional de Estadísticas), Editions of 1996, 1999, 2000 and 2002.

Oficina Nacional de Estadísticas (ONE) (2003) *Encuesta sobre el uso del tiempo* (Havana: Oficina Nacional de Estadísticas).

Popowski Casañ, Perla (1999) 'La mujer en el desarrollo económico y social cubano', *AUNA-CUBA: Análisis y Coyuntura*, no. 11, December., pp. 21–8

Reca Moreira, Inés, Mayda Álvarez Suárez, Alicia V. Puñales Sosa and María del Carmen Caño Fernández (1996) *La familia en el ejercicio de sus funciones* (Havana: Editorial Pueblo y Educación).

Rodríuez Reyes, Inalvis (1999) 'Costos del Periodo Especial para la mujer cubana', *AUNA-CUBA: Análisis y Coyuntura*, no. 11, December., pp. 8–20.

Rodríguez, Dixie Edith y Herminia (2000) 'En Cuba, mujer y poder: ¿Acceso limitado?', *Bohemia*, vol. 92, no. 5, February 25, pp. 25–34.

Rodríguez, Dixie Edith y Herminia, Isabel Candelé, Lecsy González and Menfis Benítez (2001) 'Machismo: anclado en la tradición', *Bohemia*, vol. 93, no. 5, March 9. pp. 28–34

Safa, Helen (1995) *The Myth of the Male Breadwinner: Women and Industrialization in the Caribbean* (Boulder, Col.: Westview Press), chs 2 and 5. US – Cuba Trade and Economic Council p. 38. *Eye on Cuba* (newsletter), various years.

Japan

Ito, Kimio (1993) *Otokorashisa no yukue: dansei bunka no bunka-shakaigaku* (The Future of masculinity: cultural sociology of the masculine culture) (Tokyo: Shin-yo-sha), (in Japanese).

Ito, Kimio, Minori Kimura and Junko Kuninobu (2002) *Josei-gaku, dansei-gaku: jendaron nyumon* (Feminity and masculinity: guide to gender studies) (Tokyo: Yuhikaku) (in Japanese).

Gender Equality Bureau, Cabinet Office (2003) *Danjo kyodo sankaku shakai ni kansuru kokusai hikaku chosa* (Comparative public opinion survey on the society of co-participation of men and women: 2002) (Tokyo: Gender Equality Bureau, Cabinet Office), June (in Japanese).

Statistics Bureau, Management and Co-ordination Agency (1987) *The Survey on Time Use and Leisure Activities, 1986: Whole Japan, Time Spent on Activities (2)* Statistics Bureau, Management and Coordination Agency)

Statistics Bureau, Management and Co-ordination Agency (1992) *Survey on Time Use and Leisure Activities, vol. 1.1: Time Use for Japan: Daily Time Allocation by Sex, Age and Economic Activities* (Tokyo: Statistics Bureau, Management and Coordination Agency) (data for 1991).

Statistics Bureau, Ministry of Public Management, Home Affairs, Posts and Telecommunications (1997) *Survey on Time Use and Leisure Activities, vol. 1.1: Time Use for Japan: Daily Time Allocation by Sex, Age and Economic Activities.* (Tokyo: Statistics Bureau, Ministry of Public Management, Home Affairs, Posts and Telecommunications) (data for 1996).

Statistics Bureau, Ministry of Public Management, Home Affairs, Posts and Telecommunications (2002a) *Survey on Time Use and Leisure Activities, vol. 1.2: Time Use for Japan: Daily Time Allocation by Sex, Age and Economic Activities* (Tokyo: Statistics Bureau, Ministry of Public Management, Home Affairs, Posts and Telecommunications) (data for 2001).

Statistics Bureau, Ministry of Public Management, Home Affairs, Posts and Telecommunications (2002b) *Survey on Time Use and Leisure Activities, vol. 7* (Tokyo: Statistics Bureau, Ministry of Public Management, Home Affairs, Posts and Telecommunications).

Statistics Bureau, Prime Minister's Office (1976) *Shakai seikatsu kihon chosa no gaiyo* (Summary of survey of time use and leisure activities.) (Tokyo: Statistics Bureau, Prime Minister's Office) (in Japanese).

Statistics Bureau, Prime Minister's Office (1982) *The Survey on Time Use and Leisure Activities, 1981: Whole Japan, Time Spent on Activities (1)* (Tokyo: Statistics Bureau, Prime Minister's Office).

7

Nation-state, Family and Gender: Recent Studies in Japan and Turkey

Kaoru Murakami

Introduction

Since the end of the 1980s, under the influence of postmodernism and post-colonial critiques, the relation between modern nation-state building and family and gender issues, especially in Third World countries, has been one of the focal points of debates in international feminist studies (Jayawardena, 1986; Yuval-Davis and Anthias, 1989; Yuval-Davis, 1997) The gendered construction of nation and the role played by women during the process of nation-building have been brought to agenda and Turkey has been one of the best-researched fields. The issue has been addressed in Japan too, though the frame of reference has not been taken from Third World countries, as with Turkey, but from the experiences of modern European nations. In this chapter I shall examine and compare some of the recent studies dealing with the issue in both countries.

Japan and Turkey are often referred to as good examples of non-Western countries that have succeeded in transforming themselves into modern nation-states without losing their political independence, although the historical conditions and cultural backgrounds, and thus the processes of nation-building, were quite different.

While Tokugawa Japan (1603–1867) was a modestly-sized island country, the Ottoman Empire (1299–1922), the predecessor of the Republic of Turkey, had vast territories extending on to the Asian, African and European continents. Looking at the social structure, Japanese society consisted of, roughly speaking, an ethnically homogenous people, while Ottoman society consisted of various ethnic groups, each united by religious consciousness and integrated loosely into the Empire. It may be said that Tokugawa Japan had the substance of a nation-state, while the Ottoman nation could be characterized as a World Empire in the Islamic World.

The two polities, with their different characteristics, followed different courses in the process of transforming themselves into modern nation-states under the impact of the West. Tokugawa Japan realized this process relatively rapidly. In contrast, for the Ottoman Empire it took more than a century of turmoil and struggle, as the subjects, who had been divided into ethnic groups but held a common identity through religious consciousness, awakened to nationalism, and tried to split from the empire to unite themselves under independent nation-states (Suzuki, 1993, pp. 59–64).

Considering these contrasting characteristics, it would be interesting to compare the two countries' experiences in terms of how the process of nation-building related to family and gender issues. Yet in this chapter I shall examine not the issue itself but the contentions and contexts of existing feminist studies on the issue, in order to understand their underlying concerns regarding nation-building and nationalism. In other words, the aim of the chapter is to gain deeper insight into how the contemporary feminists understand women's roles in the nationalist project in both countries.

In the first and second sections I select representative studies by native researchers in both Japan and Turkey, and look at how they approached the issue, drawing the contours of the discussion. In the final section, comparing the points of contention and the contexts of the discussion, I examine the standing grounds of feminist researchers in the two countries.

Recent studies in Japan

Reconsidering the 'pre-modernity' of the family in modern Japan

In Japan, studies relating family and gender issues to the process of nation-building started from a reconsideration of the nature of the family in modern Japan, namely during the Meiji (1868–1912) and Taisho (1912–26) periods, in the context of the findings of European modern family studies.

For a long time the main concern of Japanese family studies had been the premodern nature of the family based on the *ie* system in the modern era. *Ie*'s literal meaning is 'dwelling house', and as a derivation is used to signify the members of a patrilineal family, sometimes including non-kin members. It was a common belief that the *ie* system, as prescribed by the Meiji Civil Code of 1898, inherited and sustained a model of the family based on the traditional *ie* system of warriors (*bushi*). The family based on this *ie* system follows a Confucian criterion, that gives predominance to the *ie* family over individuals, and gives preference to the continuation and succession of the family as a patrilineal group rather than to the affections and individual freedom of the members of the family. In particular, it was thought to place women in an inferior position.

The *ie* system was considered a remnant of feudalism, obstructing the modernization of Japanese society, and as such was a target for severe criticism from academic circles after the Second World War. It still seems to be a common interpretation that the modernization of the family was made possible only after the *ie* institution was abolished with the enactment of the New Civil Code during postwar democratization (Muta, 1996a).

The Impact of modern family studies

However, with the introduction of studies of European family history in the 1980s, there was a change in the paradigm of such studies, and the common interpretation of *ie* began to be questioned. The works by social historians like Philippe Aries and Edward Shorter pointed out that the ideal of companionate, child-centred conjugal family was not universal but an historical category which emerged in modern Europe, and named it 'modern family'. The problem consisted in considering whether the *ie* family in modern Japan shared similar characteristics with the European modern family.

In Japan, modern family studies developed along with feminism, as an effective theory to explain how the idea of the woman as a private and domestic being was established.[1] It was feminist-orientated researchers who addressed this argument. They examined the family in the Meiji and Taisho periods, and illuminated the fact that the ideal of the modern family appeared in this period largely under Western influence, even though it might have been reflected in a limited way in actual conditions.

Examining articles from magazines of the period, Kazue Muta demonstrated the emergence of a new consciousness that found a desirable model of the family in the word *katei*, a translation of the English 'home' among the upper and middle classes in the early years of the third decade of the Meiji period (towards the end of the nineteenth century). The ideal of the *ie* family, which considers the continuation of the *ie* as being supreme, came to be criticized as feudal under this kind of consciousness. Instead, the aim of this consciousness was to give priority to affection and intimacy among family members (Muta, 1996a).

'Home' as the base for controlling people

What is important here is the fact that a question arose as to whether the new consciousness of the *katei* family among the upper and middle classes was linked to the establishment of the modern nation-state system in Japan. In the process of nation-building in modern Europe, it was crucial to control sexuality and morality to secure the reproduction of life and labour, and the family was seen as the basis for the state's control over the people (Donzelot, 1977 [1991]; Mosse, 1998).

With regard to debates over modern Europe, feminist-orientated researchers assume that in the case of modern Japan too the family had had a similar function. A series of studies by Muta explores the family–state (*kazoku-kokka-kan*) ideology, showing that the rule over the people in modern Japan shared some features with that of modern European nations, with both making use of the family ideal as a means of ruling their people.

Conventional understanding of the family–state ideology

Looking at modern Japan, the main argument so far has been that the *ie* family was used to maintain public order and promote rapid modernization via the oppression of family members, especially women. The family–state ideology, along with the Meiji Civil Code, has been considered to be symbolic of Japan's unique style of modernization.

The conventional theory on family–state ideology, following the traditional Japanese concept of ancestor worship of the *ie* family, included the ancestors of each *ie* as being under the umbrella of the mythological ancestors of the Imperial *ie* family. In addition, by placing the emperor as the patriarch of the people, this ideology aimed to integrate the emperor and the people by creating an image of 'one country, one family'.

This ideology had as its background the need to deal with two perceived crises: the spread of the ideologies of the Freedom and People's Rights Movement (*jiyu-minken-undou*) and of socialism; and the dissolution of the family brought about by the development of capitalism. This family–state ideology was instituted through the Imperial Rescript on Education (*kyoiku-chokugo*) in the twenty-third year of the Meiji period (1890) and had become established by the end of the Meiji period. Later, it was diffused among the people, mainly through school education. This ideology is considered to have been the ruling principle of Japan until the country's defeat in the Second World War, when the state system was reformed.

Integrating the new family consciousness into the Imperial regime

Muta's research reinterprets the family–state ideology in the light of nation-building experiences in modern Europe. Through her analysis of elementary school textbooks on moral education throughout the Meiji period, she shows that while Confucian family morals such as filial piety and ancestor worship appear as main themes, and are thus reinforced, a careful observation of the subliminal messages (meta messages) that are not clearly signalled, but rather are concealed in illustrations and anecdotes, indicates that a new family consciousness made its appearance in the latter half of the third decade of the Meiji period (late nineteenth century) (Muta, 1996a).

Concerning parent–child relations, she observes a shift from a feeling of moral indebtedness and filial piety based on vertical relationships to parent–child relationships of mutual affection that permitted the enjoyment of family life. Relatives, for their part, were originally objects of filial piety along with parents, but were later distinguished from parents and grandparents, and came to be seen as distant family members (Muta, 1996a).

In addition to the reduction of the scope of the family, and the fact that parent–child relations became closer, there was a change in the way the emperor was depicted. In the early years of the Meiji period, loyalty to the emperor was hardly referred to, but in the latter half of the third decade of the Meiji period, such loyalty became a cardinal virtue. On the other hand, affection and intimacy between parents and children, and between the emperor and the empress, who were seen as the parents of the people, were emphasized. This expression of the relationship between the emperor, empress and their people through the image of the new family, instead of an *ie* system, means that the acceptance of the absolute sovereignty of the emperor had begun (Muta, 1996a).

Consolidating the relationship between the Emperor and his people

Based on the facts discussed above, Muta argues that even though the family–state ideology can be seen as having emerged from a combination of Confucian and traditional family principles and nationalism, in some sense it made use of the new family image. This new family consciousness can be characterized as follows: (i) authority was concentrated in the power of the state, and exceeded the authority of the family, including kinship in a broad sense; (ii) the *katei* family, which involved intimacy, became the basis of nationalism; and (iii) the emperor was endowed a paternal image to bring him closer to the people (Muta, 1996a).

These three elements can also be used to describe the family–state ideology. In other words, 'pre-modern family ethics' were not the sole basis of the family–state ideology. Under the socioeconomic conditions of the time, a new family consciousness, born spontaneously within the family, played a supplementary role. Muta argues that while the family–state ideology was 'uniquely Japanese', it can be seen at the same time as a variation of the concept used for governing people through the mediation of the family, which is a universal feature of modern nations. Moreover, when the family played a part in controlling the people, through a conciliatory process imposed by the state on the family, spontaneous changes occured within the family. These changes were correlated with the process, and in some cases even promoted it (Muta, 1996a).

Respectability of women

In modern Europe, the idea of respectability emerged along with the emergence of nationalism, and the companionate, child-centred conjugal family played a key part in supporting and consolidating the idea (Mosse, 1988). Muta argues that a similar process was also observed in modern Japan, and that it was women, more than men, who supported the process enthusiastically.

Analysing the discourses of women intellectuals in various publications of the time, Muta demonstrates that their quest to improve the status and rights of women and to forge an identity for themselves took the form of the acceptance of new gender norms. Under such norms, women assumed the role of wives and mothers of the nation, and were expected to uphold a rigid sexual morality, in the context of opposing backward traditions.

In pre-modern Japanese society, regulations on sexuality were quite loose among the popular classes, and only the ruling class upheld Confucian sexual morality. Women intellectuals denied both ideas and upheld a sexual morality under which they themselves laid down the restrictions, placing absolute value on the virginity of women, in order to forge an identity as mothers and wives of the modern nation (Muta, 1996a).

'Good wife and wise mother' as an ideal for modern women

One of the notions that, along with the family–state ideology, has often been explained according to 'pre-modern family ethics' is the ideology of 'good wife and wise mother' (*ryosai kenbo*), which constitutes a model for officially recognized women's education in modern Japan.

Established theory saw the 'good wife and wise mother' as a view of women's education related to the family–state ideology and Confucianism. The concept was regarded as a conservative and reactionary ideology of the Establishment, which led to the oppression of women. It was also seen as being in conflict with the ideology of women's liberation that appeared under the democratization movement of the Taisho period (1912–26) (*Taisho Demokurashi*). However, studies by Shizuko Koyama deconstruct the ideology and add a new interpretation, referring to studies on nation-building in modern Europe (Koyama, 1991).

The indirect inclusion of women in the process of nation-building

In modern Western countries, the role of the mother has been emphasized from the viewpoint of nation-building, which was the basis for asserting the need for women's education. Koyama points out that the ideology of 'good wife and wise mother' was formed around the thirtieth year of the Meiji period (1897), and though it might have been expressed in terms of Confucianism, it played a part similar to that of the view of women's education in modern Western countries. Moreover, she shows that this ideology was inseparable from the formation of the modern nation-state and the establishment of a *katei*-type family.

Exploring the discourses over the proper role and place of women in society, Koyama points out certain changes that took place after the beginning of the Meiji period. During the preceding Edo period (1603–1867), among the upper classes, women were regarded as foolish beings in comparison with men, and what was expected most of a woman was to show devoted obedience to her husband and his parents.

However, during the following Meiji period, when efforts to make Japan into a modern nation state and to transform its people into citizens arose as national issues, women were expected to take on the role of rearing and educating children, the future citizens. For that purpose they themselves were expected to be educated. Calls began for a solid women's education under the slogan of 'good wife and wise mother' from the perspective of the establishment of a modern nation (Koyama, 1991).

The direct inclusion of women in the process of nation-building

Tracing the discourse on the idealized vision of women, Koyama further discovers that after the First World War, the ideology of 'good wife and wise mother' was revised drastically. The new vision upheld the importance of the mother's role, but added new prototypes, such as the housewife (*shufu*) who is the master (*shujin*) of the household, and can maintain a wife–husband relationship on equal terms; the type of woman who engages in remunerated work outside the household, provided that her work does not become a hindrance to household affairs and child-rearing; and the woman who strives for the improvement of society (Koyama, 1991).

Koyama points out several factors in the backdrop of the revision of the ideology. The situation of women was raised as the 'women question' (*fujin mondai*) and became a social issue first among the male intellectuals of the socialist circles who were aware of the women's suffrage movement in the West. On the other hand, the increase in the number of women who received education and got white-collar jobs prepared women to accept Western feminist ideas and make a social and political issue of their situation. Finally, and most crucially, the active advancement of European women into society in place of the absent men during the First World War roused arguments among the intellectuals that, for the country's surviving the age of imperialism, it would be a pressing issue to develop women's ability. The ideology of 'good wife and wise mother' was revised to overturn former views of women as having less capacity than men, and to encourage women to advance into society while retaining roles of wife and mother.

Koyama draws attention to the fact that some of the aspects of this argument overlapped those of the women's liberation movement. The 'good wife and wise mother' ideology of the time saw women indirectly as citizens of the modern nation, as they were given the role of rearing children, the future citizens, and supporting husbands engaging in production activities and serving in the army. In contrast, the newly reformulated ideology of 'good wife and wise mother' held the potential of women asserting a relationship within the public domain and being recognized directly as citizens. This made it attractive to women who were affected by Western feminist ideas and started to discuss their own situation. Though at this point the renewed version of 'good wife and wise mother' still remained as an ideal, Koyama sees it as beginning to function as a preparatory stage of the national mobilization in the 1930s, when Japan fully entered the total war. At that time, women including those from the masses, played a key role in cooperating with the mobilization not only as wives and mothers of soldiers, but as patriotic citizens (Koyama, 1999).

Recent studies in Turkey

Objections to the Kemalist reforms

While Japanese researchers embarked on their studies by deconstructing the ideal of family and women's role in modern Japan which had been assumed to be pre-modern and Confucian in nature, their Turkish counterparts launched discussions by deconstructing the myth of 'the liberation of women by the Kemalist reforms'.

Turkey was founded as a secular republic in 1923 by Mustafa Kemal Atatürk, a charismatic leader of the national liberation movement who became the first president, from the remains of the Ottoman Empire, after the war of national independence (1918–23) Mustafa Kemal and his followers, the enlightened governing elites, launched modernization and Westernization reforms extensively, putting a particular emphasis on the abolition of existing social institutions and mores surrounding the status of women. Soon after the republic's foundation, measures including the adaptation of a secular Civil Code (1926) which outlawed polygamy and gave equal rights of divorce to both partners, and women's enfranchisement (at the local level in 1930 and at the national level in 1934) were implemented in short order.

The reforms were, in particular, supported and defended by upper-and middle-class women who were able to take advantage of them. Mustafa Kemal Atatürk was almost sanctified as the emancipator of Turkish women. In academic circles, too, it was for a long time taboo to criticize him or the reforms he implemented. Even the ebb of modernization theories and the growing influence of Marxist perspective overshadowed the praise for the Kemalist path of modernization as the exemplar of a modernizing nation in the Western mold in the late 1960s and the 1970s, their criticisms were concentrated on the Ottoman leaders who preceded Mustafa Kemal or on those who followed him, and not on what Kemal himself attempted to do (Bozdoğan and Kasaba, 1997).[2]

Search for an indigenous feminism

It was the mid-1980s that the dogma of women's liberation by the Kemalist revolution started to be-questioned. The political vacuum after the military coup of 1980 allowed women to occupy an important space in the public gaze under the influence of the second wave of Western feminism and its criticisms.[3]

During the 1970s and 1980s, women in Third World countries began to question the direct application of Western feminism as a universal theory for liberating women in their own societies, since it had been constructed based on the situation of Western white women. Instead, they searched for the possibility of indigenous feminisms for their own cultural and political contexts.[4]

In Turkey, the search for an indigenous feminism was carried out through a reconsideration of the nature of the Kemalist reforms. While inheriting the Kemalist legacy of gender equality and women's advancement in the public domain, the feminists have proceeded to criticise the indifference of Kemalists to the women's positions within the private realm, where women are expected to be self-sacrificing mothers. They denounced the home as the very locus of women's oppression, and questioned the uncritical stance of the Kemalist women with regard to the relations within the home (Sirman, 1989).

The Symbolic importance of women's liberation

One of the earliest feminist criticisms of Kemalist reforms was lodged by Şirin Tekeli, a representative advocate of feminist. Tekeli argues that singling out women as the group most visibly oppressed by Islam, through practices such as veiling, seclusion and polygamy, was a prime consideration in Mustafa Kemal's attack against the theocratic regime of the Ottoman state. The timing of the legislation on women's suffrage in the 1930s, on the other hand, can be interpreted as an attempt by Mustafa Kemal to dissociate himself from the European dictatorships of the time (nazi Germany and fascist Italy) and claim Turkey's rightful place among Western democratic nations (Tekeli, 1981). As women's liberation was enforced 'from above' to symbolize country's development, women themselves remained passive, heavily dependent on the Kemalist state, and contented with the given place.

Women as boundary markers of the nation

Largely supporting Tekeli's remarks, Deniz Kandiyoti points out that women's emancipation under Kemalism was part of a broader political project of nation building and secularization.

From the mid-1980s, against the backdrop of the increase of interest in nationalism, in the international scene of feminist studies, attention began to be concentrated on the ways that women affect, and are affected by, nationalism (Jayawardena, 1986; Yuval-Davis and Anthias, 1989). Kandiyoti's research is one of the pioneering works in this terrain.

Tracing the discourses of reformists elites, Kandiyoti shows that the emergence of 'women question' as the central agenda among them during Turkey's period of political transition from a multi-ethnic Islamic empire to a secular nation-state, was nothing but the proof of their endeavour at constructing a national identity. The improvement of the position of women was talked over with connotations of the improvement of society. In other word, women were assigned the role of the cultural boundary markers of a collectivity (be an ethnic group or a nation).

The 'crisis' of the Ottoman Empire and the emergence of the 'woman question'

Throughout the eighteenth century, the Ottoman Empire gradually lost its power, both against Western supremacy and against the rise of nationalist, secessionist movements in its provinces. This paved the way for a period of political search and redefinition that lasted until the First World War, and culminated in the Kemalist republic in 1923. It is particularly during this period that the 'crisis' of Ottoman culture and of the Ottoman family system appeared on the political agenda. As a result, the question of women's position became a privileged site for debates concerning questions of modernization versus cultural conservatism and integrity (Kandiyoti, 1989, 1991).

During the mid-nineteenth century, when the process of full-scale modernization was launched, the restoration of the empire was discussed in terms of loyalty either to Islam or to the Ottoman cause. According to Kandiyoti, discussions on issues related to family and women were also carried out within the context of Islam. Islamists advocated a return to the unadulterated application of Islamic law, while Westernists held Islam responsible both for obscurantism and for what they saw as the debased position of women. Young Ottomans, whose position could best be defined as modernist Islamists, being situated in position somewhere between Westernists and Islamists, were in favour of marriages based on love and mutual consent, and argued that the modernization of the family was compatible with Islam (Kandiyoti, 1989, 1991).

The 'new family' as a unit of the nation

As nationalism spread among non-Muslim subjects, however, the construction of a national identity based on the 'national culture' rather than on Islam started to be raised as an issue among Turkish people.

After the Young Turks' revolution (1908), intellectuals who were in search of a national identity as Turkish people came to see the family as a basic unit of the nation-state, and family morality as the foundation of national solidarity. The traditional patriarchal Ottoman family was set aside and a family called the 'new family' (*yeni aile*) or 'national family' (*milli aile*) was idealized. It was to be a monogamous, companionate nuclear family. Women in this type of family were expected above all to be enlightened mothers taking charge of what was considered to be a duty to the nation: giving birth to and rearing children. They were expected not to be over-Westernized and to remain honourable and chaste wives. Ziya Gökalp, an authorized ideologue of Turkish nationalism, advocated 'Moral Turkism', which he justified by maintaining that the companionate nuclear family was not only compatible with the modern nation, but that its origin could be found in pre-Islamic Turkic sources (Kandiyoti, 1991).

Curiously enough, polygamy or multiple family households, which was asserted as the tradition of Ottoman families, were quite rare in reality. Kandiyoti interprets the criticisms of this type of family by the contemporary advocates as the proof of their effort to create a new moral code and a new discourse in place of Islamic ones to control women's sexuality (Kandiyoti, 1989, 1997)

The new role of women

Kandiyoti further draws attention to the fact that under Turkism, in addition to being objects of nationalist discourse, women were now mobilized as political actors in the nationalist movement. Apart from their role as mothers and housewives, women from the middle classes were expected to join the struggle for the liberation and improvement of the nation, by participating in labour and social activities. Behind such developments was the growing sense of crisis against the labour shortage and decrease in male population brought about by successive wars.

According to Kandiyoti, the new roles of women as participants in the nationalist movement were promoted as being inseparable from their roles as mothers and reproducers of the nation. For example, the 'Islamic Association for the Employment of Ottoman Women', established in 1916, employed women workers under conditions that assured them an 'honest living' by segregating them from male workers, and stipulating simultaneously that marriage for single men and women was mandatory (Kandiyoti, 1989, 1991).

When the Ottoman Empire was defeated in the First World War, the Anatolian provinces were placed under the control of the occupying Western powers. In the struggle for national independence, led by Mustafa Kemal Atatürk, not only middle-class women but also Anatolian peasant women were mobilized to serve as back up support in the war. Kandiyoti draws attention to the fact that, even on the battlefield, the protection of the sexual honour (*namus*) of women was of the prime concern of the governing elites. Women who fought side-by-side with men were expected to behave as comrade-women or asexual sisters-in-arms whose public activities never cast any doubt on their virtue and chastity (Kandiyoti, 1989).

The meanings of changes in the status of women

During the transition period from empire to republic, the status of women changed, first at the level of discourse and then in reality. However, according to Kandiyoti, it should be explained in terms of changes in the characteristics of the state ideology of political elites rather than a result of autonomous women's movements. Be it in discourse or in reality, be it for Islamist or for nationalist, the changes in the status of women were to be delimited by the prerequisite of protecting the sexual honour of women. Kandiyoti remarks, 'there appears to be one persistent concern which finally unites nationalist and Islamist discourses on women in Turkey: the necessity to establish that the behavior and position of women, however defined, are congruent with the "true" identity of the collectivity and constitute no threat to it' (Kandiyoti, 1989, p. 143).

Domesticating the passion of love

While Kandiyoti points out the integration of women into nationalist projects as icons of modernity and/or bearers of tradition and authentic culture, a series of studies by Nükhet Sirman highlight how women, as well as men, create a politics of life for constructing positive social relations between the self and collectivity – namely the family and nation – through an analysis of love motifs in modern Turkish novels.

Love motifs in the Tanzimat novel

Referring to Chatterjee's arguments concerning nationalism and nation-building in modern India (Chatterjee, 1986), she argues that the modernists' search for a new model of the family constituted a practice of constructing new models of masculinity/femininity. Using Tanzimat novels written by Young Ottomans in the 1860s and 1870s in the wake of the modern reform (Tanzimat) as text, Sirman shows that it was through this practice that a new system for governing people was devised.

In these novels, in place of the traditional household relations that were common in literary works of previous periods, feelings of love between individuals began to be depicted as elements of the social order. Often the male characters, instead of getting married to women chosen by their fathers, get married for love to an educated and wise wife, and start an independent life with her, free from the order of the traditional patriarchal family. They becomes the heads of small, independent households, and thus becomes subjects who can build a fraternal and egalitarian relationship with other young men. Through the envisioning of this image of society, a nation composed of gendered subjects and the concept of sovereignty of the nation resides in its people comes to be established at the same time, first at the level of discourse. In this way, the love appearing in novels served to examine the pre-existing order, and played the role of justifying the appearance of new actors (Sirman, 2000a, 2002).

However, once the feeling of love had accomplished this role, it became regarded as something dangerous that needed to be controlled. The feeling of love, which was an object of praise in the Tanzimat novel, soon came to be seen as a synonym for excessive Westernization, sexual desire or temptation, which would lead to the destruction of the family (Sirman, 2000a, 2002).

Constructing feminine subjectivity

While the Tanzimat novel expressed a desire to transform relations between men, rather than between men and women, and failed to depict female agency, Sirman analyses a series of works by the first Turkish woman novelist, Halide Edip Adlvar (b. 1882), who problematized female identity and generated a new discourse on women, to show how women are incorporated into the nationalist project as subjects. Curiously enough, in these novels it was not men but women who were entrusted with the control of love. She remarks that the heroine, who in early works written at the end of the Imperial period appeared as vacillating, subject to short-lived passion, and who lost her head over a lover for whom she felt sexual passion, began to be depicted in novels written after the establishment of the republic as a subject appealing to reason or to her soul, and choosing a partner who would allow a long-lasting relationship.

According to Sirman, the appearance of this kind of subjective heroine implied that the new femininity (being a chaste wife and mother of the nation), was not applied to women through force, but rather can be interpreted as an identity that women themselves desired, undertook and internalized (Sirman, 2000b, 2002). In other words, women were not always passive beings who were, as boundary markers of the nation, objects of control or manipulation, but also had aspects as supporters of nationalism.

Comparison and considerations

Similar contentions in different contexts

Since the end of the 1980s, in both Japan and Turkey, the relationship between the building of the modern nation-state, and family and gender issues has become one of the focal points of debate among feminist-orientated researchers. Japan and Turkey have different historical and cultural backgrounds, and accordingly underwent different processes of nation-building. However, as is shown above, there are some important common points of contention in the studies in both countries.

For example, feminist researchers in both countries argue that the process of nation-building was accompanied by the rearrangement of sexual moralities and codes of women's behaviour, though to a lesser extent in the Turkish case. In both countries, the ideal of the 'new family' was imagined against the 'traditional family', was conductive to controlling people and functioned as a locus where people were nurtured to be 'the nation'. They also point out that women were expected to be educated and learned as mothers and wives of 'the nation'. This means, according to the studies discussed above, that membership in the nation was not neutral but rather a gendered notion.

While these contentions are often shared in the cases of other nations, what is interesting is that they are presented in quite different contexts. In the case of Japan, it is pointed out that the family in modern Japan under the *ie* system, that has been considered a remnant of feudalism, in fact possessed features of the modern family. This new consciousness of the family, along with 'pre-modern familiar ethics', became a support for the imperial regime. The studies also point out the new role of women as master of the home, and describe them as eager subjects who were willing to take on the role of participating in the administration of the modern nation-state.

By contrast, in the Turkish case, as part of a reconsideration of the meaning of the liberation of women under the Kemalist modernization reform, it is asserted that the reform of women's status merely meant using women as symbols of a modern and democratic nation. Furthermore, it is pointed out that women were used as tools in the process of nation-building. On the other hand, it is argued that women were not always passive beings, and that the new femininity was a subjective choice of women. A search was carried on for a national subjectivity of women, different from that of men.

Highlighting women's subjectivity

It seems that while Japanese studies highlight strongly the subjectivity of women, Turkish studies question whether women were merely sexual objects or whether they were active agents. Looking at the backgrounds of the development of these studies, it seems that in neither country is the conclusion that women were either acquiescent victims or autonomous participants of nationalism. Rather, they were attempts to revise the interpretation of the position of women and restore a balance to the historical perspectives of existing studies.

With respect to this point, it seems that Japanese researchers place more emphasis on women's subjectivity than do their Turkish counterparts. This attitude may be attributed partly to their attempt to gain a balanced grasp of women's position in history. But just as important may be their reflection on the bitter memories of women's co-operation during the Second World War.

During the war, people were physically and psychologically mobilized as citizens, soldiers and workers, and the family functioned as an important device for the mobilization. It was women, consisting not only of intellectuals but also the common people, who responded most actively to this mobilization.

In the late 1980s, Japanese gender studies experienced a paradigm shift, under which women came to be considered not as simple victims of wartime mobilization but as active supporters of it. Ironically, this shift, which implied the restoration of agency in women's history, questions seriously the responsibility of women during the war. It sheds light on the fact that women's co-operation during the war was not imposed, but rather chosen voluntarily as a way to open a road to participation in the public domain as full-fledged citizens (Ueno, 1998).

These complex feelings about women's participation in nationalist projects and access to membership of the 'nation' do not yet seem to be shared by their Turkish counterparts.

Notes

1 Ochiai (1989) is the pioneering work that played a leading part in introducing the findings of European modern family studies and discussing their implications for feminist understandings of gender and family issues. One of the main arguments of the work is that the role of housewife and mother normatively assigned to women is no more than historical product that has lasted two centuries at most in Europe.

2   Besides feminist criticisms I will mention later, according to the remarks by
    Bozdoğan and Kasaba in their article published in 1997, recently in the hands of
    groups ranging from advocates of liberal economy to Islamist intellectuals, the
    criticism of the Kemalist doctrine as a patriarchal and antidemocratic imposition
    from above has become more comprehensive (Bozdoğan and Kasaba, 1997).
3   For more comprehensive and detailed explanation of the new visibility of women
    in Turkish political discourses including Islamic and leftist ones in the 1980s, see
    Sirman (1989).
4   For one of the earliest references to the difficulties in directly applying the femin-
    ism of Western societies to Middle Eastern societies, see Kandiyoti (1987).

References

Bozdoğan, Sibel and Reşat Kasaba (1997) 'Introduction', in Sibel Bozdoğan and Reşat
    Kasaba (eds.), *Rethinking Modernity and National Identity in Turkey* (Seattle:
    University of Washington Press).
Chatterjee, Partha (1986) *Nationalist Thought and the Colonial World: A Derivative
    Discourse* (London: Zed Books).
Donzelot, Jacques (1991) *Kazoku ni kainyu suru shakai* (Tokyo: Shinyosha). Originally
    published in 1977 as *La Police des Familles* (Paris: Minuit).
Jayawardena, Kumari (1986) *Feminism and Nationalism in the Third World* (London:
    Zed Books).
Kandiyoti, Deniz (1987) 'Emancipated but Unliberated? Reflections on the Turkish
    Case', *Feminist Studies*, vol. 13, no. 2, Summer pp. 317–38.
Kandiyoti, Deniz (1989) 'Women and the Turkish State: Political Actors or Symbolic
    Pawns?', in Nira Yuval Davis and Floya Anthias (eds), *Woman–Nation–State*
    (London: Macmillan).
Kandiyoti, Deniz (1991) 'End of Empire: Islam, Nationalism and Women in Turkey',
    in Deniz Kandiyoti (ed.), *Women, Islam and the State* (Philadelphia, Pa.: Temple
    University Press).
Kandiyoti, Deniz (1997) 'Gendering the Modern: On Missing Dimensions in the Study
    of Turkish Modernity', in Sibel Bozdoğan and Reşat Kasaba (eds), *Rethinking Modernity
    and National Identity in Turkey* (Seattle, Wash.: University of Washington Press).
Koyama, Shizuko (1991) *Ryosai kenbo to iu kihan* ('Good wife and wise mother' as a
    modern norm) (Tokyo: Keisoshobo) (in Japanese).
Koyama, Shizuko (1999) *Katei no seisei to josei no kokuminka* (The birth of the *katei*
    type family and the inclusion of women in the nation) (Tokyo: Keisoshobo) (in
    Japanese).
Mosse, George (1988) *Nationalism and Sexuality: Middle Class Morality and Sexual
    Norms in Modern Europe* (Madison: University of Wisconsin Press).
Muta, Kazue (1996a) *Senryaku to shiteno kazoku: kindai Nihon no kokumin keisei to josei*
    (Family politics and women in modern Japan) (Tokyo: Shinyosha) (in Japanese).
Muta, Kazue 1996b. 'Nihongata kindai kazoku no seiritsu to kansei' (The formation
    of the modern family in Japan and its pitfalls), in Chizuko Ueno, Shun Inoue,
    Masachi Osawa, Munesuke Mita, Shunya Yoshimi (eds), *'Kazoku' no shakaigaku*
    (Sociology of the 'family') (Tokyo: Iwanami Shoten) (in Japanese).
Ochiai, Emiko (1989) *Kindai kazoku to feminizumu* (Modern families and feminism)
    (Tokyo: Keisoshobo) (in Japanese).

Sirman Nükhet (1989) 'Feminism in Turkey: A Short History', *New Perspectives on Turkey*, vol. 3, no. 1, Fall, pp. 1–34.

Sirman, Nükhet (2000a) 'Gender Construction and Nationalist Discourse: Dethroning the Father in the Early Turkish Novel', in Gunes-Ayata Feride Acar and Ayse (eds), *Gender and Identity Construction: Women of Central Asia, the Caucasus and Turkey* (Leiden: Brill).

Sirman Nükhet (2000b) 'Writing the Usual Love Story: The Fashioning of Conjugal and National Subjects in Turkey', in Victoria Ana Goddard (ed.), *Gender, Agency and Change: Anthropological Perspectives* (London: Routledge).

Sirman, Nükhet (2002) 'Kadınların Milliyeti' (Women's nation), *Modern Türkiye'de Siyasi Düşünce* (Political thoughts in modern Turkey), vol. 4 (Milliyetçilik, Istanbul: İletişim Yayıncılık).

Suzuki, Tadashi (1993) *Osuman teikoku no kenryoku to erito* (Power and elite in the Ottoman Empire) (Tokyo: Tokyo University Press) (in Japanese).

Tekeli, Şirin (1981) 'Women in Turkish Politics', in Nermin Abadan-Unat (ed.), *Women in Turkish Society* (Leiden: E. J. Brill).

Ueno, Chizuko (1998) *Nashonarizumu to jenda* (Engendering nationalism) (Tokyo: Seidosha) (in Japanese).

Yuval-Davis, Nira (1997) *Gender & Nation* (London: Sage Publications).

Yuval-Davis, Nira and Floya Anthias (1989) *Women–Nation–State* (London: Macmillan).

Part III

Integrating Japan and Developing Countries in the Global Context

8
Factory Women under Globalization: Incorporating Japanese Women into the Global Factory Debate

Mayumi Murayama

Introduction

Women working in factories have been a topic of heated debate since the time of the first Industrial Revolution in Britain (Engels, 1845). In the countries that followed Britain, such as France and the USA, women again played a crucial role as industrial labourers, contributing to the successful transformation of the national economy as well as to their households' livelihoods (Tilly and Scott, 1978; Dublin, 1979; Moran, 2002). Japan was no exception. Since the establishment of the first modern silk reeling mill in 1872 and during the subsequent era of the industrial revolution, female workers constituted the majority of the industrial workforce (Hosoi, 1954; Yamamoto, 1977; Nakamura, 1985; Tsurumi, 1990; Miyake, 1991; Molony, 1991). See Murayama (2003) for a detailed bibliography.

The issue of women's factory work re-emerged as an area of academic concern again in the late 1970s, but on a much wider scale. Since then there has been a growing body of literature on women's incorporation into the industrial workforce, especially in the developing countries. The growing concern over the subject reflects the extent and velocity of the global economic restructuring in which female labour has played an indispensable part. The symbol of the 'world market factory', producing goods exclusively for export to rich countries, and where the labour force is predominantly female, has drawn the attention of all strata of society.

While the situation of female factory workers in countries undergoing the process of development has been covered extensively, relatively little attention has been paid to the current situation of women workers in factories in the developed countries. However, because of the re-emergence of sweatshops, homeworking under substandard conditions, and the engagement of immigrant workers in these types of work, there is growing academic interest, (together with the active involvement of labour unions and NGOs in Western developed countries) in female factory work in these countries (Ross, 1997; Bonacich and Appelbaum, 2000; Louie, 2001;

Featherstone *et al.*, 2002; Rosen, 2002). The lack of research in the case of Japan is therefore a matter of serious concern, particularly as Japan has been one of the major players in the global shift with regard to factories.[1] This deficiency should be rectified with empirical studies that take into account the current debate on female work under globalization. The need for rigorous academic efforts is self-evident. If the massive incorporation of female workers in the developing countries took place as a result of the shifting of production bases from the developed to the developing countries, we would naturally presume that the shift also had a substantial effect on the women employed in those relocated factories. These are two sides of the same coin.

In contrast to the dearth of studies on contemporary conditions, however, there is a substantial body of literature on the history of Japanese factory women, particularly in the pre-Second World War period, mainly in Japanese (Murayama, 2003). What is needed, therefore, is to place the cases of Japanese factory women in the mainstream of debate and to identify the areas that require further research. This chapter attempts to take the first step in filling this vacuum, drawing heavily on secondary materials in addition to some primary information acquired through interviews with entrepreneurs and trade union activists.

The chapter consists of five sections. In the second section, I shall delineate the arguments and findings of some recent studies on female factory work, especially in the developing countries. In the third section there is a review of the literature, paying particular attention to the interconnectedness of female factory workers in both developed and developing countries. I shall also look at how the experiences of Japan and Japanese factory women have been incorporated in the analysis of factory women for the sake of identifying existing analytical gaps. In the fourth section, a longitudinal story of Japanese factory women is presented by piecing together the fragmented literature, literature that has dealt with the issue in specific periods and from specific approaches. The third and fourth sections are intended to set as a start point in which to locate the case of Japanese factory women in the interrelated context of women in global factories. Preliminary findings and some recommendations for further research are summarized in the concluding section.

Debate on female factory work in the developing countries

As mentioned above, there have been extensive studies on women's factory work in developing countries, especially since the late 1970s. While these reflect divergent views and approaches to the issue, a notable general feature is that the literature on the second wave of female factory workers reflects feminist concerns, focusing on the impact of factory work on the individual woman from the aspect of gender (Kung, 1978; Elson and Pearson, 1981; Salaff, 1981; Ong, 1987; Banerjee, 1991; Wolf, 1992; Safa, 1995; Fernandes,

1997; Kim, 1997; Lee, 1998; Murakami, 1999; Kabeer, 2000 see Elson and Wright (1996) for an extensive bibliography on the subject of gender issues in contemporary industrialization.) The new literature has also evoked renewed interest in the implications of factory work for the first generation of female workers as well.[2] In this section I shall delineate the main debates and findings of the recent studies, studies that demonstrate the depth and breadth of research on female factory work.

Three contrasting views about female factory work

Views have differed with respect to the impact of female factory work. One interpretation is that factory work has benefited women in a number of ways. Workers have economic power and consequently they enjoy greater autonomy and better positions in their households. In addition, employment in factory work itself contributes to their delaying marriage, offering them more freedom in selecting spouses and a temporary escape from parental control and household chores, as well as providing opportunities to have new experiences and broaden their horizons. This positive view is often underscored by the opinion that factory work provides better wages and more economic stability to women previously viewed as being engaged in unpaid labour, or even if paid, at wages and in working conditions inferior to those in factory employment (Lim, 1983; Addison and Demery, 1988; Foo and Lim, 1989).

On the other hand, critical views of the impacts of factory work on women are echoed by a larger number of mainly Marxist or socialist-feminists. They criticize the way the state and capital, for their own benefit, take advantage of gender-based discrimination against women, and create a new pattern of female subordination in factories based on gender relations and the gender ideologies embedded in the society as a whole. Female workers are most often confined to particular types of work classified as unskilled or semi-skilled. Their wages are much lower than those of their male counterparts. Long hours of tedious work, poor working environments, conditions that are apparent violations of the law, and bans on trade union activities are characteristics commonly observed all over the world in factories where female workers predominate. These features are pointed out and criticized as evidence of the exploitation of female labour by an alliance of capitalism and patriarchy (Edgren, 1982; Mather, 1985; Goonatilake and Goonesekere, 1988; Rao and Husain, 1991).

A third opinion sees rather complex and contradictory impacts of factory work on women (Elson and Pearson, 1981; Kung, 1978; Ong, 1987; Wolf, 1992; Safa, 1995). The analysis of this point of view is wider in scope, delineating the interfaces of different forces circumscribing the lives of factory workers, although the contexts in which the proponents of this approach present their mixed conclusions vary. A much-cited work by Elson and Pearson (1981) presents a comprehensive picture in which the dialectical relationship between factory work and the gender-based subordination of women takes varied forms. They suggest distinguishing three tendencies: a tendency to intensify the existing forms of gender subordination; a tendency to decompose existing forms of gender subordination; and a tendency to recompose new forms of gender subordination. They posit these possible courses of events as 'ways of analysing particular conjunctions of forces shaping women's lives' (Elson and Pearson, 1981, p. 31). Thus each consequence does not necessarily correspond to the assessment of impact as positive or negative. The authors suggest, instead, that in each situation in which the three tendencies are intertwined in a specific manner, complex changes occur in the lives of female workers. Citing the laudatory impact of factory work in changing the form of marriage arrangement from the early arranged-marriage type to a free-choice type, Elson and Pearson argue that the change has double-edged implications for women and the system of female subordination as a whole. Though seemingly a positive change that gives women autonomy in selecting their own spouses, they contend that it is the male in fact who exercises the choice, the female having been 'commoditized' in a marriage market. Elson and Pearson thus call attention to both the explicit and implicit consequences of changes, which are contextualized in the complex web of social and cultural forces of a given society.

Other empirical studies, such as the more recent studies of Wolf and Safa, find contradictory effects of factory work that occur in different dimensions of women's lives. By taking a closer look at the lives of factory workers, they have elicited multiple effects of factory work, effects that are shaped by different economic, social and cultural factors specific to each life situation. Based on her study of Javanese female factory workers, Wolf finds that factory employment reaps some benefits for female workers in the familial sphere – for example, more participation in family decisions or the creation of new boundaries that allow longer periods of escape from parental control. On the other hand, these changes in family relationships and control do not lessen the level of exploitation in such employment (Wolf, 1992, p. 8). And Safa, from her comparative study of factory women in Puerto Rico, the Dominican Republic and Cuba, also acknowledges that positive changes have occurred more often in the household than in the workplace. She notes that 'industrial workers have begun to assume more authority in the family, though they are relatively weak at the level of the workplace and the state, where power must be exercised collectively' (Safa, 1995, p. 178).

Structuralist versus actor-orientated methodologies

The above three standpoints with respect to the impacts of female factory labour are not, however, mutually exclusive. The debate carried on so far has not dealt with precisely the same phenomena or issues, and certainly not the same study sites. Rather, the extensive literature on the subject has been produced with little effort being made to conflate the points in the debate. Thus the differences in emphases largely reflect differences in methodological framework, the individual researcher's subjectivity, and variations in the social and cultural settings of the research fields. I shall discuss these three differences below.

There are two distinctive methodological approaches used to assess the impact of factory labour on women's lives: structuralist and actor-orientated. The former approach attaches more importance to the structure and process in which existing gender relations are constructed, though conceptualizations and names for the 'structure' vary. Among such names are 'sexual division of labour', 'female subordination', 'system of patriarchy', and 'capitalism'. Despite such variations there is a common line of argument which holds that the 'structure' determines the role of women *vis-à-vis* men, femininity and masculinity (gender identity), and the relative positions of males and females (gender relations) in society. Moreover, the way in which these presumed gender conditions are transferred to the work place, to benefit capital, is also conditioned by various structural factors. Therefore, the structuralists' main area of analysis in this approach is the workplace, where there is an interplay between predefined gender relations and the profit-maximizing motives of capital, usually resulting in intensifying female subordination. Data has been accumulated on wages, working environments and management styles, and the findings from these studies tend to draw negative implications about the overall effects of industrialization on women and gender relations.

While the actor-orientated approach starts from the same notion of gender relations as the structuralist approach – namely, that women, by virtue of their gender, are in a disadvantageous position under male domination in both the household and society, it makes much more of the actions and perceptions of the female workers themselves. In this approach, female 'agency', 'capabilities', 'resistance', and 'accommodation' are key concepts to describe and analyse the changes that occur in individual women. What is distinctive in this approach is that, instead of judging the impact of factory employment, whether as positive or negative, in the light of pre-set economic or social goals such as equality and autonomy, it interprets the responses of the female workers to their work as well as the interactions between them and other actors (male family members and management, for example). Consequently, these actor-orientated studies have a wider scope as their loci of analysis, ranging from the household to the workplace, with more emphasis on the former, and their findings show that factory work has multiple effects on the workers in each social space and at each life stage.

Researchers' subjectivity

Discussing disagreements between ethnographers, Heider (1988) explains how each ethnographer's subjectivity influences the drawing of conclusions different from those of others.[3] Although it is impossible to know how biased the subjectivity factor makes the outcome of each study, it is important to keep this limitation in mind and to examine the context of the debates.[4] Here I shall illustrate two examples of the subjective evaluation of the impacts of female factory work, the one representing a positive judgement and the other, a positive interpretation.

As mentioned earlier, one of the assertions of the positive view is that factory work is, for women in the Third World, a good option as an occupation in terms of wages, working conditions and social prestige. The following remark is typical of the positive argument:

> in terms of the *consequences* of export factory labour, women workers are clearly economically better off as a result of their jobs than they were before. They are also better off compared to other, much more numerous, female wage workers employed as domestic servants, agricultural labourers, helpers in small local shops, and unpaid family labour. (Foo and Lim, 1989, pp. 215–16, emphasis as in the original)

It should be noted that the same authors acknowledge the evidence of female subordination in the workplace:

> Ideologies about women's roles do play an important role in structuring the female labour market ... These characteristics make women efficient, productive, well-behaved workers. Their short working life, for example, ensures low average seniority and hence low wages, as well as a weak commitment to the labour force and high group turnover, making labour organization difficult. Ideology also causes sex discrimination by employers in the structuring of the labour force, for example, restricting managerial and supervisory positions in female-intensive industries to males. (Foo and Lim, 1989, p. 221)

From the statements cited above, apparently the grounds for the researchers' judgement are comparison with other women and with the women's previous work experience. In other words, factory work is assessed positively on the grounds that it is 'better than nothing' or 'better than the other' work. This optimistic view that highlights the bright side of the situation may come under criticism from those who take a different stance. A re-evaluation of the positive position, especially by using quantitative measures of wage differentials among different 'female occupations', however, is absent.

The second case of subjectivity is concerned with the interpretation of changes caused by female factory work. One example is the criticism by Foo and Lim of Elson and Pearson's views about female 'commoditization on the marriage market', quoted above. They contend that 'self-selection of one's marriage partner through dating is seen by the women themselves as a progressive development, one which reflects a further exercise of personal autonomy, choice and freedom by young women' (Foo and Lim, 1989, p. 223). Implied in their arguments is an emphasis on the difference in the perception of (in this case, Malaysian) female workers and (Western) researchers. The issue of perception of female workers is very important and we have to deal with these 'perception' or 'consciousness' issues with great caution, as Wolf suggests (1922, p. 25): 'We have access to our subjects' mediated representations of themselves and can portray only our own mediated understanding and representation of them as best as we can.'

Regional variations

It is important to bear in mind regional differences in the effects of female factory work. It is difficult, however, to make an adequate comparison from the available literature because the studies of specific cases in particular countries or regions already reflect the individual authors' subjectivity and methodological inclinations. Nevertheless, it is possible to point out several significant factors underscoring regional and country differences.

One is the conditions of economic development; the level of industrialization *vis-à-vis* that of other economic sectors, in particular. The degree of industrialization is determined by factors specific to the country concerned, on the one hand, and to the state of the global economy on the other. In conjunction with the nature of the labour market, and government strategies and policies with respect to industrial development, human resource development, and the availability of formal and informal welfare systems, it determines the supply and demand of the labour force. In other words, a particular category of female workers is constructed, and particular sets of social and economic impacts are created predominantly through the interplay of those factors.

The degree and the nature of industrialization set the available employment options for the women in a society. The predominance of an export orientation in Third-World industrialization, and global economic restructuring, has caused a massive entry of women into the workforce since the late 1980s, described by the term 'the feminization of labour'. This 'feminization' varies from country to country. Also it should be noted that 'feminization' refers to the increase of females not only in formal employment but more extensively in informal sectors such as small workshops, sweatshops and homeworking. The actual job descriptions as well as working conditions, including the wage range, available to women are determined precisely by the way a country, with its economic and political endowments, is incorporated into the international division of labour. In many countries, for example, the garment industry is the first in the manufacturing sector to employ women on a massive scale. The availability of other alternatives, such as electronics and more capital-intensive industries, then provides female workers with firmer footholds in the labour market by creating space for negotiation and standing up to management, or by making it possible for them to avail themselves of other job options. The level of industrialization also affects female workers status in the female labour market. In a country where industrialization is relatively advanced, female participation in manufacturing work may no longer be a novel phenomena, whereas in another country at an early industrialization stage, the female workers are likely to be first-generation factory women, or in many cases to be the first women in their families to take employment outside the home. The different positions of female factory workers in society influence the perception of workers themselves as well as that of society as a whole regarding the occupations and those who are engaged in them. It is not surprising that first-generation women are apt to face more criticism and constraints in terms of social prestige than those who come later, since the first-comers have to challenge the pre-existing stereotypes and ideology governing female roles in the society.

It should not be forgotten that the range of employment opportunities in a country affects the male labour market too. The relative positions of male work give different meanings to female work and female labourers' contributions. In some countries where the economic marginality of men is quite visible (for example, the cases of Cuba, Puerto Rico and the Dominican Republic presented by Safa), factory work has contributed to enhancing the importance of women's work in the household (Safa, 1995, p. 179).

Differences in the level of industrialization, however, cannot fully explain the country or regional differences in the position of female workers in workplaces as well as in households and society. Comparing the status of female factory workers in Singapore and South Korea, Phongpaichit (1988) finds a marked difference between these two successful cases of industrialization. In her analysis, as well as the existence of a relatively abundant pool of potential labour in Korea, a stronger social bias against women that prevails not only in the labour market but also in general is another, and very important, factor in undermining the economic value of women's work there. Thus variations in the social, cultural and ideological backdrop against which female factory work takes place and is interpreted should be considered when attempting to understand its implications. Several authors are concerned with the influence of the family system and the females' (especially the daughters') position in it in defining the implications of factory work (Kung, 1978; Salaff, 1981; Wolf, 1992, for example). Both the studies of factory daughters of Taiwan (Kung) and of Hong Kong (Salaff) focus on the image of a filial and obedient daughter, whose work in the factory is consistent with her expected role, that of repaying the debt that she owes to her parents. Therefore, their wage earnings neither confer upon the daughters the right to control their incomes nor challenge their parents' authority (Kung, 1978, pp. 124–5; Salaff, 1981, pp. 11–12).[5] In contrast, Wolf's study on Central Java shows that factory daughters there are subject to fewer controls by their parents than are their Taiwanese counterparts (Wolf, 1992, pp. 174–5, 187–8). Wolf notes that local kinship systems, and gender and family ideologies strongly influence the effects of industrialization on women's lives (Wolf, 1992, p. 257).

One of the most visible instruments of female control exerted by males in the society is female seclusion. Female seclusion as a social norm as well as an ideology is considered to influence the impact of female factory work in two ways: by affecting both social and individual perceptions of factory work, and by embodying a social sanction against those who deviate from the norm. Female confinement to the home is widely prevalent cross-culturally. The degree of observance, however, varies with the country, region and community, as well as with the period. It also varies from class to class within the same community. Generally speaking, the countries in the region stretching from North Africa across the Middle East and the northern plains of the Indian subcontinent to Bangladesh, countries where female seclusion is quite strictly observed, have shorter histories of industrialization and, especially important, have little experience of female wage labour, much less female factory work. These differences may turn out to have significantly different implications for female factory work there than in East and South East Asia or Latin America.

Interconnectedness of women in global factories

Theoretical approaches

In the preceding section I presented the different implications of female factory work for different women and in different societies. Missing from the presentation was the aspect of the global nature of factory work and its consequent influences on workers. As the operation of factories is interconnected, changes in a factory, a company headquarters or a society affect factory women in distant locations.

Maria Mies, along with German-based feminist scholars such as Claudia von Werlhof and Veronika Bennholdt-Thomsen, has brought up the interrelatedness between women of the developed and the developing countries, drawing primarily on the new international division of labour (NIDL) perspective and the works of Rosa Luxemburg (Mies, 1986). Luxemburg argued that capitalism needs what she called 'non-capitalist milieux and strata' for the extension of the labour force, resources and, above all, the extension of markets. In the Luxemburg's analysis, the non-capitalist milieux and strata were exemplified by the peasants and artisans with their natural economy, and the concept of colony was used in conventional terms with geographical delimitations. Mies and others, however, have extended the scope of non-capitalist milieux and strata to include women's non-wage work, not only in the underdeveloped countries but also in the developed ones, thereby juxtaposing colony with the family and the domesticated housewife, and colonization with 'housewifization' (Mies, 1986, pp. 74–111). These authors have argued that capital accumulation as a result of the system of capitalist patriarchy can be understood only in the worldwide context in which the manipulation of women's labour and the sexual division of labour plays a crucial part (Mies, 1986, p. 34).

Mies states that the development of the capitalist world economy has been based on a particular international division of labour as well as the sexual division of labour. The logic governing both divisions is expressed in the zero-sum rules: the progress of one pole implies the retrogression of the other (Mies, 1986, p. 112). In contrast to the old international division of labour, in which production of raw materials and production of machine-made goods were divided between the colonies and the developed countries, in the NIDL manufacturing process, labour cost-intensive production is concentrated in the ex-colonies, or the 'developing countries', as they are now called, and the developed countries have become markets for the products.

A distinct feature of NIDL is that it is integrated with the sexual division of labour. As we know today, women have been playing indispensable roles as producers and consumers in the developing and the developed countries, respectively. The important mechanism that makes women the optimal cheap and docile labour source is the conversion of international and sexual based divisions of labour. The housewifization of women, or more precisely, the identification of women in both the developed and the developing countries as being basically housewives, places men and women on an unequal footing in the labour market – men as free wage labourers, and women as non-free housewives. Work done by women, whether they earn an income from it or not, is defined as an 'activity' rather than a job, and is thus reduced to work supplementary to that of the male bread-winner. But whereas women in the developed countries have been able to become non-working housewives because of exploitation of the colonies, the majority of women in the developing countries will never be in that position. Consequently, a division between women has been created – with those in the developing countries being mainly producers, and those in the developed countries, mainly consumers.

As we have seen, in the analysis elaborated by Mies, the developed and developing countries are depicted in their relationship as if they were situated at opposite ends of a seesaw. They cannot keep playing without each other, and the height that the one reaches is sustained only by the depth to which the other descends. Moreover, the seesaw is always tilted towards one end – the developed countries. As a result, women in the developing countries work as cheap labour in order to produce goods to be marketed in the developed countries. So what is the role of women in developed countries such as Japan? Mies states that as producers they are the first to be dismissed as a consequence of NIDL, and then they are mobilized as consumers, housewives, mothers and sex objects. Although she acknowledges the displacement of women from the workplace, mainly factories, in the developed countries, and the possibility of their being engaged in electronic homeworking or traditional piecework, she stops her discussion of those displaced women there because her main interest in women in the developed countries is in their role as consumer-housewives, rather than producers, in sustaining the present framework of the world economy.

While the debate on NIDL has dealt mainly with the movement of capital (particularly multinational corporations) since the 1970s, in the era of the 1990s and after, 'globalization' has emerged as an appropriate concept for grasping the ever wider and deeper degree of global integration. Within the globalization debate, Sassen (1998) has elucidated the linkage between the growth of export production in Third World countries and the massive increase of immigration from the Third World to the USA. She posits a number of systemic links between the two phenomena. One of the links is that both the employment of immigrant workers in the developed countries and offshore production in the developing countries are ways of securing a low-wage labour force, and of fighting the demands of organized workers in the developed countries. One example of massive employment of migrant women, women who suffer double sex and class discrimination in the developed countries, is in the growing use of sweatshops and industrial homeworking. In order to meet the demands of the higher-income social groups, which require labour-intensive services, there is a need for firms to have establishments in the developed countries, especially in the big cities. Immigrant women have emerged as a labour source for these establishments.

It is well known that the garment and footwear industries have created sweatshops in the developed countries, relying heavily on immigrant women. The increasing prevalence of sweatshops in the USA has been reported since the early 1980s (see, for example, Fuentes and Ehrenreich, 1983). From the international relations perspective, Steans (1998) has described how global restructuring in the 1980s encouraged the growth of a new proletariat in both the North and the South, with women ghettoized in assembly-line work with poor pay and prospects. In the garment industry in both Europe and North America, employers who could not relocate abroad moved to feminize their workforce and this resulted in the re-emergence of sweatshops and homeworking (Steans, 1998, p. 135).

The fact that some industries, such as textiles and garments, footwear and electronics are heavy employers of female workers in any country may indicate a possible conflict of interests between women workers in industrialized countries and those in developing countries. This problem was recognized in the early 1980s by Canadian researchers (North–South Institute, 1985). As in the USA, female factory workers in Canada have experienced adverse effects from the inflow of developing country imports. In 1982, while women comprised only 23.7 per cent of the total manufacturing labour force, they represented 63.4 per cent of the workers in six industries: textiles, knitting mills, clothing, leathers, electrical products, and toys, games and sporting goods (North–South Institute, 1985, p. 25). In those female-intensive industries, it was immigrant women who made up the major portion of the workforce. It was estimated that in Montreal, Toronto and Winnipeg, approximately half of textile workers and almost all the clothing industry workers were immigrant women (North–South Institute, 1985, p. 27). Because of the disadvantage these women suffered in terms of their sex, race and level of education, they faced the most difficulties in finding alternative employment. The measures of the Canadian government in the 1970s to combat the situation were a combination of import control and financial assistance measures for affected companies hit by import competition. Import control, however, was not very successful in terms of employment protection. After the firms introduced labour-displacing technology in order to improve their competitiveness, workers kept losing their jobs (North–South Institute, 1985, p. 38).

Incorporation of Japan in research on female factory work

A review of how Japan and contemporary factory women have been treated as subjects of research indicates that the focus of attention has shifted over time.

At the end of the 1970s and in the early 1980s, some researchers-cum-activists were concerned about the exporting of the 'tragic tales of Japanese factory women' (discussed below) to Third-World countries (Shiozawa, 1983; Hiroki, 1986). Shiozawa (1983) suggested that Japanese companies, which went into other Asian countries to escape mounting labour costs at home, brought miserable conditions for female workers that were reminiscent of the harsh conditions experienced by female workers in prewar Japan. The lives of authors such as Shiozawa and Hiroki are illustrative of a particular type of linkage between the experiences of Japanese and Asian female factory workers. They once worked in a silk industry workers' trade union in Japan and later established an NGO to support Asian female workers who were suffering under the strict control of foreign, predominantly Japanese, capital (Hiroki, 1999). They have analysed the problem mainly within the framework of North–South issues – that is, in terms of Japanese multinationals exploiting Asian workers. This approach reflects the critical views of the activities of Japanese multinational companies operating in South East Asia that were widely held by grassroots 'groups at the time.[6] And on a global scale, Third World countries were themselves condemning the unequal trade relationship between the North and the South. Their claims were represented in the forms of dependency theory and the declaration of the New International Economic Order.

Other Japanese researchers did not immediately pursue the interrelatedness of Japan and female workers as a relationship between Japanese capital and female workers in other Asian countries until another surge of Japanese foreign direct investment (FDI) into Asian countries took place from the latter half of the 1980s and in particular during the 1990s. Important studies on female factory work under Japanese management were carried out by non-Japanese scholars (Ong, 1987; Kim, 1997). Ong (1987) studied factory women at three Japanese electronics factories in Malaysia, and observed that Japanese corporate strategies controlled the workers by resorting to local communal values, such as the social obligations through which the workers were bound to their rural households, rather than by encouraging individualism among the workers, as some Western firms did (Ong, 1987, p. 174). Ong found an ethnic hierarchical relationship between Japanese management and Malay workers[7] that coincided with a gender hierarchy and supported her analytical discourse in terms of Japanese males dominating Asian women.

Kim (1997) conducted her fieldwork in the Masan Free Export Zone (MAFEZ) in Korea in 1987. Kim states that Korea's economic development based on female factory workers paralleled that of Japan in the Meiji period. The idea of mobilizing the female labour force for light manufacturing industries was transplanted by President Park Chung Hee, an ardent admirer of Japan's modernization during the Meiji period (Kim, 1997, p. 3). Being close to Japan, the factories in MAFEZ were mainly owned by Japanese capital. Kim carried out participatory observation while working for three months in a Japanese electronics factory. This was just before a nationwide labour uprising in Korea. Kim describes how the system of labour control was perceived by the workers. Although the conditions in electronics factories were better than those in garment factories, such practices as mandatory overtime, forced free labour[8] and differentiated rates of bonuses and monetary incentives were very unpopular among the workers. The management compared the company to a happy family and called for workers' loyalty, but the system as a whole encouraged the women to compete against each other for the sake of defect-free, high productivity and, according to Kim, increased tension in the workplace, as it pitted workers against each other (Kim, 1997, p. 55).

Since the end of the 1980s, there has been a massive shift of production overseas, mainly to China, by Japanese garment manufacturers. Using questionnaire surveys of workers, and interviews with management, Fujii (1997a, 1997b, 2001) examined the labour management of Japanese companies in China (three garment factories and one making electronic goods) and the female workers' responses. Fujii states that the Japanese management style, which emphasized only the low labour cost of female workers, has become increasingly unsustainable in China, especially in comparison with management styles at American and European companies, which provide better welfare facilities and wider scope for promotion. Fujii also refers to possible negative implications for Japanese women of the hollowing out of the Japanese manufacturing sector. Although she does not elaborate, Fujii mentions that displaced female workers have faced the degradation of working conditions through the liberalization of night work for women and the proliferation of part-time employment in the service sector, including care services.

The global restructuring that has taken place since the late 1980s has contributed to the diffusion of informal work, in both developed and developing countries. Ward (1990) has termed it 'triple shifts' for women. She argues that under global restructuring, defined by her as the emergence of a 'global assembly line', many women, including those in the USA, work 'triple shifts' – that is, at housework, informal-sector work, and formal labour. Ward holds that in addition to the familiar 'double shift' of housework and formal work, women's work takes on another dimension – informal work – necessitated by economic conditions caused by global restructuring. The informal work of women, together with housework, subsidizes workers' wages, lowers the risks of capitalists, and maintains the class position of households (Ward, 1990, p. 8). Despite an increase in net employment in some sectors and some countries, globalization has affected the quality of employment, in a negative way, particularly for women. Economic restructuring, together with globalization, has brought about flexibility and deregulation in the patterns of employment, leading to expansion of the informal economy in both developed and developing countries.

Goka (2003) has addressed the issue of the informal economy in the Japanese context. He concludes that the informalization of the economy is in progress at the time of writing in Japan. The number of workers in regular employment has been decreasing since 1997, especially among female workers. This implies the fragmentation of employment tenure as well as the spread of an employment pattern in which the labour contract is not very clear. One of the causes of the informalization of employment in Japan, according to Goka, is the hollowing out of industry brought about by increasing offshore production of Japanese companies as well as the reverse import of the products. Under the pressure to reduce prices, it is clear that wages and working conditions in the Japanese employment market have been dragged down by those of other Asian countries, particularly China.

Female textile workers in Japan

The textile industry in Japan

Keeping the above-mentioned theoretical as well as factual implications in mind, in this section I shall piece together the story of female factory work in the Japanese textile industry along a time line starting at the end of the nineteenth century and extending to the present.

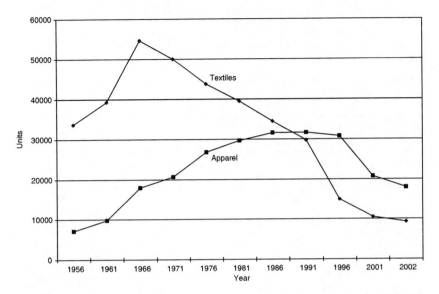

Source: Compiled from Ministry of Economy, Trade and Industry, *Kogyo tokei hyo*.

Figure 8.1 Changes in number of textile and apparel industry units, 1956–2002

As was the case in many other countries, Japanese industrialization and economic development started with the textile industry. Beginning in the 1890s, the industry grew steadily until the 1930s. It went into decline after the 1960s (see Figures 8.1 and 8.2). The textile industry's share of all manufacturing, in terms of numbers of establishments and employees, has been in continuous decline since the 1950s (see Table 8.1). As the major industry driving the Japanese economy in the 1950s, textiles gave way to heavy chemicals in the 1960s, and from the late 1970s, machinery came to the fore (see Figure 8.3).

Thus, over the twentieth century, the textile industry in Japan has experienced a dramatic transition from growth to maturity, and then to decline. Imports of textiles and clothing into the Japanese market started to increase during the 1960s and surged in the 1970s. Yet until the mid-1980s the Japanese textile industry retained some international competitiveness and import penetration of the Japanese market by foreign textile producers was moderate. Around the mid-1980s, import penetration[9] of Japanese markets by industrializing Asia[10] was 4.4 per cent and 9.4 per cent in textiles and clothing, respectively. The figures for the USA, Canada and Australia were 3.5 per cent and 16.6 per cent, 5.4 per cent and 13.6 per cent, and 12.6 per cent and 11.7 per cent, respectively (Yamawaki, 1992, p. 91). Although the Japanese textile industry, particularly for silk and

238

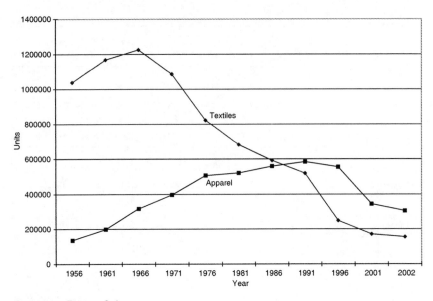

Source: as Figure 8.1.

Figure 8.2 Changes in number of textile and apparel industry employees, 1956–2002

cotton textiles, was orientated towards exporting from the beginning, the industry has been slipping in competitiveness since the mid-1970s. Synthetic products have replaced fabrics made of natural fibres as the main export items, an indication that Japanese industry has moved upstream into the highly capital-intensive production of synthetic fibres.

As mentioned above, the picture changed dramatically in the mid-1980s. The Plaza Accord, reached at a conference of finance ministers and governors of central banks of the G5 countries in 1985, accelerated the restructuring of the Japanese economy, particularly the textile industry. The rapid appreciation of the yen that followed sparked massive overseas direct investment by Japanese manufacturers as a means of reducing production costs, with investment concentrated in neighbouring Asian countries. Towards the end of the 1960s, Japanese textile and fibre firms began to invest abroad and shift production offshore. The initial places for investment were mainly newly industrializing economies (NIEs) such as Taiwan and Korea; later, the ASEAN countries and China replaced these. In recent years, some companies have been shifting their production bases from the NIEs and ASEAN to China, or moving directly to China, bypassing the NIEs and ASEAN. In the meantime, the import of manufactured commodities from those countries has increased substantially. With respect to clothing

Table 8.1 Textile and apparel industry, percentage shares of manufacturing

Share, Percentage	1956	1961	1966	1971	1976	1981	1986	1991	1996	2001
Number of establishments	100.0	100.0	100.0	100.0	100.0	100.0	100.0	100.0	100.0	100.0
Textiles	17.3	16.1	14.9	12.6	10.3	9.1	7.9	6.9	4.0	3.3
Apparel	3.6	4.0	4.9	5.2	6.3	6.8	7.2	7.4	8.3	6.6
Number of employees	100.0	100.0	100.0	100.0	100.0	100.0	100.0	100.0	100.0	100.0
Textiles	18.9	14.3	12.5	9.9	7.8	6.5	5.4	4.6	2.5	1.9
Apparel	2.5	2.4	3.2	3.6	4.8	4.9	5.1	5.1	5.5	3.9
Value of manufactured goods	100.0	100.0	100.0	100.0	100.0	100.0	100.0	100.0	100.0	100.0
Textiles	15.6	10.1	8.4	6.2	4.9	3.6	3.0	2.3	1.3	1.0
Apparel	1.2	1.1	1.5	1.4	1.7	1.4	1.5	1.4	1.6	1.0
Value added (millions yen)	100.0	100.0	100.0	100.0	100.0	100.0	100.0	100.0	100.0	100.0
Textiles	1.1	1.1	7.6	6.0	5.1	3.9	3.2	2.5	1.5	1.2
Apparel	1.1	1.1	1.7	1.6	2.2	2.0	2.0	1.9	1.9	1.4

Source: As Figure 8.1.

240

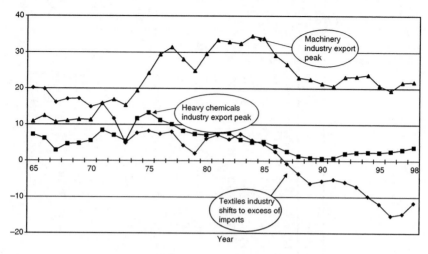

Note: The production/domestic demand (production + imports − exports) ratio is replaced with (production/domestic demand − 1)* 100. This ratio expresses the production surplus/shortage compared to domestic demand, measuring an industry's international competitiveness.

Sources: Figure 1.1.18, Ministry of Economy, Trade and Industry (2001).

Figure 8.3   Developments in Japan's industrial structure, 1965–98

Table 8.2   Japanese imports of clothing and accessories, by country, 2002

Country	Import value (US$000s)	Percentage share
China	13,705,568	78.2
Italy	996,365	5.7
Vietnam	473,006	2.7
Korea	421,016	2.4
USA	260,278	1.5
France	241,348	1.4
Thailand	239,385	1.3
Indonesia	162,068	0.9
Malaysia	120,255	0.7
UK	109,250	0.6
Other	800,933	4.6
Total	17,529,472	100.0

Source: Ministry of Economy, Trade and Industry (2003a).

and accessories, China alone accounts for almost 80 per cent of total imports (see Table 8.2).

In 1987, Japan became a net importer of textiles and clothing (Yamawaki, 1992, p. 111). The surge of imported textile commodities in the Japanese domestic market has further weakened the domestic textile manufacturers that had been losing competitiveness because of high labour costs. This has led to firm closures and employee lay-offs. The number of textile establishments, including clothing manufacturers, decreased from approximately 66,000 in 1986 to 31,000 in 2001, while employment declined by half, from over 1 million workers in 1986 to 0.5 million in 2001.[11] Import penetration[12] of textiles increased substantially over the decade of the 1990s; In the year 2000, textile imports reached 72 per cent (Yokota, 2001).

Employment issues in the prewar period

The industrial revolution took place in Japan between the latter half of the 1880s and 1907. The cotton-spinning and silk-reeling industries played a key role. As in other countries, the textile industry in Japan has been a female-led industry. Female workers constituted more than 60 per cent of all manufacturing workers, with the highest percentage, 95 per cent, in silk-reeling and 80 per cent in cotton spinning (Nishinarita, 1985, p. 12).

Although manual reeling had been done by women since ancient times, the modern textile industry began in the 1870s under the Meiji government, which promoted policies based on a 'rich country and strong army'. With the export earnings from the textile industry, the government purchased capital goods, including weapons, and built up the foundation of a machinery industry as well as a strong army (Yamamoto, 1977).

The first modern silk-reeling mill was established in 1872 as a public enterprise, with French technology and experts, including female workers, who taught Japanese women how to operate the machines. In contrast to the situation in subsequent years, the first female workers included the daughters of the ruling class of feudal Japan. Despite government efforts to recruit female workers, initial public response was fairly negative, mainly because of the fear of the unknown environment represented by a modern factory with foreign managers. The fact, for instance, that the foreigners drank wine sparked a widespread rumour that they drank human blood. In some localities, the district government resorted to legal measures to gather workers. With mounting pressure from the government, local leaders, then the ruling class, sent their own family members to the factories in order to persuade others to follow. Some of the pioneer workers, though young, were proud to learn the modern technology and later became instrumental in diffusing modern reeling technology to other parts of Japan (Kamijo, 1978; Wada, 1978; Hayata, 1997).

From the latter half of the 1890s, the rapid growth of industry as well as the rise of modern cotton-spinning mills led to a serious shortage of workers. Workers, mainly the young daughters of tenant or marginal farmers, were recruited from remote areas of Japan by middlemen. As of 1901, female workers under 20 years of age constituted 53 per cent and 66.2 per cent of all the female workers in the cotton-spinning industry and the silk industry, respectively (Nishinarita, 1985, p. 13). The terms of the contracts between workers and management were extremely disadvantageous for the workers. During the contract period, a worker was not allowed to leave, and if she did, she had to compensate the firm. On the other hand, the management could dismiss workers at will. The unilateral nature of the contract stemmed from the arrangement by which the workers, or rather their guardians, were given advances at the time of signing the employment contract. Thus the workers were not free labourers and, through the system of advances, fell into a situation similar to that of bonded slaves. Moreover, a grade-based wage system[13] and the hostels run by the companies, where most of the workers from remote villages lived, were notorious instruments of strict labour control. In the hostels, workers were provided with moral education, and exploitation was disguised in the form of traditional family values. Companies demanded devotion from the women as filial daughters and loyal workers (Yamamoto, 1977; Nakamura and Molteni, 1985). Female workers at that time worked both day and night shifts at half the wages of their contemporaries at India's cotton-spinning mills (Nishinarita, 1985, p. 14).

In 1916, the Factory Act, which prohibited the employment of children under 12 years of age, came into effect, five years after its enactment. Although there were loopholes in the law, it did indeed reduce the number of child labourers. The Factory Act was later amended in 1923 (enforced in 1926) to prohibit night work for female workers after a certain period from the enforcement of the law. This led to the replacement of female by male workers, and to technological rationalization. Along with the movement in the 1930s from the textile industry to heavy industry as the primary manufacturing sector, in 1933 the ratio of women in the total industrial labour force fell for the first time to less than half (Nishinarita, 1985, p. 20). The recruitment policy of factories had gradually shifted from indiscriminate recruitment to selective recruitment based on aptitude, and employment based on advances declined accordingly. Thus the terms of employment were slightly improved for the workers. Nevertheless, the miserable conditions of female workers as a whole did not change very much, as Wakizo Hosoi showed in his seminal book, *Joko aishi* (The pitiful history of female factory workers) (Hosoi, 1954).

During the war period between 1937 and 1945, economic activity was totally under the control of the government. Many silk factories were closed because of a shortage of raw materials, since instead of mulberry cultivation for silkworm culture, farmers began to concentrate on growing grain and vegetables. Also, many of the cotton textile factories were converted into production lines for war-related equipment such as parachutes (Shiozawa, 1971; Hayata, 1997). In the meantime, an acute shortage of male labour because of the war led to a rapid increase in female labour in the machinery industry. The number of female workers in this sector surpassed those in the silk industry in 1940, and in cotton-spinning the following year. Under the war-orientated regime, females from 14 to 24 years of age were mobilized to fill the vacancies left by male labour in various areas in the economy. It should be noted, however, that it was unmarried young women who were mobilized. Women as heads of households, as wives and mothers, were exempt, as they are were considered to be pillars of society, and were needed to safeguard traditional family values and systems (Nishinarita, 1985).

The defeat in the war in 1945 had far-reaching effects, not only for the economy but also for the value systems Japanese society had embraced. The American-led occupation forces carried out dynamic political, economic and social reforms. As part of the reforms, basic labour laws were enacted that guaranteed trade union rights for workers and promised better working conditions. However, the actual conditions of the workers did not change overnight. Let us take the example of the silk industry. The postwar government decided to make this industry the basis for the recovery of the war-damaged economy. Females, including those who had gone back to their villages during the war, were called up again to the silk factories. What they found there, however, was the same strict control through hostel arrangements, and even lower wages than they had known in the prewar period (Shiozawa, 1971, 1983).

Of course, the social and economic environment for the workers was not completely the same as before. A notable difference was in union activities. The trade union movement in the textile industry began in the 1930s – that is, in the prewar period – and leadership was in the hands of male workers, even though their numbers in the textile industry were small. Nevertheless, some female workers became aware that they were being exploited and involved themselves actively in the movement (Yamanouchi, 1975; Yamamoto, 1977; Takai, 1980; Suzuki, 1989; Hayata, 1997). In the course of their struggle, they endured various forms of harrassment from the companies' management. For example, management appealed to the female workers' guardians to make the women stop their involvement in the movement, claiming that they would be in danger sexually from involvement in trade union activities with male workers. This self-serving linkage by the management of female workers' sexual vulnerability and trade unionism was observed in both prewar and postwar periods (Yamamoto, 1977; Suzuki, 1989; Hayata, 1997). However, in the atmosphere of democratization in the immediate postwar period, the workers persistently placed their demands before the management and succeeded eventually in having them addressed. Small gains such as an improvement in meals and an end to obligatory, unpaid work, such as having to clean the factory floors before and after working hours, might seem insignificant from the perspective of the broader labour movement, but being related to the day-to-day lives of the workers, these achievements were an important step forward for them. Besides the improvements at their workplaces, the female workers also gained by broadening their social horizons through contact with young males during cultural activities (Shiozawa, 1971, 1983).

The female labour market in postwar Japan

From 1953 to 1973 the Japanese economy recorded high growth levels and over these two decades there was a fundamental restructuring of the female labour force. As was seen above, the textile industry in Japan began to lose its competitiveness because of rising labour costs and competition with the NIEs. The textile industry's share of female employment in industry as a whole decreased to 26.2 per cent in 1964 from 45.7 per cent in 1955. The textile industry had been outstripped, most notably by the machinery industry, and the share that female labour occupied in the latter in the whole grew from 19.2 per cent to 28.2 per cent over the same period (Fujii, 1997a, p. 77). Change was striking, not only in the sectoral make-up of industry but also in the characteristics of female workers. A decline in the birth rate and an increase in high school enrolment, against a backdrop of improved living standards, caused a serious shortage of young labourers. Initially, young labourers, both male and female, were mobilized in groups from less developed regions. They were referred to as 'golden eggs', denoting the scarcity of these – to management, they were lucky finds. But the wave of demographic and economic changes covered almost the whole of Japan, and it was housewives, as part-time workers, who eventually filled the gap.

The employment of housewives as part-time workers started in the electrical machinery industry from around the mid-1960s and then spread to other sectors (Fujii, 1997a, p. 79). Subsequently, a dual female labour market was created, with large-scale firms hiring young, unmarried women as regular employees and small-scale firms employing middle-aged and older women as casual or part-time employees. The two types of employment are marked by a large difference in terms of wages and other conditions. From management's viewpoint this is an efficient recycling of female workers as low-paid, unskilled labour: the young workers are retired early before they acquire any seniority, and later, when they are housewives, are re-employed as part-time workers, again at low wages. Under the Japanese system of lifetime employment, mainly for male workers, and the concept of a 'family wage' paid to a male breadwinner, salaries and wages for females have been perceived as subsidiary to those of the male mainstay of the family, thereby reinforcing gender inequality, both in the labour market and in the home.

After what is referred to in Japan as the 'oil shock' of 1973, the Japanese economy entered a new phase. In order to strengthen export competitiveness, firms rationalized production by adopting microelectronic technology, and factory as well as office automation. In the initial downturn of the economy, female workers were dismissed, but later their numbers increased at a rate higher than that of male workers. However, the increment consisted mainly of part-time workers, absorbed largely by the service sectors (Fujii, 1997a, p. 85).

Workers in the domestic textiles industry

Since the end of the 1960s, the textile industry has adopted two different strategies for survival: shifting production bases overseas, and moving to less developed areas in Japan. In both cases, the objective was to mobilize cheap labour, but in the former, young women were the targets of recruitment, while in the latter, housewives were sought for employment as part-time workers. Here I shall discuss the situation of female workers in the domestic textile industry.

From the beginning of the 1950s, the dominance of cotton-spinning as the main sector of female employment declined rapidly, and the ready-made garment industry gradually advanced. The garment industry does not require any large investment and is less subject to geographical conditions than are the spinning, dyeing and silk industries. During the 1970s, local governments in the less developed areas of Japan strove to lure investment to their areas by garment firms. Besides various incentives offered by these local governments, the abundance of labour in the form of housewives from farm households was a big inducement to investors. With the decline of agriculture and the mechanization of farming, female labour that had once been vital to sustain farm production became increasingly redundant. On the other hand, the earnings of males in farm households alone could not meet the rising cost of living. For farm-based women, garment factories established in their localities offered an alternative source of income. One observer of garment factories in rural areas in the latter half of the 1970s found strikingly low wages, long hours of work, strict control by the management, and insecure terms of employment (Hiroki, 1977, 1978). The workers were under severe pressure from the management to achieve production targets, so that even after working overtime, some women took work home to finish. Most workers suffered from health problems resulting from the hard work and poor working environment, and the rates of miscarriage and stillbirth were quite high among workers. Tables 8.3 and 8.4 show the composition of workers in 2002 in the textile and garment industries by employment status. The percentage of part-timers among female workers is considerably higher than that among male workers.

Table 8.3   Employment status of textile workers, 2002

	Male		Female	
	Number	*(%)*	*Number*	*(%)*
Total number of employees	85,208	100.0	71,116	100.0
Sole proprietors and unpaid family workers	2,544	3.0	1,534	2.2
Full-time workers	72,929	85.6	46,400	65.2
Part-time workers	6,444	7.5	21,115	29.7
Workers seconded from other companies	2,617	3.1	1,488	2.1
Temporary workers	674	0.8	579	0.8

Note: Industrial establishments with four or more employees.

Source: Compiled from Ministry of Economy, Trade and Industry (2002).

Table 8.4   Employment status of apparel workers, 2002

	Male		Female	
	Number	*(%)*	*Number*	*(%)*
Total number of employees	68,587	100.0	238,966	100.0
Sole proprietors and unpaid family workers	4,724	6.9	3,170	1.3
Full-time workers	56,915	83.0	149,562	62.6
Part-time workers	5,681	8.3	80,994	33.9
Workers seconded from other companies	802	1.1	3,525	1.5
Temporary workers	465	0.7	1,715	0.7

Note: Industrial establishments with four or more employees.

Source: Compiled from Ministry of Economy, Trade and Industry (2002).

State policy towards the textile industry

The policy of the Japanese government towards textile imports has been quite liberal; in other words, the government has not resorted to import restriction measures.[14] In contrast to the USA, Canada, and the European Union (EU), which use, or once used, tariffs and other non-tariff barriers to control imports of textiles and clothing through bilateral agreements under the framework of the Multi-Fibre Agreement (MFA), Japan does not apply any MFA restrictions on imports, although it participates in the MFA as an exporting country (Yamawaki, 1992, p. 104).

As of 2001, the general rate of duty imposed on articles of clothing and accessories ranged between 5 per cent and 17 per cent.[15] Moreover, Japan has applied the generalized system of preference (GSP) since 1971 for imports from the developing countries.[16] Under the GSP, clothing and accessories are exempt from duty. In 2001, the Japanese government announced that the GSP system would be extended for a further ten years, and that 360 items from less developed countries could be imported duty-free without quantitative ceilings. In the face of mounting textile imports, some domestic manufacturers have asked for a temporary ban on imports of certain items. The government, however, has not responded in the case of textile imports, in contrast to its attitude towards other import items such as agricultural products. The government's attitude towards textiles is partly a result of the fact that the sources of these imports include Japanese factories in the developing countries, and imposing restrictions on them would affect the interests of Japanese capital abroad.[17]

The Japanese government is not sitting idly by, however, in the face of the decline in domestic textile production. It appointed a task force to review policy, and in 2003 the advisory committee on industrial structure presented recommendations (METI, 2003b). The government recognizes the importance to the economy of the textile industry, which accounts for about 7 per cent of overall manufacturing employment, and 3.1 per cent of total manufacturing value added. Furthermore, the textile industry is deeply rooted in local and regional economies, there being some 160 regions specializing in textile production in Japan. The recommendation states categorically that the five years, up to 2008, will be the last chance for, and the last case of, large-scale state support to reform the textile industry. In a nutshell, it calls for establishing effective linkages flowing from upstream to downstream, along with developments in technology and human resources. The recommendation proposes state support for garment manufacturers to become self-reliant – that is, to relinquish their dependency on buyers and establish a fully-fledged manufacturing process ranging over product development, design and production. With respect to employment, it mentions the necessity of developing young human resources, people who have a thorough knowledge of the textile industry, including design, technology and marketing. It should be noted that already more than half the workers engaged in textile manufacturing are over 50 years of age. The report also recommends enlarging employment opportunities for elderly workers on low wages rather than increasing the number of foreign workers.

Garment workers under globalization

From the policy stand stated above, it would appear that the state's concern does not extend to workers who are currently under severe pressure. Let us take a brief look at the situation in the garment industry under the hollowing-out of the Japanese textile industry that has resulted from globalization.

Case 1: Garment factory X, Gifu Prefecture[18]

Gifu Prefecture (see the map on page xvi) is an area famous for garment production. In the years immediately after the Second World War, there were many shops selling second-hand clothes. In order to meet the growing demand, some shops started manufacturing clothing as family businesses, and later expanded to factory production. Between 1990 and 1993, garment manufacturers in Gifu and nearby Nagoya rushed into China. In 1993, these factories in China were employing around 30,000 workers, almost as many as were working at the Japanese home factories. Company X was established in 1967 by the parents of the current owner, a woman. Her company designed a coat for pregnant women that appealed to consumer tastes and sold well. As she recalls it, the garment industry in Japan peaked as early as 1973, and after that has been in continuous decline. Since then it has been very difficult to recruit young people, but until 1995, the company employed Japanese women as part-timers in addition to subcontracting out some of the work. Now the company depends on Chinese workers who come to Japan as trainees for three years. At the time of writing the company employs twenty-five workers, including ten trainees.

The trainee system was established ostensibly to provide skill training for foreigners, but in reality it is used to alleviate the labour shortage in Japan. As of the end of 2002, there were about 39,000 foreign trainees in Japan.[19] The difference in expectations between the trainees and the companies employing them is said to be responsible for serious problems, such as the exploitation of trainees. However, their problems have not been addressed by the general trade unions, since they are not categorized as 'workers' but as 'trainees'.

The fact is that Company X could not survive without the Chinese trainees. The owner says that Japanese part-time workers, housewives already past middle age, cannot compete with the young, dextrous Chinese trainees. Under the hollowing-out process, former part-time workers found alternative employment mainly in service sectors such as supermarkets and care services for the aged and the sick. But while some of those who could not adapt to such service work approach Company X for work, there are few, says the owner, whose work is worth the minimum wage.

Case 2: Garment factory Y, Aomori Prefecture[20]

Aomori is the northernmost district in Honshu, the main island of Japan (see the map on page xvi). Because of its cold winters, people from Aomori have provided seasonal migrant labour during the winter season. This was why the local government decided to offer favourable conditions to attract garment industry investment. Factory Y, however, was closed down in 2001 despite strong protests by the female workers, most of whom were housewives from fishery households. The owner said that he was under pressure from mass retailers to cut costs and could continue operations only if the workers accepted wages at the same level as in China. The local government declined to provide support on the grounds that it could not subsidize one particular company. The factory moved to China, and some of the former employees are now engaged in tomato production.

Concluding remarks

The story of Japanese textile workers reveals many similarities in the experiences of these workers with those of female workers in other countries, both developed and developing. Although they take different forms, in keeping with the specific contexts of the individual societies concerned, the innate mechanisms of capitalism and gender hierarchy have produced similar labour processes in the making of a distinct social category as female factory workers, resulting in many experiences in common among women in different countries. The case studies of two factories that were presented here have also shown that conditions at the time of writing in the domestic garment industry in Japan parallel those in other developed countries. For the sake of minimizing labour costs, the domestic garment industries in Japan have resorted to employing housewives in the less developed regions, where alternative means of income generation are limited. Just as US and European manufacturers have come to depend on migrant labour in their domestic production processes, so too has Japan become increasingly dependent on the cheap foreign labour euphemistically called 'trainees'.

A review of the literature on female factory workers in Japan shows that, in contrast to a widely held view that the 'pitiful history of female factory workers' (*joko aishi*) is a thing of the past in Japan, this is by no means an obsolete theme. Since the early 1990s a number of new articles and books have been published on female factory work (Murayama, 2003). A common feature of this literature is that it has tried to reinterpret the meaning of factory work for women, in some cases based on the narratives of workers, and in others, based on new approaches incorporating a gender perspective. Nevertheless, these studies mainly deal with women factory workers of the prewar period or, at the latest, before the beginning of the postwar era of economic high growth.[21]

Together with extending the time frame for analysis, future research should make use of the rich collection of studies on female factory workers in other developed countries as well as in the developing countries, some of which was presented in the second and third sections of this chapter. Here I would propose five areas of interest. First, is the issue of female factory work at Japanese overseas factories, the issue Ong and Kim began to explore. Second, is female factory work in sectors other than the textile industry. The third area is the problem of non-regular employment in the manufacturing sector. Fourth, the situation of foreign workers in Japanese domestic industry must be investigated in more detail. And finally, there should be a more comprehensive analysis of what impacts the hollowing-out of the Japanese economy has had on gender relations overall. In each area of research it is necessary to expand the loci of analysis to cover the multiple life dimensions of women, such as in the workplace, in the community and in the home. It is also important to listen to the voices of women them-selves as well as those of the other people who constitute the women's social environment in each of these dimensions.

The brief case studies of two factories presented here demonstrate the interrelatedness of women in Japan and other countries (in these cases, China) under the current globalization process. Their relationship is con-structed not on a zero-sum rule, whereby a loss by one means a gain to the other; rather, at least as far as their working conditions are concerned, they are compelled to pull each other down in a spiral of working conditions degrading for both parties. The experiences of contemporary women fact-ory workers in the developed countries, including Japan, give the lie to the myth that the harsh conditions suffered by women in factories in develop-ing countries will improve automatically as the industries and national economies there grow. The competition based on cutting costs always requires 'cheaper labour', creating a nested structure of cheap labour at the international, intranational, inter-firm and intra-firm levels along the lines of gender, ethnicity and other social categories.

As a solution which addresses the common interests of workers in both developed and developing countries, some advocate 'fair trade' in the broad sense of the term. As it is now, workers in the developing countries are deprived of 'fair' labour standards and wages that are commensurate with their labour, while workers in the developed countries lose their jobs because of 'unfair' competition from countries with a virtually insurmount-able advantage in labour costs. Therefore, guaranteeing workers in the developing world 'fair' wages and satisfactory working conditions benefits workers in the developed world as well (North–South Institute, 1985). I per-sonally support this strategy. However, it is not easy to put the idea into practice, since it entails additional costs for both consumers and factory owners. In order to gain wider public support, it is necessary to identify where conflicts as well as the intersection of interests lie among workers in different locations and at different points in time.

Notes

1 Despite the apparent importance in terms of its massive capital outflow and resultant domestic economic restructuring, Japan has often been left out of books compiling case studies of concerned countries. See, for example, Rothstein *et al.* (1992), Bonacich *et al.* (1994) and Chow (2002). Elson and Wright (1996) compiled about 270 articles and books published from the early 1970s to the mid-1990s on gender and industrialization, among which are only three articles on Japan.

2 Miyake (2001) has criticized earlier studies on female factory workers in Japan for their lack of a gender perspective in their analyses.

3 Some of the elements of subjectivity that Heider refers to are: personalities, value systems, cultures, other traits (such as gender, age, race, sexual preference, family status, personal health and height), and the theoretical orientations of the ethnographers.

4 Heyzer and Tan also point out that different perspectives illustrate that the writers' views are influenced by their experiences, interests and values, though they do not elaborate (Heyzer and Tan, 1988, p. 4).

5 Joekes's study on Moroccan factory daughters also reveals a similar relationship between parents and daughters. Parents can claim the right to income earned by their daughters until their marriage (Joekes, 1985, p. 207).

6 The late prime minister, Kakuei Tanaka, faced large-scale, anti-Japan riots in both Indonesia and Thailand during his official visits in 1974. Anti-Japanese and nationalist feelings were running high in countries witnessing the flooding of their markets with Japanese products, arrogant behaviour on the part of Japanese businessmen, and the use of Japanese official development assistance to benefit Japanese companies rather than the people of the recipient countries.

7 There were Chinese as well as Indian Malaysians in smaller numbers than Malays, and these workers occupied positions between the Japanese and ethnic Malays.

8 According to Shiozawa (1971, 1983), the practice of compulsory unpaid labour was prevalent in silk factories even as late as 1960. The starting-up and cleaning of the machines, and the cleaning of the floor had to be done before and after the stipulated working hours and without pay. Ending compulsory unpaid labour was one of the demands of the silk workers' trade unions.

9 Here import penetration is expressed as a percentage of imports over domestic sales.

10 This includes China, Hong Kong, Korea, Taiwan and the ASEAN.

11 Figures are taken from various issues of *Census of Manufacturers* (METI, various dates).

12 Degree of import penetration = import value/(domestic production + import value – export value) × 100.

13 A grade-based wage is a kind of piece-rate system. However, grade and wage are determined in relation to the average for all workers. Therefore, the increments in wages for skilled workers were provided by the deduction from the wages of workers with inferior skills. The system promoted severe competition among workers, while the company did not have to pay any extra wages.

14 See Yamazawa (1988) for details of government policies towards the textile industry before the early 1980s.

15 Yokota (2001) remarks that the Japanese government has not been very active in protecting the domestic textile industry, as indicated by the low tariff rates for textile commodities in comparison with those of the USA and EU countries.

16 See http://www.mofa.go.jp/policy/economy/gsp/index.html. for details of Japanese GSP.

17 Information based on an interview with a trade union official.

18 Based on interviews with a factory owner.

19 An article published in *Asahi Shinbun*, 22 June 2003.

20 Based on interviews with a trade union activist.

21 Except for an anthropological study by Roberts (1994) on female workers in a garment factory, few studies are available on contemporary factory women in Japan.

References

Adachi, Mariko (1994). 'Keizai no gurobaruka to rodoryoku no joseika' (Economic globalization and feminization of labour) in Emiko Takenaka and Yoshiko Kuba (eds), *Rodoryoku no joseika: 21 seiki e no paradaimu* (Feminization of labour: a paradigm for the 21st century) (Tokyo: Yuhikaku) (in Japanese).

Addison, Tony and Lionel Demery (1988) 'Wages and Labour Conditions in East Asia: A Review of Case-Study Evidence', *Development Policy Review*, vol. 6, pp. 371–93.

Banerjee, Nirmala (ed.) (1991) *Indian Women in a Changing Industrial Scenario* (New Delhi: Sage Publications).

Bonacich, Edna and Richard P. Appelbaum (2000) *Behind the Label: Inequality in the Los Angeles Apparel Industry* (Berkeley, Calif.: University of California Press).

Bonacich, Edna, Lucie Cheng, Norma Chinchilla, Nora Hamilton and Paul Ong (eds). (1994). *Global Production: The Apparel Industry in the Pacific Rim*, (Philadelphia, Pa.: Temple University Press).

Carney, Larry S. and Charlotte G. O'Kelly (1990) 'Women's Work and Women's Place in the Japanese Economic Miracle', in Kathryn Ward (ed.), *Women Workers and Global Restructuring* (Ithaca, NY: Cornell University Press).

Chow, Esther Ngan-Ling (ed.) (2002). *Transforming Gender and Development in East Asia* (New York: Routledge).

Dublin, Thomas (1979) *Women at Work: The Transformation of Work and Community in Lowell, Massachusetts, 1826–1860*, 2nd edn 1993 (New York: Columbia University Press).

Edgren, Gus (1982) *Spearheads of Industrialisation or Sweatshops in the Sun? A Critical Appraisal of Labour Conditions in Asian Export Processing Zones* (Bangkok: ILO-ARTEP).

Elson, Diane and Ruth Pearson (1981) 'The Subordination of Women and the Internationalisation of Factory Production', in Kate Young, Carol Wolkowitz and Roslyn McCullagh (eds), *Of Marriage and the Market: Women's Subordination in International Perspective* (London: CSE Books).

Elson, Diane and Caroline Wright (1996) *Gender Issues in Contemporary Industrialization: An Annotated Bibliography*, Labour Studies Working Papers No. 10. Centre for Comparative Labour Studies, University of Warwick.

Engels, Frederick (1845) *The Condition of the Working-Class in England* in Karl Marx and Frederick Engels *Collected Works, vol. 4* (1975) (Moscow: Progress Publishers).

Featherstone, Liza and United Students Against Sweatshops (2002) *Students Against Sweatshops* (New York: Verso).

Fernandes, Leela (1997) *Producing Workers: The Politics of Gender, Class and Culture in the Calcutta Jute Mills* (Philadelphia, Pa.: University of Pennsylvania Press).

Foo, Gillian H. C. and Linda Y. C. Lim (1989) 'Poverty, Ideology and Women Export Factory Workers in South-East Asia', In Haleh Afshar and Bina Agarwal (eds), *Women, Poverty and Ideology in Asia: Contradictory Pressures, Uneasy Resolutions* (London: Macmillan), pp. 212–33.

Fuentes, Annette and Barbara Ehrenreich (1983) *Women in the Global Factory* (Boston, Mass.: South End Press).

Fujii, Harue (1997a) 'Nihon gata kigyo shakai to josei rodo' (Japanese-style corporate society and female labour), in Mitsuo Fujii (ed.), *Higashi Ajia no kokusai bungyo to josei rodo* (International division of labour in East Asia and female labour) (Tokyo: Mineruba Shobo), pp. 77–121 (in Japanese).

Fujii, Harue (1997b) 'Kokusai bungyo no shinten to rodoryoku no joseika: Chugoku nikkei kigyo no kesu o chushin ni' (Progress in the international division of labour and feminization of labour: with a focus on Japanese companies in China), *Ohotsuku sangyo keiei ronshu* (Journal of Okhotsk Business Science) vol. 8. no. 2 pp. 1–29 (in Japanese).

Fujii, Harue (2001) 'Chugoku apareru sangyo no romu kanri' (Labour management in the apparel industry in China), in Mitsuo Fujii (ed.), *Higashi ajia ni okeru kokusai bungyo to gijutsu iten* (International division of labor and technology transfer in East Asia) (Tokyo: Mineruba Shobo), pp. 234–55 (in Japanese).

Goka, Kazumichi (2003) 'Disento waku kara mita Nihon no koyo to rodo' (Employment and labour in Japan from a 'decent work' perspective), *Josei Rodo Kenkyu* (The bulletin of the society for study of working women), vol. 43, pp. 20–30 (in Japanese).

Goonatilake, Hema and Sabitri Goonesekere (1988). 'Industrialisation and Women Workers in Sri Lanka: Working Conditions Inside and Outside the Investment Promotion Zone', in Noeleen Heyzer (ed.) *Daughters in Industry: Work, Skills and Consciousness of Women Workers in Asia* (Kuala Lumpur: Asian and Pacific Development Centre), pp. 184–208.

Hayata, Ritsuko (1997) *Kojo e no tabi: Tomioka seishijo kara Omi kenshi e* (A journey to factory women: from Tomioka mill to Omi silk spinning) (Kyoto: Kamogawa Shuppan) (in Japanese).

Heider, Karl G. (1988) 'The Rashomon Effect: When Ethnographers Disagree', *American Anthropologist*, vol. 90, no. 1, pp. 73–81.

Heyzer, Noeleen and Tan Boon Kean (1988) 'Work, Skills and Consciousness of Women Workers in Asia', in Noeleen Heyzer (ed.) *Daughters in Industry: Work, Skills and Consciousness of Women Workers in Asia* (Kuala Lumpur: Asian and Pacific Development Centre).

Hiroki, Michiko (1977) 'Gorika no naka no fujin rodosha: seni sangyo ni hataraku fujin rodosha no koyo to bosei hogo no jittai' (Female workers under rationalization: employment and maternity protection of female textile workers), *Gekkan rodo kumiai* (Trade union monthly), April, pp. 34–7 (in Japanese).

Hiroki, Michiko (1978) 'Fukyo no naka no seni joshi rodosha' (Female textile workers under economic depression), *Gekkan rodo kumiai* (Trade union monthly), March, pp. 52–7 (in Japanese).

Hiroki, Michiko (1986) *In the Shadow of Affluence: Stories of Japanese Women Workers* (Hong Kong: Committee for Asian Women).

Hiroki, Michiko (1999) *Ajia ni ikiru josei tachi* (Women in Asia: fifteen years' experience of association with female workers) (Tokyo: Domesu Shuppan) (in Japanese).

Hosoi, Wakizo (1954) *Joko aishi* (The pitiful history of female factory workers) (Tokyo: Iwanami Shoten) (in Japanese).

Joekes, Susan (1985) 'Working for Lipstick? Male and Female Labour in the Clothing Industry in Morocco', in Haleh Afshar (ed.), *Women, Work and Ideology in the Third World* (London and New York: Tavistock), pp. 183–213.

Kabeer, Naila (2000) *The Power to Choose: Bangladeshi Women and Labour Market Decisions in London and Dhaka* (London: Verso).

Kamijo, Hiroyuki (1978) *Kinu hitosuji no seishun: Tomioka nikki ni miru nihon no kindai* (My youth for silk: modern Japan seen in Tomioka diary) (Tokyo: Nihon Hoso Shuppan Kyoukai) (in Japanese).

Kim, Seung-Kyung (1997) *Class Struggle or Family Struggle? The Lives of Women Factory Workers in South Korea* (Cambridge University Press).

Kung, Lydia (1978) *Factory Women in Taiwan* (Ann Arbor, Mich.: UMI Research Press) (New edition published 1994 by Columbia University Press).

Lee, Ching Kwang (1998) *Gender and the South China Miracle: Two Worlds of Factory Women* (Berkeley, Calif.: University of California Press).

Lim, Linda Y. C. (1983) 'Capitalism, Imperialism, and Patriarchy: The Dilemma of Third-World Women Workers in Multinational Factories', in June Nash and Maria Patricia Fernandez-Kelly (eds), *Women, Men, and the International Division of Labor* (Albany, NY: State University of New York Press), pp. 70–91.

Louie, Miriam Ching Yoon (2001) *Sweatshop Warriors: Immigrant Women Workers Take on the Global Factory* (Cambridge, Mass: South End Press).

Mather, Celia (1985) ' "Rather Than Make Trouble, it's Better Just to Leave": Behind the Lack of Industrial Strife in the Tangerang Region of West Java', in Haleh Afshar (ed.) *Women, Work and Ideology in the Third World* (London and New York: Tavistock).

Mies, Maria (1986) *Patriarchy and Accumulation on a World Scale: Women in the International Division of Labour* (London: Zed Books).

Ministry of Economy, Trade and Industry (METI) (2001) *White Paper on International Trade* (Tokyo: METI).

Ministry of Economy, Trade and Industry (METI) (2003a) *White Paper on International Trade* (Tokyo: METI).

Ministry of Economy, Trade and Industry (METI) (2003b) *Nihon no seni sangyo ga susumubeki hoko to torubeki seisaku* (Directions and policies Japan's textile industry should take) Sub-Committee on Textile Industry, Advisory Committee on Industrial Structure (Tokyo: METI) (in Japanese).

Ministry of Economy, Trade and Industry (METI) (various dates) *Kogyo tokei hyo* (Census of manufacturing) (Tokyo: METI) (in Japanese).

Miyake, Yoshiko (1991) 'Doubling Expectations: Motherhood and Women's Factory Work under State Management in Japan in the 1930s and 1940s', in Bernstein, Gail Lee, (ed.), *Recreating Japanese Women, 1600–1945* (Berkeley, Calif.: University of California Press).

Miyake, Yoshiko (2001) 'Nihon no shakai kagagu to jenda' (Social sciences in Japan and gender: an analysis of the discourse on *Joko aishi* [The pitiful history of female factory workers]), in Yoshiko Miyake (ed.), *Nihon shakai to jenda* (Japanese society and gender) (Tokyo: Akashi Shoten) (in Japanese).

Molony, Barbara (1991) 'Activism among Women in the Taisho Cotton Textile Industry', in Gail Lee Bernstein (ed.), *Recreating Japanese Women, 1600–1945* (Berkeley Calif.: University of California Press).

Moran, William (2002) *The Belles of New England: The Women of the Textile Mills and Families Whose Wealth They Wove* (New York: St. Martin's Press).

Murakami, Kaoru (1999) 'Toruko no kojo josei rodo to jenda kihan' (Factory daughters and gender norms in Turkey), *Ajia keizai* (Asian economies), vol. 40, no. 5, pp. 24–48 (in Japanese).

Murayama, Mayumi (2003) 'Nihon ni okeru josei kojo rodosha kenkyu' (Studies on female factory workers in Japan: with a focus on the textile industry), in Mayumi Murayama (ed.), *Nihon ni okeru kaihatsu to jenda: Tojokoku kenkyu no tame no bunken kaidai* (An annotated bibliography on development and gender in Japan) (Chiba: Institute of Developing Economies), pp. 103–41 (in Japanese).

Nakamura, Masanori (ed.) (1985) *Gijutsu kakushin to joshi rodo* (Technological innovation and female labour) (Tokyo: United Nations University and University of Tokyo Press) (in Japanese).

Nakamura, Masanori and Corrado Molteni (1985) 'Seishi gijutsu no hatten to joshi rodo' (Development of silk-reeling technology and factory labour) in Masanori Nakamura (ed.) *Gijutsu kakushin to joshi rodo* (Technological innovation and female labour) (Tokyo: United Nations University and University of Tokyo Press), pp. 33–70 (in Japanese).

Nishinarita, Yutaka (1985) 'Joshi rodo no shoruikei to sono henyo' (Types of female labour and their evolution: 1890s to 1940s), in Masanori Nakamura (ed.), *Gijutsu kakushin to joshi rodo* (Technological innovation and female labour) Tokyo: United Nations University and University of Tokyo Press), pp. 7–31 (in Japanese).

North–South Institute, The (1985) *Women in Industry: North–South Connections* (Ottawa: The North–South Institute).

Omi, Naoto (2001) 'Kozui teki yunyu kara seni sangyo o mamorou' (Let's protect the textile industry from the flood of imports) *Zensen kompasu*, vol. 51, no. 5. pp. 2–11 (in Japanese).

Ong, Aihwa (1987) *Spirits of Resistance and Capitalist Discipline: Factory Women in Malaysia* (Albany, NY: SUNY Press).

Phongpaichit, Pasuk (1988) 'Two Roads to the Factory: Industrialisation Strategies and Women's Employment in Southeast Asia', in Bina Agarwal (eds), *Structure of Patriarchy: State, Community and Household in Modernising Asia* (London and New Delhi: Zed Books and Kali for Women), pp. 151–63.

Rao, Vijay Rukmini and Sahba Husain (1991) 'Invisible Hands – The Women Behind India's Export Earnings', in Nirmala Banerjee (ed.), *Indian Women in a Changing Industrial Scenario* (New Delhi, Newbury Park London: Sage Publications), pp. 133–200.

Roberts, Glenda S. (1994) *Staying on the Line: Blue-Collar Women in Contemporary Japan* (Honolulu: University of Hawaii Press).

Rosen, Ellen Israel (2002) *Making Sweatshops: The Globalization of the U.S. Apparel Industry*, (Berkeley, Calif.: University of California Press).

Ross, Andrew (ed.) (1997) *No Sweat: Fashion, Free Trade, and the Rights of Garment Workers* (New York: Verso).

Rothstein, Frances Abrahamer and Michael L. Blim (eds) (1992) *Anthropology and the Global Factory: Studies of the New Industrialization in the Late Twentieth Century* (New York: Bergin and Garvey).

Safa, Helen I. (1995) *The Myth of the Male Breadwinner: Women and Industralization in the Caribbean*, (Boulder, Col.: Westview Press).

Salaff, Janet W. (1981) *Working Daughters of Hong Kong: Filial Piety or Power in the Family?* (Cambridge University Press).

Sassen, Saskia (1998) *Globalization and its Discontents* (New York: The New Press).

Shiozawa, Miyoko (1971) *Kekkon taishoku-go no watashitachi: Seishi rodosha no sonogo* (How we are after retirement on marriage: the lives of former silk workers) (Tokyo: Iwanami Shoten) (in Japanese).

Shiozawa, Miyoko (1983) *Meido in tonan ajia: gendai no joko aishi* (Made in South East Asia: pitiful contemporary history of female factory workers) (Tokyo: Iwanami Shoten) (in Japanese).

Steans, Jill (1998) *Gender and International Relations* (New Brunswick: Rutgers University Press).

Suzuki, Yuko (1989) *Joko to rodo sogi* (Factory women and labour disputes) (Tokyo: Renga shobo shinsha) (in Japanese).

Takai, Toshio (1980) *Watashi no joko aishi* (My pitiful factory work history) (Tokyo: Sodo Bunka) (in Japanese).

Tilly, Luise A. and Joan W. Scott (1978) *Women, Work, and Family* (New York: Holt, Rinehart & Winston).

Tsurumi, E. Patricia (1990) *Factory Girls: Women in the Thread Mills of Meiji Japan* (Princeton, NJ: Princeton University Press).

Wada, Ei (1978) *Tomioka nikki* (Tomioka diary) (Tokyo: Chuko Bunko) (in Japanese).

Ward, Kathryn (1990) 'Introduction and Overview', in Kathryn Ward (ed.), *Women Workers and Global Restructuring* (Ithaca, NY: Cornell University Press).

Wolf, Diane L. (1992) *Factory Daughters: Gender, Household Dynamics, and Rural Industrialization in Java* (Berkeley, Calif.: University of California Press).

Yamamoto, Shigemi (1977) *Aa Nomugi toge* (Ah! The Nomugi Pass) (Tokyo: Kadokawa) (in Japanese).

Yamanouchi, Mina (1975) *Yamauchi Mina jiden: 12 sai no boseki joko kara no shogai* (The autobiography of Mina Yamauchi: my life from the time I was a twelve-year-old cotton-spinning factory girl) (Tokyo: Shinjuku Shobo) (in Japanese).

Yamawaki, Hideki (1992) 'International Competition and Japan's Domestic Adjustments', in Kim Anderson (ed.), *New Silk Roads: East Asia and World Textile Markets* (Cambridge University Press), pp. 89–118.

Yamazawa, Ippei (1988) 'The Textile Industry', in Ryutaro Komiya Masahiro Okuno and Kotaro Suzumura (eds), *Industrial Policy of Japan* (Tokyo: Academic Press Japan), pp. 395–423.

Yokota, Takaaki (2001) 'Nihon no seni sangyo to meido in Chaina' (The Japanese textile industry and 'Made in China'), *Nicchu keikyou janaru* (Journal of Japan-China Economic Co-operation) June, pp. 6–15 (in Japanese).

Index